"This book presents a strong challenge to the contemporary church to rethink her attitudes toward and practices of community prayer. I thought I knew a thing or two about praying together. But I found myself being challenged and learning more about the practice of prayer in my own life and ministry team."

Ajith Fernando, Teaching Director, Youth for Christ, Sri Lanka; author, *Discipling in a Multicultural World*

"*A Praying Church* is a 'page turner'—richly biblical, wonderfully practical, and chock-full of engaging testimonies and helpful illustrations. It is convicting but filled with pastoral love and concern. Paul Miller writes brother to brother, leader to leader. Without boasting, Miller clearly practices what he preaches. Several chapters are worth the price of the book. My favorite is the chapter on fasting and prayer."

John F. Smed, Director, Prayer Current; author, *Prayer Revolution: Rebuilding Church and City through Prayer*

"Churches that are true change agents in their communities are congregations for whom prayer is a way of life. My good friend Paul Miller has written a thoughtful and challenging appeal in *A Praying Church*. Read this wonderful book, and you'll discover how to partner with the Spirit of Jesus in transforming your community for the kingdom of Christ!"

Joni Eareckson Tada, Founder, Joni and Friends International Disability Center

"Paul Miller is on a quest to return prayer to its rightful central place in everyday life and ministry. Read this book to be challenged to pray. Study it for tips on how to make prayer second nature. Ponder it for a refresher on the Bible's testimony to prayer, on prayer in countless settings today, and on myriad impediments to prayer. Most of all, rediscover how Christ and the Spirit equip the saints for the work of the ministry—through prayer. This is an enormously informative and encouraging book."

Robert W. Yarbrough, Professor of New Testament, Covenant Theological Seminary

A Praying Church

Other Crossway Books by Paul E. Miller

J-Curve: Dying and Rising with Jesus in Everyday Life

A Loving Life: In a World of Broken Relationships

A Praying Church

Becoming a People of Hope in a Discouraging World

Paul E. Miller

Foreword by Dane C. Ortlund

∷ CROSSWAY®

WHEATON, ILLINOIS

Library of Congress Cataloging-in-Publication Data

Names: Miller, Paul E., 1953– author.
Title: A praying church : becoming a people of hope in a discouraging world / Paul E. Miller ; foreword by Dane C. Ortlund.
Description: Wheaton, Illinois : Crossway, [2023] | Includes bibliographical references and index.
Identifiers: LCCN 2022017665 (print) | LCCN 2022017666 (ebook) | ISBN 9781433561641 (trade paperback) | ISBN 9781433561665 (mobipocket) | ISBN 9781433561658 (pdf) | ISBN 9781433561672 (epub)
Subjects: LCSH: Prayer—Christianity. | Church.
Classification: LCC BV640 .M55 2023 (print) | LCC BV640 (ebook) | DDC 242/.4—dc23/eng/20220907
LC record available at https://lccn.loc.gov/2022017665
LC ebook record available at https://lccn.loc.gov/2022017666

Crossway is a publishing ministry of Good News Publishers.

LB		32	31	30	29	28	27	26	25	24	23
15	14	13	12	11	10	9	8	7	6	5	4	3	2	1

To Bob Allums,
a Barnabas, whose gentle leadership and kind laughter
have been catalysts for a million prayer stories

and

To faithful friends in Polk County, Florida,
whose generosity made this book possible

Contents

List of Illustrations

Figures

Tables

Foreword

THE BATTLE TO PRAY IS not mainly a battle against prayerlessness but a battle against discouragement, cynicism, and unbelief.

If this is true of our individual lives—and it is, including mine—how much more of the life of our local churches. This magnificent book is a winsome and utterly compelling rallying cry to step out of the smiling unbelief infecting and dampening our churches, where prayer is one dutiful activity among many. The wondrous alternative that Paul Miller gives us, according to Scripture, is to move prayer into the nuclear core of all we do—which is to say, to do church *as if God is there.*

This book defies neat categorization. On the one hand, it takes us deep into the inner workings of Pauline theology and how the New Testament speaks of the Spirit and the dawning of the new age in Christ's resurrection. On the other hand, this book is supremely earthy and practical, using real-life examples and stories of how prayer has worked (and hasn't) in the author's own life and ministry.

A Praying Church is chock-full of deeply probing insights into what prayer is and how it sets aglow an entire church community. For example:

What I pray over lasts, and what I don't pray over doesn't last.

I've seen what happens when the Spirit of Jesus inhabits a community—everything starts to sparkle.

Paul never mentions "the gift of prayer." Why? Because there is no gift of breathing.

If you grasp the simplicity of *prayer → Spirit → Jesus → wonder*, then praying together won't be just another burden; it will be the activity that transforms all your burdens.

Insights like these abound. Taking the book as a whole, however, here's the real genius of it: Paul Miller brings prayer into the messy reality of our actual lives. Not the cleaned-up lives we're all walking around presenting to others, but the lives we're really living, with all their failures and discouragements and tears and numbness and fatigue. In other words, Paul understands prayer in a gospel way—just as the gospel is power for us at the precise place of our need, so too prayer is deep power and help at the very place where we have need and weakness. It's the whole point.

And what this book has managed to do is to take that gospel reality of prayer—the way prayer is for us *now* in our *need*, not later once we've got it together—and make prayer actionable for a church body. Paul coaches us into praying our way forward together. Noting that the early church leaders insisted that "we will devote ourselves to prayer and to the ministry of the word" (Acts 6:4), Paul Miller wants us to do church by prayer.

In other words, *A Praying Church* is not a book telling us to scurry faster on our hamster wheel of prayer. It is an invitation to step off of that hamster wheel by looking to the Spirit of Jesus and letting him lead us forward as we commune with him. Wonderfully simple, widely neglected, deeply liberating.

A church with rich history, flawless music, powerful preaching, amazing childcare, a paid-off mortgage, and stellar attendance but sleepily operating out of the resources of the flesh instead of prayer is headed toward tragic inconsequentiality.

A church riddled with dysfunctions, embattled and beleaguered, unimpressive in preaching, off-tune musically, small in numbers, and without resources but quietly collapsing into the freefall of faith-fueled praying that this book outlines is a church that will bless this world in a thousand surprising ways and leave a mark that reverberates through eternity.

This book may be the wardrobe door into Narnia your church has been needing and longing for. For it is not, finally, a book about prayer. It is a book about God, and how we move through life as a church as if he is actually there. I commend it wholeheartedly, and I thank Paul Miller for giving it to us.

Dane C. Ortlund
SENIOR PASTOR
NAPERVILLE PRESBYTERIAN CHURCH
NAPERVILLE, ILLINOIS

PART 1

———————

WHY PRAY TOGETHER?

1

A Glimpse of a Praying Community

FOR MOST OF US, PRAYER IS SOLITARY, which means that when it comes to corporate prayer, we aren't exactly sure what it even feels and looks like. So I begin this book by letting you peek in on my three prayer meetings this morning. Before we lament the loss of praying together, we need to know what we've lost!

My first prayer time in the morning is with my wife, Jill. Beginning at 5:45, we take forty-five minutes together to read the Bible and pray together. Jill punctuates our time with fervent prayers for our family, friends, and world. It's also interrupted by job duties for me: "Oh, Paul, would you move all the boxes off your office floor before you leave for work? The carpet cleaner is coming today." (Technically this is a question, but relationally it's an order!) Then back to more fervent prayer for our family, which is interrupted by Jill asking if she can call our handyman to hang pictures, since I'm so backed up with other projects. "Yes, that's fine." Then back to more prayer for our grandchildren.

Jill freely admits she has ADD. Recently, I suggested she hold off on the job ideas for me until we'd finished praying. In her defense,

I've been painting the house, and we've redone the kitchen, so not only is she managing lots of loose ends, but I'm behind in my to-do list, and it's just easier to tell me stuff as it comes to her mind.

This is my most disorganized prayer time of the day, and yet it is the most powerful. Jill usually leads. It took me about ten years to realize that if I wanted to pray with her, I couldn't organize her. Not only that: she prays better than I do. By that I mean, her prayers are almost on the verge of lamenting—she talks to God like she's talking to me when I've promised to paint a room and keep postponing it. She feels the growing evil of our day and prays passionately against it. She's a fighter. Jesus's repeated command to *ask anything* gives us freedom to ask for even seemingly impossible things. Because of the loss of our beloved daughter Ashley to cancer, we especially pray for people battling cancer. We do have one systematic stretch of ten to fifteen minutes when we pray for our more than twenty-five children, spouses, and grandchildren.

Next I pray with our adult daughter Kim, who is affected by disabilities. We pray together barely five minutes, but I love hearing her "voice." Using her speech computer's icon language, she thanks God for multiple things. This morning she thanked God for our Thanksgiving dinner four days ago. (Dinner with our extended family was canceled due to the pandemic, so we went to a restaurant similar to the one in *Lady and the Tramp*, which absolutely charmed her.) Usually she slips in a prayer for our very bad golden retriever, Tully, who's always stealing her things. If I'm biking to work, she prays that I won't crash. If I'm skiing at night, she prays I won't hit a tree. She prays for her ninety-seven-year-old grandmother in London. I usually encourage her to pick one niece or nephew to pray for. She often picks one she feels is too noisy or bad. Kim looks at her nieces and nephews like wine—they get

4

better with age. Kim struggles with anger—it's a symptom of her disability—but we try not to let her "diagnosis" define her, so she prays regularly for God to help her with anger. Lately, we've been visualizing her day together and praying for the parts where she might be tempted to get angry. That has helped. And then, as often happens, I notice my struggle with impatience, so Kim and I close by praying for each other's struggle with impatience.

My third prayer meeting is mid-morning with the ministry I direct, seeJesus. About thirty of us gather on Zoom for about an hour. We spend the first half hearing reports from around the world on our seminar and training ministry. It's an open mic, so we also hear updates on personal and family needs.

As we pray together, it feels like we are weaving a tapestry: We begin by praying for Felicia, who, the day before Thanksgiving, lost her sister to COVID. Our prayers wander through Felicia's life with her sister, enjoying the good things that God had done, and lamenting the hard things. Then we pray for Mafdi's work in the Arab world. Someone circles back to praying for Felicia; then we pray for Mafdi's online Arabic *The Person of Jesus* study. We pray for Miguel, our Spanish-speaking trainer in Chile, who has been sick. With only five minutes left, prayers pick up their pace slightly, a bit like the fourth quarter of an American football game. We don't want to forget anything, so the conversation style of the prayer meeting disappears, and short, quick prayers emerge to cover what we've not yet covered. I close our prayer time by inviting the Spirit of Jesus into our work to shape and lead us.

Our prayer time is the high point of the day. You can tell because hardly anyone misses and people start gathering early. The feel of the prayer time is *resurrection*. We pray boldly and expectantly, not just because that's what resurrection people do but because we've seen God work in so many amazing ways. Prayer fuels prayer.

The hopeful, resurrection *feel* of each of these three prayer meetings does not happen automatically. It has taken time to cultivate. With Jill, I'm attentive to her and her world. With Kim, I prompt her with ideas—her limit is about five promptings. Any more and she gets irritated because *SpongeBob* awaits! With seeJesus, I try to be attentive to each person in the prayer meeting and to his or her story. For example, I talked with Felicia ahead of time to hear more of the story of her sister, so in our "open-mic" time, I prompt Felicia with questions to plumb the depths of suffering that her family has been through, but also to highlight some amazing ways that God worked through Felicia in her sister's life. Attentiveness to resurrection keeps us from getting stuck in sadness.

These three prayer meetings are completely ordinary. Jill's language to God is no different from her language to me when I've forgotten to take out the trash. I say this because we tend to think of prayer as somehow a *higher life*, when it's actually *real life*. Each of these three prayer times is strikingly different from the others, based on the focus and who is involved, but that's true of all our conversations. We shape our dialogue based on who we are talking to.

Why Pray Together?

You likely agree that prayer is important, but let's be realistic; not many of us have the luxury of praying for an hour and a half in the morning. Life comes at us too fast.

Actually, I slow down to pray with other believers *because* life is coming at me so fast. Instinctively, I respond to life's speed with my own speed. That creates a ten-car pileup not only in my outward life but also in my soul. I can't imagine leading my family or community without corporate prayer. I do these morning prayer times not from discipline but from *learned desperation.* I am constant in corporate prayer because the Jesus communities I'm in are *constant in need.* I have no interest in doing anything that hasn't been prayed for and prayed over. What I pray over lasts, and what I don't pray over doesn't last. But there's more: A Jesus community is characterized by wonder, and the conduit to that is prayer. I've seen what happens when the Spirit of Jesus inhabits a community—everything starts to sparkle.

Praying together is not a luxury, nor is it something just for "spiritual" Christians; it's the very *breath of the church.* Most of us don't have the faintest idea of what that means. That's what I hope to show in this book: how integral prayer is to a Jesus community.

God has used my earlier book and seminar *A Praying Life* to help many *individuals* pray, but without a supportive, praying *community*, it's easy to lose hope, to wear out in the work of prayer. Unless entire churches learn to pray together, individual prayer can lose steam. And that isn't just in official prayer meetings but in our families and small groups too, and even in that random phone conversation. That's the passion of this book—to foster praying communities.

Creating Praying Communities

Here's an overview of what we'll cover in the pages ahead:

- In part 1, we answer the question Why pray together? We'll discover why prayer is critical to the church's life. My template is Luke and Acts. I hope to capture your imagination with a new vision of how prayer ignites the Spirit of Jesus in his church.

- In part 2, we examine what the church is. This book isn't just about praying together; it's about how a Jesus community works. Using Ephesians, we'll discover who runs the church (the Spirit of Jesus) and exactly what the church is made of (saints), which helps us see why prayer is fundamental to how we *do* church. If I can fill you with wonder, with a new, richer way of looking at the church, you'll find your heart enlarged—and that will do its own work.
- In part 3, we explore the interface between the Spirit of Jesus and a community at prayer. We turn our eyes outward and discover where the church is going and how it gets there. If you miss the journey and the goal, then prayer becomes either merely therapeutic or a power trip.
- In part 4, we focus on *how* to pray in community, and the multiple subcommunities that make up a family, mission, or church, and how to cultivate prayer in them.
- In part 5, we look at how integral prayer can be to the subcommunities of the church.

I opened this chapter with three morning prayer meetings to give you a feel for what a praying community looks like; then I briefly shared *how* I lead those prayer meetings; and finally, I paused to share my heart as to *why* praying together is so vital. Once you grasp *why we pray* (part 1), *what the church is* (part 2), and *how the Spirit works* (part 3), then *how we pray* (parts 4–5) will come alive in fresh ways. But no matter what, you must begin to pray together—even if just with a good friend. Some things are understood only from the inside. For example, you can study love all you want, but until you've endured in love, you won't understand love.

When I say "a praying church," I mean the local church, but also the multiple layers of friendship we have with other believers. Some of my examples of a praying community come from the mission I lead, seeJesus, but the principles of praying together are the same in any Jesus community, whether it's the local church, your family, or a friendship.

My Hope for This Book

I've written this book for the whole church, because it's the whole church that prays. When Luke gives us a sermon in the book of Acts, we get a preacher: "But Peter, standing with the eleven, lifted up his voice and addressed them" (Acts 2:14). But when Luke describes a prayer meeting, we get the whole church: "All these with one accord were devoting themselves to prayer, together with the women and Mary the mother of Jesus, and his brothers" (Acts 1:14). This book is for everyone. Anyone can ask a friend in the middle of a conversation, "Could we stop and pray about that?"

That's what five Williams College students did in 1806 while taking shelter from a thunderstorm in a haystack: they started to pray for world missions. The five students were relatively wealthy, busy, and faced with a society that was increasingly cold of heart. Because of the impact of Enlightenment secularism, American church attendance was at an all-time low. And yet the haystack prayer meeting ignited a groundswell of prayer that led to the greatest period of growth the church has ever seen. Over the next hundred years, professing Christians went from 10 percent to 30 percent of the world's population.[1] And it all began with five college students praying together.

I had a front-row seat in watching and participating in the development of two praying churches over a period of twenty years where I was a deacon and then an elder—Mechanicsville Chapel and New Life Church, north of Philadelphia. But the heart of this book is my experience in cultivating communities of prayer within my family and in my ministry, seeJesus. I've worked in over two hundred churches encouraging them to become praying communities. I've mentored hundreds of pastors in cohorts, in counseling, and just in friendships. I know the slowness of cultural change, but I also know, as many of you do, the power of the Spirit of Jesus to do beyond all that we can ask or imagine!

As in all my writing, I write only about what has become a part of my life. I'm not a spiritual guru; I'm a discipler. When I was a young man, I noticed that Christians *dabbled*—bouncing from book to book, trying to stay current with the latest idea. In a world saturated with Christian values, you might get away with dabbling, but in a post-Christian and increasingly anti-Christian world, we need discipleship that produces change into the image of Jesus. That only happens when we concentrate on some aspect of Jesus long enough that we begin to look like him. My desire is to help the church look like Jesus, to have his heart, his cadences—in short, to have his prayer life. We are now his praying body.

A church hosted a gathering of artists to talk about their work: a musician, a painter, and a writer. I was the writer. When it came my turn, I explained that I was more of a craftsman than an artist, like the unnamed architects who created the soaring Gothic cathedrals. These architects weren't trying to create art for art's sake; they designed something that transported people into the heavenlies. That's my hope for this book, that the Spirit will use it to help create "virtual spaces" that draw the church into the heavenlies.

In order to craft this cathedral, I share stories from my own life. My desire is not to boast of my successes or glory in my failures but to put shoes on the ideas I'm sharing. Ideas need to connect with reality. We aren't "brains on sticks."[2] We need to see things enfleshed in the nitty-gritty of real life so we can imagine what they might look like in our own communities. I hope this makes praying together easier, as natural as asking a friend to meet for coffee. When praying together becomes perfectly normal, frequent, and filled with love, the Spirit will have given us a praying church.

2

Who Killed the Prayer Meeting?

AN EAST INDIAN EVANGELIST described his first experience at an American prayer meeting. He was visiting a megachurch known, even in India, for the pastor's outstanding preaching. He was thrilled when the pastor invited the three thousand Sunday worshipers to the midweek prayer meeting. The pastor even shared that something was "heavy on his heart" for prayer.

The evangelist couldn't wait. In India, the prayer meeting was the heartbeat of the church, where you stormed the heavens, often far into the night. The designated prayer chapel seated only five hundred, so he arrived early to get a seat. But at the designated 7:00 p.m. start time, he was alone. At 7:15, puzzled and still alone, he wondered if he had the wrong location, so he went outside to check the name. Yes, it was the same chapel the pastor mentioned on Sunday. Finally, at 7:30 a few people straggled in, chatting about sports and weather until the leader arrived at 7:45. The leader shared a short devotional with the seven attendees, prayed briefly, and closed the meeting.

The evangelist was stunned. No worship. No crying out to God for help. No senior pastor. What was heavy on the pastor's heart? What about prayer for the sick, for the lost?[1]

No one in this story thought that corporate prayer is important: not the senior pastor (he didn't show up), the congregation (only seven came), or the prayer leader (he was forty-five minutes late and only had one brief prayer). Prayer was a mere window dressing. If you doubt something, you don't think it works, so you don't use it. No one here thought prayer works. Unbelief is as practical as faith.

The State of Prayer in the Church

When we descend from the formal prayer meeting down to the smaller parts of a Jesus community and into our families and friendships, we encounter the same corporate prayerlessness that the evangelist experienced. Christians are praying, but they are doing it by themselves. According to a recent Barna study, 94 percent of American adults who have prayed at least once in the last three months do so by themselves. Barna's researcher writes:

Prayer is by far the most common spiritual practice among Americans. . . . [But] people pray mostly alone—it is a solitary activity defined primarily by the immediate needs and concerns of the individual. Corporate prayer and corporate needs are less compelling drivers in people's prayer lives. . . . But what would it look like to begin to broaden the scope of those prayer lives? To consider the power of corporate prayer—when more than one are gathered in God's name?[2]

The American church is functionally prayerless when it comes to corporate prayer. Of course, a remnant does the hidden work of prayer, but in most churches corporate prayer doesn't function in any meaningful way. How big is that remnant? In our prayer seminars, we ask several confidential questions about a participant's prayer life. In hundreds of seminars, we've found that about 15 percent of Christians in a typical church have a rich prayer life. So when someone says, "I'll keep you in my prayers," 85 percent of the time it is just words. This isn't a pastor problem; it's a follower-of-Jesus problem.

The prayer meeting, which used to function at the heart of a praying church, is all but dead. Wednesday night prayer meeting used to be the core meeting, where the most dedicated, spiritual people attended; now for many, the prayer meeting itself is a distant memory. At a recent A Praying Church seminar, I asked participants what they don't like about prayer meetings. One young man nailed it: "It's boring." Someone else added, "It's depressing." But the most poignant comment was "I don't know where I'd go to attend a prayer meeting." I asked the pastor of a three-thousand-attendee church if he knew of any prayer meetings in his church. He said, without a hint of concern, "No, I'm not aware of any."

How Secularism Killed the Prayer Meeting

Which brings us to the unique challenges of praying together in much of our modern world. We are a busy, and often wealthy, people. We didn't reach our career goals and attain the comforts we enjoy by sitting around, and yet praying together feels like we are *sitting around*. We can be so intent on building and producing that we don't pause to reflect on *what* we are building.

Behind our busyness and wealth is a philosophy called *secularism*, which doesn't just deny God's existence but denies the existence of any spiritual world. This is strange, because every culture in the history of humanity has openly acknowledged the spiritual world. You ignored God or "the gods" at your own peril. Given this history, it would be normal for every news program to open with a prayer of thanksgiving. We don't, of course, because secularism defines *normal* for us. Talking openly about God or to God feels odd.

It's no coincidence that the prayer meeting has declined simultaneously with the rise of secularism, which sees the spiritual world as mere illusion, true for you, but not true for everyone else. That comes from the eighteenth-century Enlightenment. Immanuel Kant, the Enlightenment's leading thinker (and regular church goer!) called prayer a "superstitious delusion" that God has no need to hear and that therefore accomplishes nothing.[3] Kant's god is distant, nonpersonal. Ignoring God is a far more effective than denying his existence. If you ignore him, he disappears.

Secularism remained confined largely to our universities and our elites until the rise of mass media (radio, TV, etc.) in the mid-twentieth century. Endlessly portraying a world without God and without meaning, it created a new normal. Modern agnostics are not just unsure of God's existence; they no longer care. God is a nonissue. As one young man who'd walked away from his faith said to me, "What difference does it make?"

Kant killed prayer by dividing the world into the spiritual and the physical (see fig. 2.1). The spiritual (the top half of the circle) is the realm of faith, inner feelings, and what is true only for you—it cannot be verified by sense experience. The physical (the bottom half) is the realm of facts, what can be tested by the five senses, what is true for everyone—in other words, hard reality.

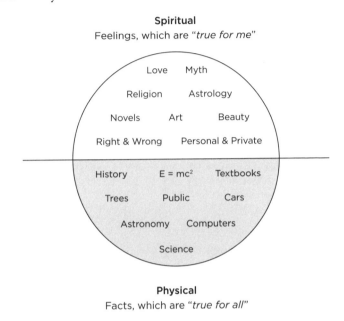

Spiritual
Feelings, which are *"true for me"*

Love   Myth

Religion   Astrology

Novels   Art   Beauty

Right & Wrong   Personal & Private

History $E = mc^2$ Textbooks

Trees   Public   Cars

Astronomy   Computers

Science

Physical
Facts, which are *"true for all"*

Figure 2.1. How most people divide the world

Figure 2.2 shows another way of looking at prayer. For the modern secularist, life is lived only on a physical plane, but prayer assumes a vertical dimension as shown by the "prayer" arrow. Prayer assumes an unseen connectedness in life. For example, Jill and I had been praying for a young man for years, that God would break down the barriers between him and his family. Just this week, we saw a remarkable breakthrough. We never mentioned a word to him about our prayer or even our desire, and yet God broke through. The connection was completely unseen. Our prayer (where the arrow starts) had no visible connection with the answer (where the arrow ends).

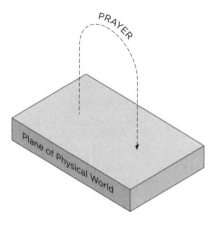

Figure 2.2. Prayer assumes an unseen connection

That unseen connection is fundamental, because the church is a three-dimensional Spiritual community. The capital *S* in "Spiritual" is deliberate. We aren't a yoga community, burning candles to get in touch with our feelings; we are a praying community, living in a personal world where the Father, by his Spirit, is constantly making Jesus come alive in our midst.[4]

When we relegate prayer to the world of feelings, prayer becomes mere therapy. If it is simply the world of feelings, then praying together feels awkward. When you talk with someone about sports, typically your conversation feels fluid—you share a common interest, language, and knowledge. You enjoy watching football and rooting for your favorite team. You both know that sports exist. But what if everyone in your life who sounded smart and powerful, and everyone you saw on TV, told you that sports are fake, that no one is really playing, and the games you see in person are just elaborate dramas? After you'd heard this nonstop, year after year, it would get into your blood.

When we combine a prayerless church with a prayerless culture, it creates a "feelings world" where God feels exalted but distant. Then when hardship comes, God feels impotent and uncaring. This is especially true if you've prayed about something difficult and the heavens have been like brass. Eventually, you don't feel anything about God. He's merely peripheral.

Because our flat, two-dimensional world rules out prayer at the outset, spontaneously praying with friends at mealtime or on the phone feels odd. We've lost the fluidity of prayer that you see in children, where in one breath they are talking to you and in the next breath they say, "Thank you, God, for no bad dreams."[5] We'll hear sermons on prayer, listen to a pastoral prayer, and begin meetings with prayer, but prayer seldom happens naturally in conversation. It just feels too religious.

That's one reason why it's a delight to fellowship with Africans or Asians, who are largely unaffected by the eighteenth-century Enlightenment. For example, for years Ugandan churches have had monthly all-night prayer meetings. They are keenly aware of the spiritual world, so prayer flows easily.

But secularism alone didn't kill the prayer meeting.

"I Killed the Prayer Meeting"

My father, Jack Miller, had recently joined the faculty at Westminster Theological Seminary when, in 1968, he decided to visit Francis Schaeffer in Switzerland. Schaeffer was already well known from his writing and the impact of his lived Christianity at L'Abri Fellowship. At L'Abri, Dad encountered something he'd never seen before: prayer operated at the center of L'Abri; the community orbited around prayer. Here are Edith Schaeffer's reflections on what a praying community looks like:

To live without prayer being woven into every part of every day is stupid, foolish, senseless, or is an evidence that your belief in the existence of the Creator, who has said we are to call upon Him, is an unsure belief. Common sense Christian living takes place in an atmosphere where prayer is as natural as breathing, as necessary as oxygen, as real as talking to your favorite person with whom there is no strain, as sensible as reaching into the bag of flour for the proper supplies for making bread.[6]

Dad was a professor at a leading seminary, an ordained minister in the Orthodox Presbyterian Church, a pastor at a local church, and a newly minted PhD, yet prayer operated at the periphery of his life. He didn't have a deep prayer life, nor had he cultivated a praying community. And yet the Spiritual power coming out of the Schaeffers and L'Abri was striking.

After Dad and Mom visited L'Abri, they also visited a ministry to former priests in Holland and an inner-city ministry in London. All three of these ministries had prayer at the center. I was fifteen at the time, but I still recall Dad puzzling over these three Jesus communities at prayer. He knew something was missing from how he "did church" and how weak our church's prayer life was. He later wondered, *Who killed the prayer meeting?* Then it dawned on him: *I killed the prayer meeting by talking too much.* So Dad stopped talking at prayer meeting and started praying.

Dad was not alone in his struggle with corporate prayer. Multiple pastors have told me how difficult it is for them to be faithful in prayer. Recently at lunch several Southern Baptist church planters said to me, "Planting a church killed my prayer life."

Something is off with how we view the church.

A Peculiar Danger

I went to dinner with a young pastor and his wife after one of our prayer seminars for pastors. As a homeschooling mom with three kids, this wife shared with me how she did life through prayer. Then she leaned over and asked her husband, with a puzzled expression on her face, "Isn't that how you do church?" He shook his head. She was so surprised, she asked him again. "No," he said. "We pray at the beginning of meetings, but it tends to be official and lack depth."

The megachurch pastor who announced the prayer meeting as if it were a high value but didn't show up didn't just devalue the prayer meeting. He sent a mixed message to the congregation. His words said one thing, but his actions another. Jesus calls that hypocrisy. In the Sermon on the Mount, Jesus singles out prayer as a "hot spot" for hypocrisy (Matt. 6:5–6). There is nothing worse for a Jesus community than looking Spiritual on the outside but being hollow on the inside. Hypocrisy in leaders creates cynicism in followers.

After I've reflected with a group of pastors on their struggles to have a consistent life of prayer, I'll ask, "How good are you at public praying?" They usually say, "Pretty good." I query again, "So, what does it do to your heart to be outwardly good at prayer but inwardly bad?" They groan, because they are good men. Of course, this applies to all of us. Any time we cultivate an outer appearance of maturity but mask inward weakness, we corrupt our soul. That weakens our best gift we offer to others—a soul that walks with God.

Now that we've reflected on why we *don't* pray, the question remains: Why *should* we pray? Why is the death of the prayer meeting in the American church even a problem? Why bother praying together? Our failure to address the *why* has resulted in the virtual death of prayer in the church. But if you get the *why*, it will transform your view of how the church works. That's the next chapter.

A Word to Pastors

Life as a pastor in a post-Christian world is overwhelming. With the moral breakdown in our culture and the resulting fracturing in our families, pastors have far more needs coming at them than they did fifty years ago. With faith burning low, people's inner core has weakened, making them thin-skinned, easily triggered. And yet they obsess over "relationships" but have little capacity for the basics, like forbearance and forgiveness. So when pastoring, you need to be slower, more careful with your words. In addition, with perfectionism on the rise, pastors are getting a lot more free advice and criticism. Pastoring has never been more difficult.

Consequently, you might feel like a camel walking through the desert, burdened with a load of bricks, and now I've just tossed on another brick called prayer. It's a particularly heavy brick because it has *guilt* written all over it. But I hope by the end of this book, you'll realize you don't need to be the camel, that you were never meant to carry a load of bricks. I hope to renew your excitement about the presence and leadership of the Spirit of Jesus in your community, possibly even making pastoring in a post-Christian world actually fun. In short, I hope to increase your faith, to restore the original wonder that led you into the pastorate in the first place.

3

The Missing Spirit of Jesus

AFTER EXPERIENCING A PRAYING community at L'Abri in 1968, Dad began to take prayer seriously. He stopped talking at prayer meeting and started praying. But he didn't know *why* prayer was important, until two years later, on a summer sabbatical in Spain, he discovered that the end times had already begun. It began on Easter morning with the resurrection of Jesus and the outpouring of the Spirit.[1]

Dad saw the close connection between the giving of the Spirit and the presence of Jesus. He was captured by Ezekiel's vision of the river of grace flowing out of the new temple in Ezekiel 47. Everything the river touches comes alive. The further out the river goes, the deeper it gets.

Jesus refers to Ezekiel's vision when, on the last day of the Feast of Tabernacles, huge vats of water are poured out in the temple, symbolizing the outpouring of the Spirit in the last days. And he stands up and cries: "'If anyone thirsts, let him come to me and drink. Whoever believes in me, as the Scripture has said, "Out of his heart will flow rivers of living water."' Now this he said about the Spirit" (John 7:37–39).

Dad realized like never before that Jesus is the new temple, with rivers of grace flowing out of him. The Spirit is now alive in his church, pouring rivers of grace into and out of us. Dad's rediscovery that the Spirit is the real, functioning center of the church transformed how he did ministry.

At the time, the church where Dad pastored part-time had only about eighty people. I was only seventeen, and my own faith wasn't particularly strong, but I remember watching my dad preach and thinking, *You can't be that excited about Jesus and not have God do something big.* Over the next year our church began to fill with the "counterculture": hippies, druggies, and just needy folks. Dozens came to know Christ.

For the next twenty years, I saw God pour out his Spirit on Dad's life. Not only was his ministry transformed; so was he. He became warmer and more joyful; he started smiling more. He also became bolder, more daring in sharing Jesus with others. It was a delight to see.

In this chapter we'll take a closer look at the connection between prayer and how the Spirit of Jesus works in his church. This understanding is crucial if you want to be a praying church.

A Typical Church versus a Praying Church

Dad's blueprint of the local church had, prior to his sabbatical, looked like figure 3.1. At the core of the typical church are important ingredients: the pastor, preaching, plans, worship, and so on. Every element in the chart is important and good. The arrows on the outside show the church reaching out with mission. The one oddity is how weak prayer is, which I've represented by graying out *prayer.*

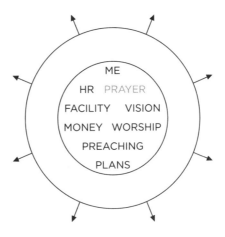

Figure 3.1. A typical church, weak in prayer

This blueprint is flawed. If you have the wrong blueprint, you'll build the wrong thing. If these were the plans for a car, I'd say that the car looks great and is comfortable, but it lacks an engine, transmission, and steering. Here's the scary thing: the blueprint of a typical church fits the narrative world of secularism, which denies the existence of any spiritual world.

This blueprint might create a business, but the church is not a normal business. It's a *Spiritual* business. It's the only business where, uniquely, the Spirit of Jesus functions at the core.

Figure 3.2, "A praying church," has the same elements as figure 3.1, "A typical church," but in a praying church the elements don't operate at the core—the Spirit of Jesus does. Prayer becomes central because the Spirit, who carries Christ to us, is central. An attentiveness to the Spirit of Jesus is the missing key to the church's prayerlessness. We struggle with prayerlessness primarily because of the way we've been taught to view the church.

Figure 3.2. A praying church, centered on the Spirit of Jesus

Below, I offer five insights to help us understand how prayer interacts with the Spirit of Jesus. Some of these insights are from another Westminster professor, Richard B. Gaffin Jr. What my dad developed practically, Gaffin developed in biblical studies.[2]

The Church's Power Train

Insight 1: Prayer accesses the Spirit of Jesus. The apostle Paul articulates a specific pattern I call the church's power train: *prayer →
Spirit → Jesus → power.* Our car's power train moves power from the engine to the transmission and then the wheels. Paul prays the church's power train in Ephesians 3: he prays to the Father for the gift of the Spirit to make Jesus present.

For this reason *I bow my knees before the Father*, from whom every family in heaven and on earth is named, that according to the riches of his glory he may grant you to *be strengthened with power through his Spirit* in your inner being, *so that Christ may dwell in your hearts* through faith—that you, being rooted and grounded in love, may have strength to comprehend with all the saints what is the breadth and length and height and depth, and to know the love of Christ that surpasses knowledge. (vv. 14–17)

Here's a paraphrased version showing the Trinity at work:

I pray to the Father ("I bow my knees before the Father") for the Spirit to continuously re-create resurrection in our lives ("that . . . he may grant you to be strengthened with power through his Spirit in your inner being"), so that Jesus possesses us ("so that Christ may dwell in your hearts through faith"), in order that we overflow with the love of Christ ("that you . . . know the love of Christ that surpasses knowledge").

Prayer is the critical spark that brings this Spirit engine to life. Consequently, prayer is not one more activity of the church—it lies at the heart of all the church's ministry. This explains something unusual about Paul's gift lists. Some people are clearly better at praying than others, and yet Paul never mentions "the gift of prayer." Why? Because there is no gift of breathing. Prayer is not an option; it's the engine. Prayer is so fundamental to the life of the church that it is not a gift given to a few.

Insight 2: Jesus now lives by the Spirit. After Dad's visit to L'Abri in 1968, he grasped the first part of the drivetrain, *prayer*, but he didn't understand the heart of the power train. His power train looked like this: *prayer → ??? → power.* It wasn't until his sabbatical that he discovered *Spirit → Jesus* at the center of the power train, that we now live in the age of the Spirit.

To understand how the Spirit works in the church, we need to understand how the Spirit works in Jesus; after all, the church is his body. Let's go back two thousand years to Easter morning to a garden tomb just outside the western wall of Jerusalem. It's still dark, and the lifeless body of Jesus lies on a cold, limestone slab inside the tomb's outer chamber. The apostle Paul gives us X-ray vision to see what happens next. "Thus it is written, 'The first man Adam became a living being'; the last Adam became *the life-giving Spirit*" (1 Cor. 15:45 AT). What does Paul mean that Jesus became life-giving Spirit? The Spirit unites with Jesus so intimately that, without losing their separate identities, Jesus and the Spirit become functionally one.[3]

Most translations obscure how radical Paul's description of Jesus's resurrection is. Here's a typical translation: "The last Adam became *a life-giving spirit.*" That doesn't say much. Jesus was already a life-giving spirit. But to say that Jesus became life-giving Spirit means that Jesus was so transformed by the Spirit that his body had become a Spiritual body.[4] Here's Gaffin's summary:

> In his resurrection he [Jesus] has been so thoroughly trans-formed by the Holy Spirit . . . that consequently they are one in the work of giving resurrection life. . . . The presence of the Holy Spirit in the church and as he indwells all believers is the indwelling presence of the exalted Christ in his resurrection life and power.[5]

Jesus and the Spirit are so united that Paul easily interchanges "Spirit" and "Lord" or joins them in a single phrase, "the Spirit of the Lord": "Now the *Lord is the Spirit,* and where the *Spirit of the Lord* is, there is freedom. And we all, with unveiled face, beholding the glory of the Lord, are being transformed into the same image from one degree of glory to another. For this comes from the *Lord who is the Spirit*" (2 Cor. 3:17–18).

Insight 3: The Spirit solves the problem of Jesus's limited body. Why did Jesus need the Spirit? As the incarnate Son of God, Jesus could be in only one place at a time.[6] The Spirit now carries Jesus to us. Or to put it simply, the incarnate Son of God is dependent on the Spirit not only for his life but also to "get around." In figure 3.3, the left side captures the constriction that Jesus experienced when he took on a human body and was obedient to the point of death on the cross. It's the constriction of love. The right side depicts the Spirit's work of "spreading Jesus out"!

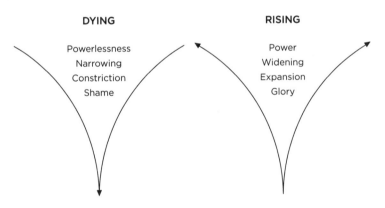

Figure 3.3. Dying and rising by the Spirit

What does this have to do with us? What does this have to do with prayer? That's the next insight.

Insight 4: If the fully human Jesus lives by the power of the Spirit, so do we. One of the Bible's most basic rules is that what happens to Jesus, happens to us. Early in Ephesians, Paul uses the pattern of the power train to pray for the Ephesians. He prays that the "Father of glory" would give them a "Spirit of wisdom" so that they would see "the immeasurable greatness of his power toward us who believe," which is identical to "his great might that he worked in Christ when he raised him from the dead" (1:16–17, 19–20). The Spirit made Jesus's body come alive, and now he continues to make Jesus's body on earth (the church) come alive. The Christian life, then, is a continual experience of the resurrection Spirit of Jesus.[7] When we pray together, the Father responds with the Spirit of Jesus, who re-creates mini-resurrections in our families and communities.

The resurrection itself is an answer to prayer. On Friday afternoon, as he was dying, Jesus cried out, "My God, my God, why have you forsaken me?" (Matt. 27:46). On Sunday morning, the Father responded with the gift of the Spirit to his Son. Then, fifty days later, at Pentecost, Jesus turned around and gifted the Spirit to us. Peter says, "Having received from the Father the promise of the Holy Spirit, he [Jesus] has poured out this that you yourselves are seeing and hearing" (Acts 2:33).

So praying together *is* good for us, and our Father *does* answer our prayers, but the Bible's vision is much bigger: we are talking about the very life of Jesus by his Spirit flowing into our lives, our families, and our communities, reflecting "the immeasurable greatness of his power."

That's why corporate prayer is so critical: *prayer is not a ministry of the church—it is the heart of ministry through which the real, functional leadership of the intimate union of the Spirit and Jesus, formed at the resurrection, operates.* Or to put it more simply: *prayer accesses the Spirit of Jesus. He runs the place.* It will take us the rest of this book to begin to see how stunning this statement is.

If you miss the Spirit of Jesus, then prayer becomes a dreary work. I'm in about eighty prayer meetings a month, but you'll seldom hear me talk about the "power of prayer." I couldn't sustain prayer if I were focused on prayer. It's the Spirit of Jesus who I want to run my life, my family, and my ministry. It's how a Jesus follower does life. My dad never made prayer central, but prayer filled his life because prayer opened the door to making the Spirit of Jesus central for large portions of his life.

Insight 5: The church at prayer lights the explosive power of the Spirit. The last word of the Spirit's power train is *power.* In Ephesians 3:14–21, Paul first prays that power would explode on the inside, that the Ephesians would be strengthened with power through his Spirit in their inner being (v. 16). Then Paul concludes by asking that the Spirit's power would explode on the outside: "Now to him who is able to do far more abundantly than all that we ask or think, according to the *power* at work within us" (v. 20). Paul strains to contain the immensity of the Spirit's power—"far more abundantly than all that we ask or think." Nor is it just power. The Spirit brings *life, glory, love,* and *wisdom.*[8] It's like an immense fireworks show with a thousand colors, brilliant lights, and one surprise after another.

The immensity of the Spirit's work was on display in Jill's conversion. Jill was one of the counterculture kids that Dad reached out to in the early 1970s when he was pastor at Mechanicsville Chapel. She had grown up in the church, but because of hypocrisy she saw in the church, her heart had become distant. She didn't want to have anything to do with preachers. She'd become friends with my sister Barb, who was going through her own rebellion.

The first time I met Jill, in fall 1970, she'd come over to our house to get help in math from Barb. In frustration, Jill threw her math book out the third-story window, not far from where I was standing. She cheerfully greeted me when she came down to retrieve it. That should have been a warning to me that life would not be boring with Jill!

The following spring Jill shared with Barb some struggles her boyfriend was having. Barb suggested that our dad might help him. Jill agreed, but she wasn't about to go into this preacher's house, so when she dropped off her boyfriend, she warned him, "He loves to talk." Waiting outside in her Mustang, Jill grew increasingly impatient. *This preacher is taking forever.* After an hour, she stormed out of the car, ready to extract her boyfriend. When she came into the house, Dad greeted her warmly and offered her a seat. When she was seated, Dad asked her: "How are you doing? How can we pray for you?" Jill burst into tears and said, "I'm not good." In that moment, Jill became a believer. It was that simple.

Notice the range of the Spirit's work. The Spirit moved with *power*, bringing *life* to Jill, all while preserving his *glory.* Dad did nothing. Notice also how surprising the Spirit's work is. It shatters our categories and expands our imaginations. The Spirit works in the box, he works outside the box, and he blows up the box! Jill's conversion was a wonder!

The mysterious working of the Spirit's power train is hidden from us. There is no visible connection between Dad's praying for two years and what happened to Jill. Jill didn't know Dad was praying for her. Dad didn't know Jill's heart struggles. Our unbelieving age looks for a reason for Jill's change other than prayer: "Jack was reaching out" or "Jill was open."

And yet, when it comes to a conversion like Jill's, we generally know the Spirit has to work, but what if the Spirit of Jesus so saturated the church that our managing, our pastoring, and our hiring all had the same flavor as Jill's conversion? What if that flavor was in our families and our friendships? That's a goal of this book, for the entire church to be *in step with the Spirit*, to feel his wonder.

We have a lot more to learn about praying together, but if you grasp the simplicity of *prayer → Spirit → Jesus → wonder*, then praying together won't be just another burden; it will be the activity that transforms all your burdens.

A Word to Pastors

Earlier I reflected that you might feel like a camel with a load of bricks. The message of this chapter is that you aren't the camel. Yes, bricks are in abundance, but they aren't yours to carry. They are the Spirit's. It seems simplistic, but it is remarkably freeing. Of course, you'll daily bear the burdens of your congregation, but if yours becomes a praying church, increasingly you'll feel like a spectator following what the Spirit is doing.

My dad used to encourage people to resign from being the third person of the Trinity. When I first got serious about prayer in my late thirties, the Spirit prompted me to write out "letters of resignation" like the one below, where I invited God to take possession of my life. It may help you to write out a resignation letter along these lines:

I officially resign from my role as the third person of the Trinity.
I submit my resignation as the Spiritual head of ___ Church (or

my family). I want Christ, by his Spirit, to be the Spiritual leader of this congregation. I no longer want to be the center. I want Christ to be the real, functional Spiritual head. I repent of any desire to control or be prominent in his body. I realize that he has entrusted me to teach and guard the flock, but I recognize it is his flock. I am merely an under-shepherd. I commit myself to being a praying pastor who desires to lead a praying congregation.

4

A Short History of the
Praying Church

BECAUSE CORPORATE PRAYER HAS FALLEN on hard times, we
don't have a sense of what it looks like. We lack context, a way of
seeing what is normal. By telling you briefly the story of prayer
in the Bible, I hope to give you some context, to show you that
praying together is not optional for the church—it's essential. In
the last chapter, we discovered prayer's inner process (the power
train); now we look at prayer's outer life.

Ancient Israel: A House of Prayer

The first mention of the people of God in the Bible states only
that they were praying. It introduces us as a praying people:
"At that time people began to call upon the name of the LORD"
(Gen. 4:26). Before even the mention of Abraham's faith, he
"called upon the name of the LORD" (Gen. 12:8). The very
name *Israel*, means "one who contends or struggles with God."
Of course, Israel's book of prayers, the Psalms, was without

parallel in the ancient world. To be an Israelite was to be a *pray-er*.

The temple itself was dedicated as a "house of prayer" (Isa. 56:7). Multiple things happened in the temple: sacrificing animals, giving tithes, and eating showbread, yet Solomon's prayer of dedication in 1 Kings 8 focuses only on prayer. Why? To understand Solomon's temple, it helps to understand the broader context of the surrounding pagan world, which also had temples. For everyone, including the pagans, a temple was the "house of god," the meeting point between heaven and earth. By definition, it was a place of prayer, the communication link between "the god" and his people. The sacrificial system repaired the damage to communication with the god by gaining the god's favor so your prayers could be heard.

At the dedication, Solomon climbs the steps to the great altar, lifts up his hands to the heavens, and prays. His prayer describes seven different problems that Israelites might encounter. Each prayer ends with something like "whatever prayer, whatever plea is made by any man or by all your people Israel . . . then hear in heaven your dwelling place and forgive and act" (1 Kings 8:38–39). Solomon's God is no mere tribal deity. He is the Creator God who has bound himself in covenant love to his people, so *he hears from heaven* (see Isa. 64:4).

Solomon's vision of the temple as the house of prayer permeates Israel. So Jonah prays in the belly of the fish, "My prayer came to you, into your holy temple" (Jonah 2:7). But all is not well. The Israelite pray-ers themselves are broken, praying to false gods. Yet even when taken captive to Babylon, Daniel prays three times a day toward the house of prayer. At the end of his life, Daniel invokes Solomon's prayer, as he repents for the sins of his people.

The prophets look forward to a day when God will transform these broken pray-ers by giving them "a new heart" (Ezek. 36:26). God himself will get inside them by "pour[ing] out my Spirit" (Joel 2:28). Even the nations will come to this house of prayer, "For my house shall be called a house of prayer for all peoples" (Isa. 56:7).

The Gospels: A Praying Person

Luke is particularly attentive to the theme of prayer. He opens his Gospel with a prayer meeting in the temple (1:10). In the parable of the Pharisee and the tax collector, the two men go "up into the temple to pray" (18:10). In Acts, Peter and John encounter a lame man when they go "up to the temple at the hour of prayer" (Acts 3:1). When Paul arrives at Philippi, he goes to the "place of prayer" to find his fellow Jews (Acts 16:13, 16). The temple is still a house of prayer.

But something is off. The opening prayer meeting in the temple is the only prayer meeting in Luke's Gospel. Jesus clears out the temple because it has ceased to be a house of prayer. The disciples never pray together; Jesus, however, will "withdraw to desolate places and pray" (5:16). We see a praying person, not a praying community.

Prayer saturates Jesus's life, but prayer for Jesus is no mere discipline. It's how the fully human Jesus does life in step with the Spirit. Jesus receives the gift of the Spirit while he is praying. "When Jesus also had been baptized and was *praying*, the heavens were opened, and the *Holy Spirit descended* on him in bodily form, like a dove; and a voice came from heaven, 'You are my beloved Son; with you I am well pleased'" (3:21–22).

As Jesus prays, "the heavens [are] opened." Jesus is the interface between heaven and earth, the place where divine-human communication happens. Notice the power train of *prayer → Spirit → Jesus → power.* Prayer leads to the descent of the Spirit, which confirms the Father's pleasure in his beloved Son. At Jesus's baptism and transfiguration, we glimpse the Trinity in conversation. That's what the drivetrain is—a divine prayer meeting.

Luke especially emphasizes that Jesus's prayers create breakthroughs. Before he selected his disciples, "all night he continued in prayer to God" (6:12). Insight emerges out of Jesus's praying life: "As he was praying alone, the disciples were with him. And he asked them, 'Who do the crowds say that I am?'" (9:18). At the Mount of Transfiguration, as Jesus "was praying, the appearance of his face was altered, and his clothing became dazzling white" (9:29). Power and wisdom flow effortlessly from Jesus's praying. Clearly, Jesus is the praying temple.

Jesus Shapes a Praying Community

In Jesus's final journey to Jerusalem, he teaches his disciples to pray by praying: "Now Jesus was praying in a certain place, and when he finished, one of his disciples said to him, 'Lord, teach us to pray, as John taught his disciples'" (Luke 11:1). The result is the Lord's Prayer:

And he said to them, "When *you* pray, say:

"Father, hallowed be your name.
Your kingdom come.
Give *us* each day *our* daily bread,
and forgive *us our* sins,
    for *we ourselves* forgive everyone who is indebted to *us*.
And lead *us* not into temptation." (Luke 11:2–4)

Notice all the plurals (italicized). Jesus is showing his disciples how to pray together. We assume that the disciples meant "Teach us to pray *individually*," but clearly Jesus was responding to the missing request "Teach us to pray *together*." What we call the Lord's Prayer is *our* prayer for praying *together*.

After showing the disciples *what* to pray, Jesus shows them *how* to pray. In the parable of the friend at midnight (Luke 11:5–8), he encourages them to ask boldly and persistently. When Jesus applies the parable, he applies it to us praying together. Seven plurals in the Greek pronouns and verbs are hidden in English: "*Ask*, and it *will be given* to *you*; *seek*, and *you will find*; *knock*, and it *will be opened* to *you*" (Luke 11:9). Here's the sense in English: *When you ask together in prayer, all of you will be given to; when you seek together in prayer, all of you will find; when you knock together in prayer, it will be opened to all of you.*

Then Jesus gets to the heart of praying—the *why*. We can pray together because Jesus's Father is our Father. He loves to give good gifts: "If you then, who are evil, know how to give good gifts to your children, how much more will the heavenly Father give the Holy Spirit to those who ask him!" (Luke 11:13). The Father's best gift is the Holy Spirit. Jesus invites his disciples into how he does life: a prayerful, waiting dependence on the Spirit.

As Jesus approaches Jerusalem (where he will be treated badly by an unjust judge), he doesn't hesitate, in the parable of the unjust judge (Luke 18:1–8), to encourage us to be like a widow who asks boldly and persistently. In the parable of the Pharisee and tax collector (Luke 18:9–14), Jesus describes two fundamentally different ways of praying. In contrast to the Pharisee's arrogance and self-sufficiency, the tax collector is childlike, aware of his frailty, saying, "God be merciful to me, a sinner." Like Jesus, he can do nothing on his own.

Change Must Happen on the Inside

I've just summarized Jesus's "course" on prayer. Even though preaching plays a significant part of his ministry, the disciples *never* ask Jesus to teach them to preach.[1] They can *preach*; they don't know how to *pray*.

At the darkest moment of Jesus's life, at Gethsemane, he tries but fails to get a prayer meeting going.[2] He pleads with Peter, James, and John, "Pray together that *you* may not enter into temptation," but he "found *them* sleeping for sorrow" (Luke 22:40, 45 AT).[3] Again, notice the plurals. Jesus pleads for his three closest disciples to pray together. They fail from sorrow. We fail from busyness and unbelief.

Gethsemane reminds us that Jesus's example and teaching, by themselves, do not produce change. His example gives us a track to run on, but without his atoning death and the gift of the Spirit, examples only depress us. You can feel Jesus's frustration. "Simon, are you asleep? Could you not watch one hour?" Later he checks on them: "And again he came and found them sleeping, for their eyes were very heavy, and they did not know what to answer him." Finally, he comes a third time, "Are you still sleeping and taking your rest?" (Mark 14:38–41). For Jesus's disciples to become a praying community, he has to get inside them.

Acts: Jesus Gets Inside

After his resurrection, Jesus gets inside his disciples: "He breathed on them and said to them, 'Receive the Holy Spirit'" (John 20:22). Immediately, we see Jesus's Spiritual presence. After his ascension, the disciples lead a ten-day prayer meeting: "All these with one accord were devoting themselves to prayer" (Acts 1:14). Just weeks before, even with Jesus right next to them, they couldn't pray. Now with Jesus on the inside, they can't stop praying. The Spirit of Jesus doesn't just respond to our prayers; he prompts us to pray.

On the tenth day of their prayer meeting, the Spirit descends "like a mighty rushing wind, and it filled the entire house where they were sitting" (Acts 2:2). Peter explains what is going on: "Having received from the Father the promise of the Holy Spirit, he [Jesus] has poured out this that you yourselves are seeing and hearing" (Acts 2:33). What Jesus got at the resurrection (the Spirit), he now gifts to his church.

Now filled with the Spirit of Jesus, Peter preaches about "this Jesus . . . [whom] you crucified and killed. . . . God raised him up." As a result, "about three thousand souls" are saved (Acts 2:23–24, 41). You can see the power train at work: *prayer* for ten days → descent of the *Spirit* → preaching about *Jesus* → *power* in conversion. Here's the point of the power train: We don't get the Spirit in the abstract. The Spirit brings Christ to us. So now, what Jesus has done individually in prayer, the disciples do corporately as the Spirit continually makes Jesus present. The praying person has become the praying community. Jesus has gotten inside.

You can see Jesus all through Acts. Like Jesus, the apostles select their leaders during an extended time of prayer: "And they prayed and said, 'You, Lord, who know the hearts of all, show which one of these two you have chosen'" (1:24). Like Jesus, they recognized prayer as a cornerstone of their lives: "And they devoted themselves to . . . the prayers" (2:42). Like Jesus, they had all-night prayer vigils when threatened by evil: "So Peter was kept in prison, but earnest prayer for him was made to God by the church" (12:5). Like Jesus, leaders saw things happen when they devoted themselves to prayer. While praying, Cornelius receives a vision from an angel, who said, "Your prayer has been heard" (10:31). While praying, Peter sees "a vision, something like a great sheet descending, being let down from heaven" (11:5). Acts should be called "The Acts of Jesus Christ, Part 2."[4]

Praying together is so fundamental that the first description of Christians recalls the words of Genesis 4:26, "people [who] began to call upon the name of the LORD" (cf. Acts 2:21; 9:14, 21). Jesus's praying heart has become the church's praying heart.

To this day, in the Arab world, when Christians go to church, they say, "I'm going to pray." Why does the Arab church, the oldest continuous church, single out prayer among all the activities of the church? Why not say, "I'm going to church"? The Arab church preserves the centrality of prayer because that's what the early church did. It saw itself as a house of prayer.

The story goes on—in every period of church history, you discover a praying church. In fact, up until the last fifty years, corporate prayer in some form has been a central feature of the church. You might find the medieval liturgy constricting, but at least they were praying. You might chafe at the coldness of some Reformed orthodoxy, but at least they were praying. You might be bothered by the legalism of American fundamentalism, but at least they were praying. We (America and the West) are the first generation in two thousand years to have lost this vision of the church as a house of prayer.

Some Reflections for Today

It's clear from this story of prayer that praying together is not optional for the church—it's fundamental. Solomon didn't preach a sermon on prayer; instead he prayed about prayer. The disciples didn't have a ten-day speaking conference; they had a ten-day prayer meeting. It's how we do church.

When I'm mentoring pastors with prayer, they become excited and want to do a sermon series on praying together. I discourage them. I want them to pray about prayer, not teach about prayer. I encourage them to slow down the horizontal (talking to people), and increase the vertical (talking to God). When our talking gets ahead of our obedience, it shuts down the Spirit's work—which lies at the very heart of effective praying.

Several years ago, I led our A Praying Church seminar with a group of pastors. We read the early church's job description for pastors when they selected the first deacons: "Therefore, brothers, pick out from among you seven men of good repute, full of the Spirit and of wisdom, whom we will appoint to this duty. But *we will devote ourselves to prayer and to the ministry of the word*" (Acts 6:3–4). Their job description is divided evenly between praying and preaching. So forty-five minutes into our first session, I asked, "How much training do you have in ministry of the word?" Hundreds of hours. Then I asked, "How much training do you have in prayer?" One pastor yelled from the back, "About forty-five minutes!" Everyone laughed, but it is a serious miss.

Then I showed them a photoshopped picture of a man whose right side bulged with muscles (ministry of the word) but whose left side was emaciated (ministry of prayer) and asked, "Do we look like this man?"

Why so little training on prayer? Partly because prayer is considered "spiritual," a vague word for floaty, positive feelings about God. Consequently, outside of the charismatic movement, little attention has been paid to the theological and biblical structure of prayer.

Like never before, our churches are increasingly discouraged and dispirited. Like never before, the church needs to be connected to the glowing power center at the core of our faith. So God's strange gifts, like the COVID-19 pandemic, slow us down and help us listen to God. We become teachable. Wouldn't it be just like the Spirit of Jesus to use the church's current weakness to make it a praying power center and thus a beacon of hope to a dying world?

PART 2

WHAT IS THE CHURCH?

5

Saints in Motion

WHEN WE TALK ABOUT THE NEED to become a praying church, no one really disagrees. Nods all around. Yep, we need to pray more. But "doing more prayer" is not the crux of it. You can't take our modern way of doing church, add more prayer, and get to a praying church.[1] Remember the megachurch where the senior pastor lauded the prayer meeting but didn't show up? The church isn't just weak in prayer; its current way of functioning makes it *prayer resistant*.

To help us see the church better, in part 2 we turn to Paul's opus on the church, his letter to the Ephesians. Paul opens Ephesians by greeting "the saints who are in Ephesus" (1:1). "Saints" are the forgotten front line, the missing key to understanding the church. When saints are overlooked, prayer is overlooked.

Let me acquaint you with three saints—Jill, Sean, and Rachel—and their experiences from a recent weekend.

Saints, the Cutting Edge

Saint 1. Jill has been quietly helping a family whose son Brian has Down syndrome. She's worked especially hard to get him work.

Joblessness is a huge problem in the world of disabilities. Workshops help, but a job gives dignity and gets kids out in the real world. Jill has been partly successful with getting work for Brian. She's also befriended Brian's mom, Morgan, an intellectual unbeliever with an allergy to Christianity. Jill's conversations with her are 99 percent love and 1 percent about faith. So Jill peppers me with questions as to what books Morgan might be willing to read. We see some seeds sprouting—Morgan has started praying. On Friday, Jill called me all excited: "Morgan is thinking of sending Brian to our church's disability ministry!"

Saint 2. On Saturday, I had breakfast with Sean, who expressed his concern for reconciliation in his family. We reflected on some tentative plans to reach out to some of the estranged family members, hoping to encourage the more mature ones to absorb the immaturity of the others. We prayed together and then committed to a time of waiting and praying.

Saint 3. On Sunday, I heard about a friend of ours, Rachel, who is in a nursing program in Philadelphia. Rachel had a patient who was dying. Her arms were filled with needle marks. The medical staff were focused on the dying woman's body, but no one was caring for her as a person—she was a prostitute. Rachel sat by the bed, held her hand, and told her, "It will be okay." Just a simple extension of love.

Jill, Sean, and Rachel are the cutting edge of the kingdom. *They are saints in motion, doing Jesus in small but costly and potentially powerful ways.* No formal mission or donation could ever pay for the work they are doing. I suspect Jill has spent a couple hundred hours befriending and helping Brian and Morgan. Of course, it's not quantifiable—Jill loves Morgan, enjoys her, and prays for her. In our own family, Jill and I are thankful for social services' help for Kim over the years, but as much as agencies want to love, it's almost like they are incapable of it. You can't monetize love.

Saints who are in motion energize praying together. Jill and I frequently pray for Brian and Morgan. Now I'm praying with Sean for his family. When you listen to and value saints like Jill, Sean, and Rachel, you feel the weight of the needs they bear. Prayer becomes a necessity. Energy and passion ripple through the kingdom. The saints are up against things they can't handle, driven by dreams they can never achieve in their own strength, so they naturally pray better. The rest of us pray better, too, by being part of their stories. Every week I could tell you a dozen saint stories. For example, Melissa posted this on Slack on a Saturday for our staff prayer meeting:

> My husband and I have the honor of hosting his family for Christmas tomorrow afternoon. None of the people celebrating with us attend church, love Jesus, or have their lives together in any recognizable way. Drugs, alcohol, bankruptcy, shame, divorce, pornography, sexual identity: you name it and it is at play here. Would you pray with us that Jesus would shine brightly tomorrow? I plead regularly that God would work his redemption among our ranks. After watching the remarkable answer to prayer last week, we wait with renewed hope.

On Monday, when we gathered for prayer, someone asked, "Melissa, how did it go?" Notice also her reference to a "remarkable answer to prayer." We saw God bring someone from death's door last week, which encouraged Melissa's faith. Faith begat faith.

When the saints are on the move, prayer times actually become interesting. So, what might have begun as feeble, even tedious prayer in time becomes a story that the Spirit shapes. Watching for those stories, and enjoying them unfold in community, in turn, fuels powerful praying. In contrast, churches tend to collect and share requests, but you seldom know what comes of them. That gap can foster that awful cancer of the soul—cynicism.

The Forgotten Front Line

No church program can duplicate the impact of a Jill, a Sean, or a Rachel. Their networks of friendships penetrate the world like no church program or paid staff can. Their lived Christianity, their authenticity, can break through walls of unbelief and cynicism like a hot knife through butter. They are the hands, feet, and mouth of Jesus.

And yet, on Sunday we hear announcements like this: "We really want you to get involved with the church. We need volunteers to take up the offering." Both sentences are correct and good, but repeatedly linking two sentences like these unwittingly equates the life of the body of Christ with institutional roles. Of course, the church needs staffing, much as the Pentagon needs staffing, but the Pentagon exists to recruit, equip, and send out the frontline solider. We want to hear what is happening on the beaches of Normandy, not the Pentagon. In fact, people like Jill, Sean, and Rachel are likely already taking up the offering, but we seldom hear about their critical frontline work. What about giving them space on Sunday morning to (discreetly) share their work of love? What about enjoying and celebrating their stories? Our churches are filled, maybe even overflowing, with these quiet lovers of people. Our surrounding community, like most, is dying for love.

Typically, we miss the glory of the saints around us. If we notice it at all, we might think, "Jill's in a hard relationship" or "Rachel is reaching out." Our inability to see the glory prevents us from listening to, valuing, and celebrating them. When you walk through a redwood forest or come upon a mountain stream, you need to stop talking, to be still in front of beauty—otherwise you miss it.

To make matters worse, the would-be therapist might tell Jill she is overextended. The therapist is right of course, but she's likely unaware that, by definition, saints overextend themselves. Look at how overextended Paul was: "I will most gladly spend and be spent for your souls" (2 Cor. 12:15). I'm not diminishing the importance of rest—I'm talking about a way of seeing and celebrating people that's missing.

The difference between the therepeutic vision and the "saints vision" is subtle. Is Sean, with his family struggles, someone who needs a good counselor, or is he a saint doing the good but hard work of love as he dives into a tough problem? Perhaps both. But if we miss the latter, we will neuter the saints' natural passion, born of faith.

A godly mom, who is free from any spirit of complaining and loves her church, shared this with me without a trace of animosity: "The saints' stories often seem so minor that I think the saints don't even see the story themselves. Many pastors I know don't know much if anything about the details of people's personal lives of love, so they don't have access to enjoy and celebrate stories." Of course, there are many exceptions. Especially in smaller churches, the pastors know the saints. I know a pastor of a midsize congregation who takes a day to job shadow each member of his congregation.[2]

Our inability to see saints as they are engaged in their daily callings distorts our view of the church and neuters prayer. Prayer stories never take root and grow. No one is sharing the wonder because no one beckons,

Come and hear, all you who fear God,
> and I will tell you what he has done for my soul. (Ps.
> 66:16)

Lives become lackluster. The story becomes stale. But when we see and celebrate saints at work, praying together comes alive in vibrant and fresh ways. Prayers are enlarged from purely personal needs (health, safety, success) to tuning into what the Spirit is doing in multiple lives.

"Saint Lumber"

So, what is the church? What's the point of contact of the Spirit's power with reality? Paul's answer: *the saints!* After all, we are his body. In Ephesians 2, Paul helps his Gentile readers see the church as a living temple.

> So then you are no longer strangers and aliens, but *you are fellow citizens with the saints* and members of the household of God, built on the foundation of the apostles and prophets, Christ Jesus himself being the cornerstone, in whom the whole structure, being joined together, grows into a holy temple in the Lord. *In him you also are being built together into a dwelling place for God by the Spirit.* (vv. 19–22)

The entire structure is built out of "saint lumber": "you are fellow citizens with the saints." Paul does mention the role of leaders: "the apostles and prophets" lay a foundation; this likely refers to the original apostolic church planters and/or the New Testament itself. But even the apostles build on Christ, the chief cornerstone, which in the ancient world would stabilize and align the entire building. The cornerstone (Christ) and foundation stones (apostles) are usually hidden.[3] When we step back and look at the entire building, we see saints. "In him you are also being built together into a dwelling place for God by the Spirit."

Paul's vision of the church in Ephesians, as well as what we see in Acts, has three major functional elements:

- The most important thing is the *Spirit of Jesus.*
- *Praying together* accesses the Spirit of Jesus.
- This empowers the *saints* and pushes them out into mission.

When the church's power train (*prayer* → *Spirit* → *Jesus* → *power*) empowers the saints, the whole church comes alive. People experience a reality of the risen Christ that kills unbelief and cynicism. The Spirit's energy empowers the little people, allowing the kingdom to come in real time. Jesus is enfleshed.

Saints or Consumers?

In contrast to Paul's vision in Ephesians, here's a functional description of the modern evangelical church:

- The most important part of the week is *Sunday morning.*
- *Good preaching* is the most important part of Sunday morning.
- Consequently, the *preacher* is the most important part of the church.[4]

Each of these three elements above is not just good but excellent, but by having them at the center, where the Spirit of Jesus should be, this model can be prayer resistant. Saints unwittingly become consumers. In megachurches, they consume experience, and in more theologically in-tune churches, they consume theology.

Let's look at each of these three elements in turn, beginning with Sunday morning. First, let me clarify. If I had to pick the single most important *signal* that someone is not doing well Spiritually, I'd say lack of church attendance. Prior to the pandemic, my car mechanic told me that he and his wife had stopped attending church. They hadn't rejected the faith; they just didn't have a reason to go. I was so surprised, I said nothing, but the next time I brought my car in, I told him, "I've decided not to do any more maintenance on my car since it's running fine." He smiled, but he didn't change his behavior.

Neglecting the Sunday gathering is a signal of trouble. But there is a difference between something being *a signal* and something being *central*. Church attendance is a metric, not a goal. While many New Testament texts presuppose the importance of gathering to worship, the fact remains that we have only one exhortation in the entire New Testament for church attendance (Heb. 10:25). Following the collapse of church attendance in America, if we were Puritans, we would *not* say, "How do we get people to come back?" but "What's wrong with us?"

Likewise, regarding the second major element—preaching. Again, let me clarify. Like the apostles in Acts 6, we need the dual ministry of the word and prayer. My father taught me as a child that heresy is *truth out of balance.* That is, we need both columns in table 5.1. The table shows how prayer and preaching operate together. (These are broad generalizations, subject to multiple nuances.)

Table 5.1. How preaching and prayer work together

	Preaching the Word	Praying Together
Who does it?	Pastors/teachers	Whole body
What are the saints doing?	Listening	Speaking
Effect on the saints	Feeds the saints	Empowers the saints
What if it's solely emphasized?	Truth without power; doctrine without life. Can tend to legalism and coldness of heart.	Power without truth; zeal without knowledge; life without doctrine. Can tend to lawlessness and is led by feelings.
What does it create?	Categories and content for becoming like Jesus.	Power and life for becoming like Jesus.
How to improve it	Saturate with prayer.	Saturate with God's word.

I'm emphasizing the right column—praying together—because the church is weaker here. *Truth is out of balance.* Jesus's life is saturated with Scripture, but still Jesus leans on the right column. We have no record of the disciples asking Jesus, "Teach us to preach." We have a sample prayer given to show us how to pray, but we have no sample sermon given specifically to show us *how* to preach. We have multiple parables valuing the importance of prayer, but none specifically on the value of preaching. (The parable of the sower is on the effect of preaching on various hearers, like seeds on various soils.) Jesus pleads with his disciples at Gethsemane to pray together, not to preach together. Possibly, we see this leaning in Jesus's teaching because we leaders lean toward talking. Schools of public speaking were everywhere in the Greco-Roman world—speaking was a high value in that culture.

Those of us in speaking ministries need a ministry of prayer like flowers needs rain. The ministry of God's word, regardless how Christ-centered, is delivered by us. We are visibly at the center. Everyone is looking at us. But in a prayer meeting, no one is looking at us. Seldom do we see immediate results. In fact, there is no visible link between the activity of praying and what the Spirit does. At multiple levels, a prayer meeting is an exercise in dying. We need the dying of prayer to balance the rising of preaching. This applies to all of us. The godly mom I mentioned earlier told me: "I am praying for a praying community to develop in our home. Learning to die to my 'control' has been an antidote to my 'preaching' to my kids!" Even good "preaching" (like this mom's) needs good praying, or we begin to rely too much on the power of our horizontal words, when what we need is more vertical words.

Preaching, if done well, also has a dying side, as the preacher first pours himself out in study and then in the preaching. Nevertheless, preaching requires getting people's attention. In the dying of prayer, few if any notice. Good preaching exalts Christ and not the preacher, but the act of preaching itself (the pastor is higher up so people can see; he's talking and everyone is listening) increases the *potential* for pride. Jesus points out that prayer, too, can be turned into a show that puts you at the center, but even here Jesus is referring to a public prayer where everyone is looking (Matt. 6:5–6).

I'm not denigrating preaching. Some activities are just potentially more dangerous for the soul. Jesus's caution about turning fasting into a show doesn't mean he opposes fasting (Matt. 6:16–18). The problem isn't preaching but the *potential* sins that preaching can set us up for. Praying together, by being so hidden and so slow, potentially kills those sins. And while it's also true that the results of preaching are often not immediate, the preacher often gets immediate positive feedback. Prayer needs time to develop, often over many years.

Now let's look at the third element—the preacher. Paul's functional description of how a church works in Ephesians barely mentions leaders and leadership gifts. When Paul does mention leaders, they are primarily servants of the saints. "And he gave the apostles, the prophets, the evangelists, the shepherds and teachers, to *equip the saints* for the work of ministry, for building up the body of Christ" (4:11–12).

Every pastor I know affirms this text, but I see five distinct "misses" in how the modern church relates to this task of equipping the saints.

Five Equipping Errors

First, we may assume that the sermon alone equips. Later (chap. 24), I tell the story of discipling two young men struggling with sexual temptation by teaching them to pray. When I shared this story with the same godly mom mentioned above, her response touched my heart. "Could you address the man who will respond to this story by saying, 'Nice for them to have five years of discipling, but I don't have that option in any community in my life.'" Her lament describes most churches—most do not have a discipling structure. Preaching by itself hadn't changed these young men. When it came to the sins that gripped their lives, they had become *preaching resistant*. They needed the close work of equipping-by-discipling, where someone tenaciously focused on the goal of a Christ-like purity. Preaching might inspire them, but they needed the ongoing "grunt work" of accountability along with the daily grind of faithful praying for them. Jesus told his disciples (about their failure to cast out a demon), "This kind cannot be driven out by anything but prayer" (Mark 9:29). Jesus had prayed. They hadn't.

Second, preaching can lose an equipping goal and become an end in itself. A leader in a church-planting movement told me recently,

"All our church planters really want to do is preach." He wasn't being negative or critical, just commenting on their desire. Notice he didn't say, "All our church planters really want is for Christ to be formed in their churches." I've often heard comments that focus on the process (preaching) and not the product (saints who reflect the beauty of Jesus).

By my third year of teaching in urban Christian schools, I'd become a good teacher, that is, until I started teaching math. My students did miserably on their first test. Their low grades measured my equipping ability, not their intelligence. So I completely revamped how I taught. I began to teach less, come alongside them as they worked, and give them a short weekly test on Fridays. I even stopped using colorful illustrations, because I noticed that they'd enjoy a story but miss the point. My teaching actually got a little flatter, but their learning improved dramatically because I was focused not on my teaching but on the goal of teaching. In other words, I shifted from what I thought was teaching to *teaching to equip*.

I will never forget seeing, as a young man, my dad's preaching overflow with love for Jesus and his ache that saints enter that love. Paul's prayers in Philippians 1, Colossians 1, and Ephesians 1 overflow with this goal of Christlikeness. Of course, a love of preaching potentially includes multiple good loves—love of Scripture, love of communicating well—but, still, a love for preaching can easily become a love for a process, not an end, a *telos*.

Third, without this equipping goal, focusing on preaching and the preacher can breed a celebrity culture. Celebrity culture has bedeviled the evangelical church. In Paul's Ephesians paradigm, the primary task of leaders is to equip the saints, to seek out these hidden warriors, train them, honor them, encourage them, and pray with and for them. That involves a radical decentering of the role of the leader. Leaders exist for the people we serve, not for ourselves or even our church's expansion (as good as that is!).

Fourth, the saints, then, can be forgotten. Pastors and leaders are appropriately on the inside—and every culture needs insiders. So, instinctively, we want to bring the outside in, to minister to more and more people on Sunday morning. Maximizing Sunday attendance becomes a benchmark for how well we are bringing outsiders in, and it's tempting to view them as validating the pastor. Paul flips that. He turns the organization chart upside down by putting leaders at the bottom, as equippers, and *saints* at the top, as the leading edge to the world. The *inside* exists for the *outside*.

Paul is not trying to include the "little people" as an expression of love—the gifts of leadership *exist* to equip these frontline warriors—not the other way around. The Spirit of Jesus empowers the saints, not the institution. Of course, the church is both organism and organization, both in need of the Spirit and all his fruit, but the Spirit of Jesus builds up saints, not disembodied structures, statistics, or leaders' egos. Jesus is more concerned about heads, hearts, and hands serving in his name than about head counts that bolster the church's name. A failure to value and equip the "little people" verges on institutional idolatry.

The Gospel of Luke especially focuses on the "little people." In the first two chapters we meet a village priest and his wife (Zechariah and Elizabeth), a carpenter and his pregnant fiancée (Joseph and Mary), some grungy shepherds, and a couple of old folks praying in the temple (Simeon and Anna). Even before Jesus can speak, the little people are the conduit to the coming kingdom. Jesus himself embodies this pattern as he honors and empowers the outcasts and the marginal, but Jesus isn't merely honoring the little people; the kingdom comes in and through the "least of these" (see Matt. 25:40, 45).

The quiet people in our churches are enmeshed in multiple relationships. When they are equipped, empowered, and honored, the Spirit takes them in amazing directions—as he took Jill first to a disabled young man and his mom, Rachel to a dying prostitute, and Sean to work on family reconciliation. Each is on mission. The unseen wind of the Spirit enables the "least of these" to do beyond all that we can ask or think (Eph. 3:20).

Fifth, if the saints are marginalized, the church can become prayer resistant. When the Barna Group asked pastors to rank their twelve top priorities, prayer was at the bottom of the list. Only 3 percent identified prayer as a major priority.[5] Prayer resistance is not just a bad habit; it's a resistance to the vision, direction, and power of the Spirit of Jesus. Prayer meetings are peripheral because without supernatural passion, you don't need supernatural means.

When the Spirit of Jesus moves to the functional center of the church, everything at the center (pastor, facility, etc.) moves slightly to the periphery. That allows the Spirit to empower the outer edge of the church, where Jill, Rachel, and Sean come alive (see the arrows in fig. 5.1). All of us who are leaders must say, "He must increase, but I must decrease" (John 3:30).

Here's my point: When the Spirit of Jesus becomes the captain, the ship itself begins to change. Instead of a professional and program-driven ministry, the saints are energized and equipped for mission. This takes enormous pressure off pastors. The entire dynamics of the congregation are reshaped around mission—which many are already doing!

Figure 5.1. A praying church unleashes the saints

Saints are natural dreamers, enticed by the Spirit to work and live in daring ways; but without an encourager calling them to greatness and pulling them out of the doldrums, that all withers, and passion never takes flight. But when it does, then prayer becomes critical, because the saints need help. When the power train is connected to kingdom vision and passion, all heaven breaks loose.

6

Feeding the Saints

I KNOW OF THREE LARGE CHURCHES in southeastern Pennsylvania whose attendance is down 50 percent. They've all responded with a sermon series on the vision of their particular church. Their logic is simple: "Lots of our people aren't going to church anymore. Let's inspire them with how important the church is."

I know three mature Christians in these churches who have reacted to these vision series. I was at lunch with one of them. He put his head between his hands, let out a sigh, and said, "It's so '90s." Another businessman told me his wife—a successful businesswoman herself—somewhat playfully has been trying to remember their new two-word mission statement on their way to church. Every Sunday for the last four months, they've repeated these two words. Before each sermon, a video pulsates the two words. She's bright, but still finds it elusive. The third person, also a businessman, has felt the same "selling" but has befriended and prayed with his pastor (who is near collapse from the pressure of the pandemic).[1]

These three Christians have been faithful to their churches despite the drop in attendance. All of them have extensive marketing experience in their work. What are they reacting to? They are recoiling from their churches unwittingly feeding people church. You can eat Christ, but you can't eat church. These churches have missed what saints are: Spiritual beings who can sustain love only by feeding on Christ. *Marketing the church* doesn't energize love. *Faith* energizes love (Gal. 5:6). Plus, it makes no sense: If your business is failing, why spend energy telling your remaining customers how good your business is? These churches' power trains look like this: *marketing → church → powerlessness.*

The three Christians I've described are reacting to a subtle form of idolatry that I call "soft idolatry," where the church itself is worshiped. It's not classic idolatry, where you worship a false god; it's what Augustine calls a "disordered love." So, for example, a family who regularly misses church because of sports. The parents' love for their kids' success in sports is elevated above love for the body of Christ. Enjoying success in sports isn't bad, but in this case it's a love that is out of order.

Prayer and soft idolatry don't mix well. God hasn't designed prayer as a means of making idols work. The prophets seldom criticized Israel for their prayerlessness; the problem was their idolatry, which radically misdirected prayer (Ezek. 14:7–8).

I believe one reason why God permitted the COVID pandemic was to expose this disordered love—suffering always exposes our true loves. The Spirit wants us to shift our gaze from looking at ourselves to looking at Jesus.

A poignant description of soft idolatry comes from my mom, who wrote Dad this letter in 1983:

As I watch you in your struggles and labors and your desire to be God's man in this 20th century, I also see the mission work and the church taking your time and energies. They are the source of your deepest joys and greatest fears. You nourish and cherish them as a bridegroom his bride. When we wake up in the morning your thoughts are usually on the church, the discipleship group, neighbors, church, your writing, the missions team, and your teaching and preaching.

Your daytime energies are directed in these areas, and at night, they are still with you. I don't mean to imply that this is all in the energy of the Flesh. No one could do all these things unless empowered by the Holy Spirit. I am saying that, as I study Ephesians 5, I read that there is a holy energy that goes into marriage from the husband to the wife.

The other day when I asked if we could have tea together or just go out, I wanted to say some of these things, but your response was: "I thought we had enough of problems." I forgive you, and I forgive you for making the church and the mission your first love, but I'm not sure I am helping you by keeping quiet.

I have learned to accept this as a way of life, but is it God's norm? You often say you want to be a man controlled and compelled by the promises of Scripture, a man of prayer and patience, and a perpetual learner. God is making you all of this, but I rarely hear you desire to be taught how to nourish and cherish your wife as Christ does the church.

I tell the story behind this letter later in part 3, but notice how, at this point in his life, soft idolatry had weakened Dad's ability to love. Dad had discouraged a saint.

Idolizing the church is extraordinarily hard to see because it has *Jesus* plastered all over it. As God poured out his Spirit on New Life Church, at times we began to think we were special.

We struggled, for example, to enjoy people leaving the church, even when it was for good reasons. Our love for our church kept us from blessing people that God called elsewhere. Our loves, at times, were disordered.

Idols, like black holes, suck in everything around them. They demand allegiance. So the saints move from being the church to being *resources* for the church. Saints function merely as feeders. They feed the church by attending, giving, and helping. Praying together then becomes superfluous. If you are doing human things in human strength, there is little need for the Spirit's "magic."[2]

But the saints are uncomfortable with this. The three Christians above didn't like being treated as objects of marketing campaigns. My mom recoiled from a lack of being cherished.

So, what do saints need? What do Jill and Sean and Rachel need on Sunday morning? How do we equip these front-line warriors? Let's see how Paul fed the saints in Ephesians 1–3.

Paul Feeds the Ephesians by Praying over Them

In Ephesians 1, Paul feeds Christ to the saints by praying over them. In the fashion of the early church, Paul lifts his hands over his brothers and sisters and pours Jesus into them.

> <u>Blessed</u> be the God and Father of <u>our</u> Lord Jesus Christ, who has <u>blessed us</u> *in Christ* with every [S]**piritual** <u>blessing</u> *in the heavenly places*, even as he chose <u>us</u> *in him* before the foundation of the world, that <u>we</u> should be holy and blameless before him. (vv. 3–4)

Notice four things about this prayer that I've emphasized with underlining, boldface, and italics.

First, this is an ancient Hebrew blessing. Paul emphasizes this by repeating forms of the word "bless" three times (underlined). Blessings are sideways prayers—spoken to other believers but indirectly to God. So in Psalm 103:1, David addresses his soul, "Bless the LORD, O my soul."

Blessings are specialized prayers that convey divine energy. So Isaac blessed Jacob; Jacob blessed his sons; Aaron blessed all of Israel. Because my dad preached a sermon on blessings many years ago, I began to regularly put my hands on each of our six children after story time at night and bless them. They all still remember it. They were blessed.

Why a blessing? The saints are exhausted. Our trio of Jill, Sean, and Rachel are weary. Morgan never got back to Jill about Brian possibly coming to our church; Sean's family is still brittle; and Rachel lost track of the woman in the hospital. That's the life of a Jesus follower on the front lines. We all need regular infusions of divine energy.

Second, Paul feeds the saints by giving them a window into the immensity of God's love for them "in Christ" (and equivalents, italicized). The entire blessing goes from Ephesians 1:3 to 1:14.[3] It's the longest blessing in the New Testament. If you look at Paul's entire blessing, he points them to some version of all that we have in Christ eleven times. The saints' greatest need is to know the immensity of the Father's love for them in Christ. That knowledge constantly leaks and needs to be replenished. Paul builds their faith by taking them into a cascade of the Father's love for them in Christ.

Third, Paul emphasizes that he too is one of the saints. In verses 3–14 he uses fourteen plural Greek pronouns (see "us," "we," "our," also underlined in the quoted sample), laboring to include himself in the "we." He stands with his fellow saints. He, the great apostle Paul, needs to see Jesus too.

Finally, hidden in Paul's blessing is the church's power train: *prayer* → *Spirit* → *Christ* → *power* (bold). Paul doesn't teach the power train; he prays it over the church. He doesn't tell them about the car; he takes them on the ride of their life. Paul equips the saints by being a conduit of *Spiritual* power and life to them. That's what praying together does.

Paul Feeds the Ephesians by Being Constant in Prayer

Now that he's prayed over the Ephesians, Paul will preach, right? Nope. He is just warming up. He shifts his prayer from blessing to asking. The church's power train (bold) once again forms the structure of Paul's prayer as he prays to the Father (1:16–17) for the gift of the Spirit (1:17–19) to open their eyes to see the immensity of the resurrected and enthroned Christ (1:20–23). Paul's vision of the exalted Christ so captures him that he begins to worship (1:21–23). Here's Paul's opening:

> I do not cease to give thanks for you, **remembering you in my prayers,** that the God of our Lord Jesus Christ, **the Father of glory, may give** you the **Spirit of wisdom** and of revelation in the knowledge of him, having the eyes of your hearts enlightened, that you may know . . . what is the immeasurable greatness of his power toward us who believe, according to the working of his great might **that he worked in Christ** when he raised him from the dead and seated him at his right hand in the heavenly places. (1:16–20)

Paul doesn't teach the church about prayer; he breathes the Spirit's life as he prays by leading them in a virtual worship service. The apostle isn't modeling prayer; his prayer is the Spirit's conduit to bring the life of Jesus into the Ephesian community. Paul is doing church even as he teaches the foundation of the church—the love of God in Christ Jesus. Almost the entire first chapter (vv. 3–23) is a prayer of blessing, asking, and worshiping. Now you have some sense of why I was surprised when one of the senior leaders of a megachurch told me he was unaware of any prayer meetings in his church. This man loved the Lord, but he and the other leaders weren't doing church—they had a speaking and worship business.

Paul breaks off his prayer in Ephesians 2 and then picks it up in 3:1—"For this reason I, Paul, a prisoner of Christ Jesus on behalf of you Gentiles"—only to interrupt himself and describe yet more wonders in the gospel. Finally, Paul brings his prayer to a close by praying the church's power train once again:

> For this reason **I bow my knees before the Father,** from whom every family in heaven and on earth is named, that according to the riches of his glory he may grant you to be **strengthened with power through his Spirit** in your inner being, **so that Christ may dwell in your hearts through faith**—that you, *being rooted and grounded in love, may have strength to comprehend with all the saints what is the breadth and length and height and depth, and to know the love of Christ that surpasses knowledge, that you may be filled with all the fullness of God.* (Eph. 3:14–19)

This is now the third time in Ephesians 1–3 that Paul has prayed the power train. So the complete power train looks like this: *prayer → Spirit → Jesus → power → saints.* Paul prays the power train because the *saints* have a capacity problem (see italics in quote). We don't have enough capacity "to know the love of Christ that surpasses knowledge," so we need to be "rooted and grounded in love." Paul is referring not to our love for others but to our awareness of God's love for us. We call that faith.

Why pray for faith? Because life drains faith. If your spouse gives you a steady diet of criticism, that can drain your faith. Criticism says you aren't worthy. Faith says you are. If you have a dead-end career, going to work every day drains your faith. If you are a single woman, the longing to be married when there are no prospects on the horizon can drain your faith. When life's raw evidence says you aren't worthy of love, faith says you are loved more than you can imagine. Paul feeds the saints because the saints are famished.

Notice how prayer flows effortlessly throughout Ephesians 1–3:

- Ephesians 1: introduction → prayer of blessing → prayer of asking →
- Ephesians 2: sermon →
- Ephesians 3: short prayer → short sermon → closing prayer

Paul isn't interrupting himself; he's *constant in prayer*. Maybe the best analogy is our cell phones. Many of us are *constant in cell-phone use*. Phone checking has become a primary rhythm of our lives. It's so ubiquitous, people are seldom offended when you glance down at your phone in a meeting. Everyone does it. That's exactly what constant in prayer is like.

Why pray? Why not just teach faith? Paul isn't shy about teaching faith, but ultimately faith is Spiritually discerned. We need the Spirit's magic touch in order to know the immensity of our Father's love for us in Christ. So when Paul teaches the Ephesians about the church, he leads a prayer meeting. He prays his letter: 45 percent of Ephesians 1–3 is Paul praying. It's almost perfectly balanced between praying and preaching. He doesn't just instruct the Ephesians; he does church, "sparking Jesus" in their midst.

Strikingly, Paul's opus on the church centers not on the church but on Christ. We do church best when we don't look at church but gaze at Christ. Nor does Paul center on prayer. He centers on Jesus and all he is for us. Prayer is the church's lifeblood because it's the conduit to the Spirit continually renewing in us Jesus's resurrection life. I get itchy when people talk almost exclusively about the power of prayer or how amazing prayer is. Prayer merely accesses the Spirit, who makes Jesus present. That's why we go to church. To eat Christ. He's the center. He's everything.

In closing, table 6.1 summarizes two different ways of *doing church*.

Table 6.1. Contrasting ways of "doing church"

	Typical Evangelical Church	Paul's Ephesians Model
What is the church's power train? What makes a good church?	Good preaching + pastoring + vision + generosity. *(Each of these is wonderful, but they aren't the power train.)*	In response to prayer, the Father continually pours out his Spirit so that the saints overflow with Jesus's love.
What does the power train move?	The answer is not clear. Growth? Attendance?	The saints and their beautification!
What place does prayer have in the church?	Prayer is good, but we are all so busy. Prayer is delegated to a few prayer warriors.	Prayer at all levels continually ignites Spiritual wisdom, power, love, and glory.
What is the church?	The gathering on Sunday for worship, fellowship, and preaching. *(Sunday is critical, but it's not the church.)*	The saints, attentive to their "head," overflowing with love for Jesus and one another, who then love to gather Sunday to be filled with prayer and the preaching the word.

Table 6.1 *(continued)*

	Typical Evangelical Church	Paul's Ephesians Model
Who are the primary ministers?	The pastors, elders, and ministry leaders. *(Thank God for pastors, who labor tirelessly especially with the critical saints! But they are not primary.)*	All the saints. *(We wear out our pastors if we make them primary.)*
What's the role of pastors and staff?	To provide the structures to make the church happen, especially preaching. *(Good preaching is critical! But there's more.)*	To equip, encourage, and enjoy the saints in their countless ministries. To feed Christ to the saints with preaching and prayer.
What is the leadership attitude toward the saints?	The laity are encouraged not to be consumers, which they often act like.	The saints are the church! They need to be encouraged to be what they are—saints!
What is the role of programs?	The staff makes sure five to ten crucial programs are staffed. *(Programs are important, but the informal ministries are powerful.)*	Each saint runs five to ten informal ministries (like Jill's, Sean's, and Rachel's). Leaders focus on equipping, thus multiplying the saints' effectiveness.
How is outreach done?	By programs. *(It is good to have several outreach programs. But programs cannot duplicate the saints' hundreds of relationships.)*	The entire congregation reaches out into their families and communities.
How do we measure success?	Sunday attendance, budget, and a strong lead pastor. *(Growth in numbers is wonderful, but it's a secondary metric to love and faith.)*	Are we growing in love and unity, overflowing with the love of Christ? Do we look more like Jesus?
What if there is a pandemic and we can't meet Sunday?	The church stops being church because we aren't meeting together.	We consciously enter a fellowship of his suffering. Fewer programs allow for more in-depth discipling.

A Word to Pastors

Rediscovering the *saints* is remarkably liberating. It gives you less to do and more to celebrate. You'll do more discovering and enjoying of what the Spirit is doing instead of trying to make things happen. Instead of trying to create waves, you ride them. If the gospel liberates our conscience, rediscovering the *saints* liberates our ministry. Plus, it encourages the saints, giving honor and dignity to their work. I continue to be impressed with the multiple burdens that many saints cheerfully bear. Treating them as saints, calling them to greatness of faith and love, gives them clear tracks on which to run.

7

Are Saints Real?

IN CHAPTER 5, WE DISCOVERED that the saints are often not valued. Consequently, they are not enjoyed, honored, or equipped. In chapter 6 we discovered why saints aren't valued—at times, we've idolized the church. Feeding saints *church* as an end in itself leaves them starving and weak, while praying Christ into saints energizes them for ministry. Now we look at a deeper reason why saints are overlooked: a failure to believe that saints are even real. Let me explain.

Why Jill Jumped

At our annual staff retreat I read Richard Gaffin's insights on saints:

> At the core of their being, in the deepest recesses of what they are—in other words, in the "inner self"—believers will never be more resurrected than they already are. God has done a work in each believer, a work of nothing less than resurrection proportions that will not be undone. Such language . . . is not just a metaphor.[1]

Jill just about jumped out of her chair and asked, "Where is that?" She was so startled, everyone laughed. I told her Gaffin was reflecting on the verse "Therefore, if anyone is in Christ, he is a new creation. The old has passed away; behold, the new has come" (2 Cor. 5:17).

I knew why Jill jumped. First, most of her life she had been immersed in solid Reformed teaching, but she'd never heard that at the core of her being, her heart, she would never be more resurrected than she already was. In other words, Jill had never heard that she *really* is a holy person, a saint. We don't see *saints* among us because we don't believe they are real. If our identity as saints is true only *positionally*, but not *actually*, then the word *saints* is almost meaningless, like a participation award.

Second, Jill had experienced the implications of this missing category of saints. When Kim was young, Jill didn't feel enjoyed or celebrated when, as a young mom, she dropped out of church ministry to do the hidden work of love, where you give and give, and fewer and fewer results are noticed. Jill jumped at Gaffin's insights because she immediately sensed how encouraging this forgotten truth is. She'd felt the sin-guilt-forgiveness side of her faith, but not the resurrection-hope-saint side. She'd experienced the church program side, but not the enjoying-the-saints side. One side isn't better than the other—we need both!

If saints don't exist, if holy people really aren't holy, then the pews are filled not with front-line warriors like Jill and Sean and Rachel but with consumers. Consumers need to be catered to, entertained. They can also be cranky, so Sunday morning needs to be slick. All of which leaves pastors tense and exhausted. This, of course, makes prayer merely peripheral, because praying together requires discipline, work, and faith—all of which are weak in consumers. This might describe the modern church but, thank God, not Paul's vision of saints.

Saints Are Lovers: Lovers Are Pray-ers

In Ephesians 4, Paul tells the saints what they should do. In a world gripped by evil (vv. 17–19), he calls saints to an exuberant love dripping with humility that absorbs slights, overlooks insults, and extends forgiveness.[2] Paul calls his fellow saints to a 24-7 love because he assumes they are capable of it. You see that assumption in verse 1: "Walk in a manner worthy of the calling to which you have been called." It's a constant theme in Paul's writings: "For at one time you were darkness, but now you are light in the Lord. Walk as children of light" (Eph. 5:8). Paul assumes a definitive work of the Spirit in our hearts.

When Paul looks at the Ephesians, he sees what they really are—saints. That shapes his call to greatness: he repeatedly encourages the church to be what they already are. Of course, this side of heaven, we continue our fight with the flesh, but Paul's affirmation that we are saints gives a positive, encouraging tone to his call to maturity.

The reality of our saintliness aligns perfectly with the work of love. The Jill, Rachel, and Sean stories show that we define *ministry* too narrowly. Once you broaden your definition of *ministry* to "saints in motion," then Paul's emphasis on doing love in Ephesians 4–5 makes sense. What do saints do? They love. So love defines what they do (living with a difficult spouse) and how they do it (persistently, gently, faithfully, humbly).[3] We've not gone from theology to application, but from doing faith (Eph. 1–3) to doing love (Eph. 4–5). Saints are both believers (1:1) and lovers (4:1).[4] When doing love becomes mere application, it weakens the church, relegating love to a backwater.

If ministry is love, that greatly expands our definition of ministry. All of life for a Christian is ministry. So the person enduring in a difficult marriage is doing the ministry of humility. The person enduring with a disabled child, likewise, is constantly being drawn down into the death of Jesus so Jesus's life can come in and through him or her. Living and working with not-yet-perfected saints requires incredible patience, forgiveness, and forbearance. Paul himself was "a prisoner for the Lord" (4:1)—many, many saints are in prison-like situations, stuck but still loving.

"Become what you are" is a radically different perspective from "Stop being what you are." Even when Paul goes negative, he tends to say, "Stop being what you *aren't*." He reorients how we see ourselves as saints. That reorientation needs to begin with how we see one another.

What does this have to do with prayer? In our prayer meetings, I often connect people's seemingly mundane requests with their sainthood. So when Melissa asked for prayer for her dysfunctional family at Christmas, I cheered her on, telling her that she isn't just unloading another prayer request, but she is a saint on the cutting edge of the kingdom. When I do this, the saints light up. With a little encouragement and lots of prayer, saints blossom.[5]

The Spirit has imprinted our souls with the image of Jesus. Consequently, we really and truly are saints. The only way we can sustain superhuman love is by asking our Father to keep doing what he did at Jesus's resurrection and now has done permanently at the core of our being. So when we pray, we are asking the Father to give us the Spirit yet once again in order to bring us Christ so that he will resurrect something broken in our lives. That's why prayer is like *breathing* for a working saint. When most Christians start praying, they think they are moving *out* of who they are naturally, but they are actually moving *into* who they most deeply are.[6] We are never more ourselves than when we are praying.

Invisible Saints

Why do we fail to see saints? Why this theological swing-and-a-miss? I believe three badly resolved tensions keep us from seeing saints.

First, our Reformation heritage has an inner tension in how the church functions. On the one hand, the Reformers rediscovered that we are all saints: there isn't a special category of super-spiritual people called "saints"—the gospel creates a radically leveled community where we are all sinners justified by faith and thus now all saints. And yet, the Reformers, because of their love for Scripture, elevated the sermon. Preaching replaced Communion as the focal point of the worship service. This inadvertently promoted the preacher, creating a new kind of clergy-laity distinction. America's celebrity culture began not in Hollywood in the 1900s but in the 1700s. George Whitefield, whose preaching united the colonies, was America's first celebrity. So while we might say that every Christian is a "minister," preaching is regarded as the central load-bearing ministry. It's how we function, and what we do trumps what we say.

Second, Luther articulated a tension at the heart of our faith: we are simultaneously justified and sinners.[7] These two truths go hand in hand, and yet, in time, the sin side overwhelmed the saint side. Seeing sin comes easily, but seeing saints takes work. Practically, that meant that the flesh loomed larger than the Spirit's resurrection work at the core of our being. The gospel became, at times, a "one string guitar," and we just muddle through life.[8]

Third, as we've seen, the modern church's therapeutic bent emphasizes the sufferer or victim, so when Allison groans about being with her broken family at Thanksgiving dinner, instinctively we see her as a suffering person who might benefit from counseling. The therapist might tell her to give herself a break. There is a time for that, but such counsel can blind us to recognizing Allison as a saint on a mission of love. Maybe all Allison needs is her faith-tank filled up by friends who enjoy her sainthood and pray with her; so when Uncle Billy dominates the conversation and complains about the food, she can smile, knowing she's a saint, reflecting Christ's beauty with the virtue of patience.

Consequently, we are blinded to the beauty of these hidden saints. It's as if we're entering a medieval cathedral with sunglasses on—it's too dark. We see sinners, but not saints. If we miss saints, then we neuter the church's life of prayer, and the weight of doing church falls on pastors. Pastors—and anyone else, for that matter—are not meant to function at the center of the church. We miss that saints are the physical earthly body of Christ, Jesus's ministers to a dying world.

A Word to Pastors

Pastors rightly grieve over the consumer mentality in the pew, which asks, "What's in it for me?" Here's my encouragement: don't give Satan the high ground. Yes, many believers act like consumers, but if Ephesians is correct, then your congregation is made up of saints on the cutting edge of life. Tell them they are saints; hunt for their stories and celebrate them. Some are enduring difficult marriages or laboring with depressing jobs. Many have children estranged from the faith. Seek out their stories, and then ask God to create openings or venues where others can enjoy saints' stories.

Prayer meetings give the saints a venue to share those stories. What a joy to hear from the saint who overlooked the cranky relative at Christmas dinner, or to hear about the woman who encouraged the weary UPS driver by offering him coffee and donuts. When people feel our pleasure over the very real work of Jesus in them, they just glow.

8

Saints Unleashed

WHEN I WAS WRITING THIS CHAPTER, our prayer group had been praying for Howard's family reunion.

No Soldier Fights Alone

Howard is as levelheaded as they come, but he and his wife sensed the power of darkness at multiple levels within their extended family. As the reunion approached, they found their spirits sagging, but Howard shared that he was determined to not give in to evil.

When Howard shared his determination at prayer meeting, I told him that he reminded me of Gandalf in *The Lord of the Rings* telling the evil Balrog, "You cannot pass!"[1] I also reflected on Ephesians 6 where, confronted by evil, Paul repeatedly says, "Stand." So I read Paul's description of the armor of God out loud:

> Finally, *all of you* be strong in the Lord and in the strength of his might. *Together*, put on the whole armor of God, that *all of you* may be able to stand against the schemes of the devil. For we do not wrestle against flesh and blood, but against the rulers,

against the authorities, against the cosmic powers over this present darkness, against the spiritual forces of evil in the heavenly places. Therefore *all of you* take up the whole armor of God, that *together* you may be able to withstand in the evil day, and *together* having done all, to stand firm. *All of you* stand therefore, *together* having fastened on the belt of truth, and *together* having put on the breastplate of righteousness, and, as shoes for *all* your feet, having *together* put on the readiness given by the gospel of peace. In all circumstances take up *together* the shield of faith, with which *all of you* can *together* extinguish all the flaming darts of the evil one; and *together* take the helmet of salvation, and the sword of the Spirit, which is the word of God. (vv. 10–17 AT)

As I read, I added the plurals back in, which are easy to miss in English.[2] Every Sunday school image of the armor of God shows an individual soldier. But Paul isn't equipping an individual soldier: he's equipping an army of saints. No soldier fights alone.

Howard wasn't alone. We were all praying for his family. Over the weekend, he texted us with a charming series of mishaps, but best of all, by the end of the weekend, the secular family members remarked on how well the Christians loved. At every point, the saints were washing feet, reaching out, and loving. Jesus won the day.

Prayer as Armor

Prayer—the seventh piece of Paul's armor—was the thread that held evil at bay and energized them for love.

. . . praying *together* at all times in the Spirit, with all prayer and supplication. To that end, *let the entire church* keep alert with all perseverance, making supplication for all the saints, and also for me, that words may be given to me in opening my mouth boldly to proclaim the mystery of the gospel, for which I am an ambassador in chains, that I may declare it boldly, as I ought to speak. (Eph. 6:18–20 AT)

Paul spends more time on prayer than on almost all the other armor combined. It's that powerful. He has no Roman armor equivalent for prayer, but the modern soldier does—the radio. In warfare, good communication means everything; the absence of it, Carl von Clausewitz famously called "the fog of war."[3]

What makes the radio so powerful is not intrinsic to the radio; it's what the radio is connected to—overwhelming power. My dad's brother, Sergeant Leroy Miller, fighting in Italy with the Tenth Mountain Division, was operating as a forward artillery observer when the Germans spotted and killed him with a mortar barrage. Why did the Germans bother to launch a mortar barrage on a lone soldier? Leroy had a radio connecting to overwhelming power. In the Battle of the Bulge, the entire northern sector of the American line held, largely because of the radio. The US Army had three hundred artillery pieces zeroed in (called Time-On-Target), so whenever German tanks threatened a breakthrough, they encountered a barrage. On several occasions the Germans overran American units, but American officers called down artillery on their own position, blunting the attack. All because of the radio.[4]

Prayer is by far our most powerful weapon because it connects us to the Spirit's power. But it won't be used effectively if the saints aren't properly equipped. Behind the scenes at our prayer meeting, I was equipping the saints. Before our prayer meeting, I asked Howard how the weekend had gone. So, going into the prayer meeting, I knew his story. But by the end of our sharing time he was quiet, so I asked him to share. Then after Howard shared, I read Paul's armor of God. I equipped the saints by praying, listening, putting their stories in the center, and feeding their faith. The result? Their shields of faith were up; their gospel shoes fastened; and helmets of salvation on. Howard and the rest of us stood shoulder to shoulder—a line of Christian warrior-saints.

The same week, Mafdi told of a breakthrough with a young Arab man, Abdullah. Abdullah had expressed interest in Jesus, but he was still hesitating, even after three visions of Jesus! To our delight, he had a fourth vision, this time from Moses. Moses told him to put his trust in Jesus. We were thrilled he'd begun moving toward Christ, but absolutely charmed that it took Moses. I don't know to what extent these were visions or dreams, but I do know this kind of thing is happening all over the Muslim world. Both Howard and Mafdi were on the front lines. Mafdi's needs weren't more "spiritual" than Howard's. Every saint counts.

Seeing saints as front-line warriors, at multiple levels, transforms prayer meetings and even worship services. Praying together is no longer boring. It's fascinating to follow a prayer story through its ups and downs, and see what God does. You can feel people's spirits lift after they've been prayed for. Just last night, at the end of one of the monthly prayer meetings I'm in, several people said how encouraging praying together had been for them in the last year. A praying community energizes and encourages the front-line warriors. They aren't alone in their critical work.

Here's a report from a woman who's been leading a prayer movement at her church:

Interestingly, we hosted our community prayer service last night. As we were praying for an Assistant Principal who is on the front lines, doing the light-into-darkness work of bringing Jesus into crazy hard situations, I kept thinking, *this woman is on the front lines. We are equipping the saints as we pray tonight.* I could literally see her whole outlook changing and her hope rising up as Jesus led His church to pray away the discouragement. It was so amazing!

All Paul's prayers in Ephesians build to the unleashing of the saints on the kingdom of darkness—not a few professional missionaries, but a vast army of praying saints who, energized by faith, engage evil with love. Only then does the sleeping giant awaken. We are in this to win.

A Word to Pastors

Sometimes I forget that I'm a *saint first* and *pastor second.* That insight hit me thirty years ago as I was rushing to my discipling training on Sunday morning. I passed my friend David Powlison in the hallway, and he was listening intently to a woman with psychological problems. He was attentive, leaning in, his whole body bent slightly in her direction. I saw a woman with schizophrenia; David saw a saint. I was a poster child for the managerial (rushing by her) and the therapeutic ("she's schizophrenic").

Fast forward twenty years. We'd gotten to know Makena through a Bethesda Bible study class that Jill taught for her teenage daughter (who struggled with disability). Makena, an African emigrant, had just gotten off the phone with two pastors in her church. Her daughter had become defiant, and as a single mom (abandoned by her husband), Makena was at her wit's end. The first pastor told her to call the pastor in charge of counseling. The second pastor, the counselor, listened to her and said, "I'm not really equipped to handle your daughter with disabilities." When Makena called me in tears, she was as upset with the pastors as she was with her daughter. "Why couldn't they even just pray for me over the phone?" It was a triple miss of the Hebrew "big three" needs: Makena was functionally a widow and an alien, and her daughter, an orphan. The pastors, in this instance, were efficient managers but missed an opportunity to be what they are—*saints*.

Jill and I prayed with Makena, made some suggestions about her daughter, and followed up over the next several months. Her daughter has been through some rough spots, but in general she is doing well.

9

The Parable of the Missing CEO

ALL OF US CAN GET "STUCK" IN our own little worlds and miss big, obvious things. King David was stuck in the sin of adultery and murder, likely because both were considered normal for an ancient king. The prophet Nathan "unstuck" David by telling him a parable of a selfish king who robbed a poor man of his beloved lamb. David was enraged at this selfish king—that is, until Nathan in effect told David, "You are that selfish king!" (2 Sam. 12:7). David was brokenhearted. The parable had pulled him out of his world and created a mirror where he could look at himself. That's what Jesus did with the teacher of the law who had a narrow view of who was his neighbor. The parable of the good Samaritan created an alternative world that allowed the teacher to see his world better.

A Modern-Day Parable

I hope the following modern-day parable helps us all see ourselves a little better as well.

———

Imagine a company with a superb CEO. He is widely praised for his visionary leadership inside and outside his company. His insights into marketing and product design are second to none. Plus, he has a unique ability to attend not only to tasks but also to people. His imprint on the company since he founded it is such that the company is almost synonymous with him—his person and his work sit at the center of the company. Some even say that he's sacrificed so much for the company, it is almost like he's died for it.

The respect for him runs so deep that the company gathers weekly to celebrate him. Some even write songs extolling him. This remarkable CEO has even written a book about how to run the company, and this book has become a worldwide bestseller. People regularly study the book, quote it, and model their lives on it. It is such a part of the employees' lives that everyone calls it "the Book." At their weekly gathering, one of the leaders gives a talk on some part of the Book. Many of the leaders even have gone to a school where they've studied the Book.

And yet something is amiss. The company's market share is dwindling and profits are down. Wall Street analysts have marked the company's stock as a "sell." The company is struggling to recruit younger people, and gray hairs fill the offices. Things are not going well, but no one knows why. Some leaders have even become cynical. A few prominent ones have done the unthinkable: they've left the company and said they no longer follow the Book. The leaders who remain are discouraged.

Oddly enough, the one bright spot is how clean the company offices are. Even with budget cuts, the building literally sparkles. The janitors themselves are relentlessly cheerful. Whenever a janitor enters a room, people's spirits are lifted because the janitors sing as they work. A few onlookers, though, find their constant singing irritating.

In desperation, the company's leaders gather. What are they missing? Should they study the CEO's Book more? Should they invite more people to their weekly celebration of the CEO? Attendance has been down lately. They are puzzled.

Then one of the older leaders recalls a time many years ago when she and other leaders actually met with the CEO each week and talked directly to him. Others are puzzled by this idea. It seems like a waste of time, since they all have so much to do for the CEO. Plus, they aren't sure what to say in a meeting with him or how to organize it. Those who recall talking with him say it was strange, because he listened well but didn't always answer right away. And to run a company, you needed answers—quickly. Someone mentions hearing that some of the janitorial staff are still meeting with the CEO, but the eavesdropper isn't sure when or how. The idea seems strange.

The leaders decide to consult the Book. Sure enough, the Book says that the company will thrive only if the leaders talk to the CEO regularly. In fact, the Book says that the company was designed so it works only when there is regular communication with him. The Book is filled with stories of janitors talking to and listening to the CEO. The leaders ponder this. They respect the Book, but when it comes to running the company, you need a book that tells you what to do. Someone suggests asking the janitors how to talk with the CEO, but that is dismissed out of hand for obvious reasons. They are janitors, after all. They don't know how to run a company.

The leaders end their meeting with a renewed commitment for all of them to write books on how to run the company. That seems like a good idea. But a few of them decide to find the janitors' meeting room. They begin their search in the company's executive offices but find no trace. A search of sales and marketing comes up empty, too. They search the entire building but find nothing. Finally, someone remembers that in the far corner of the basement, behind the furnace room, there's an empty supply room. As they approach the room, they hear a quiet murmuring. When they peek in, they have trouble seeing, because the room is so bright. After their eyes adjust, they see a room filled with janitors speaking to the CEO. The leaders are puzzled. The janitors are talking to the CEO as if he is present, but the leaders don't see or hear him.

Some of the leaders leave. This is clearly a waste of time. Nothing is happening. And honestly, they are uncomfortable listening to the janitors going on and on. They even talk to the CEO about their physical ailments! One janitor even describes her hip problems. Plus, they find the brightness of the room jarring. As leaders, they have been trained to see what is important, and this clearly is not.

The remaining leaders wonder, *Have we missed something about how to run the company?* After all, the only part of the company that is going well is the work done by these janitors. The bathrooms sparkle! So they stay and listen.

Week by week, the leaders descend into the far corner of the basement and listen to the janitors talk to the CEO. Soon some of the leaders join the janitors. It feels odd, because the CEO doesn't seem to be listening. As weeks turned into months, though, strange things begin to happen: They begin to get brief glimpses of the CEO. His image flickers briefly in the center of the room, or they see his hand out of the corner of their eyes. They hear his voice. Sometimes they just sense his presence. He never shows up the same way twice. You definitely can't control how or when he shows up. He is his own boss.

The leaders who talk to the CEO begin to notice unusual, random things happening in their work. An unseen hand seems to shape it in surprising and subtle ways. Their work begins to sparkle, just like the bathrooms. At the same time, these leaders find their own plans falling apart. Most begin to experience suffering. Some are demoted—some even became janitors. They can see that the CEO is beginning to take control of their lives. He has his ways, and no one can stop him.

Surprisingly, these leaders also change. They start greeting the janitors, thanking them for their work, learning their names, and asking about their lives. They begin listening to the janitors and asking them questions about how to run the company. It is remarkable how much the janitors know. Other people in the company notice how their lives sparkle, just like the bathrooms.[1]

———

This parable sums up much of what I've shared so far. Prayerlessness in a Jesus community (a family, a church, a friendship) simply reflects a way of doing church without the Spirit of Jesus. It's hard for leaders to see this because they genuinely love and honor their "CEO." And yet, the leaders in this parable aren't just weak at talking to the CEO; they feel they don't need to. He doesn't fit into their system. Their system is *prayer resistant.* They are on their own.

The janitors in this parable descend to the basement not because they want to "talk to the CEO" as an end in itself. They are attentive to the CEO so he can help them in their work. They can find purpose in the otherwise dreary, unappreciated work of cleaning the bathrooms only by regularly meeting with the CEO. They can't do their jobs without being directed and energized by their leader. Similarly, praying together isn't disconnected from reality;

it connects us with the church's deepest management need—the executive power and wisdom of the Spirit of Jesus. A praying community makes space for the Spirit, who in turn brings us Jesus. He's the boss.

Learning the Art of Decreasing

The parable only hints at a positive vision of what's it's like to let the CEO run the company. The 2017 musical film *The Greatest Showman* helps us see what it feels like to let the Spirit of Jesus run his church.

Prior to filming, the producers did a run-through of the script in New York City to get a green light from investors. At the last minute, Hugh Jackman, the lead actor, had surgery to remove skin cancer on his nose. Doctors forbade him to sing. The producers made do by having a stand-in from the choir sing while Hugh gestured awkwardly up front. At least that was the plan. The song that captured both the heart of the movie and Hugh's own life story was "From Now On." As the stand-in painfully sings, you can see Hugh fighting the urge to sing. Finally, he can take it no more; beginning softly at first, he gradually lets loose the full power of his magnificent voice. He electrifies the room. The choir joins in, and it becomes almost a worship service. It is breathtaking to watch.[2]

Those of us who are pastors and leaders are the stand-ins. No one comes to hear *us* sing. When Hugh takes off, the stand-in retreats, beaming as he rejoins the choir. As Hugh comes alive, the stand-in comes alive too, along with the whole choir. The stand-in is so captivated by Hugh's singing that he and the rest of the choir start dancing, and in his exuberance, the stand-in repeatedly points to Hugh.

A stand-in who "gets it" is John the Baptist. His disciples sense their ministry weakening—the crowds are leaving and going to Jesus. The disciples see failure. They tell John, "Rabbi, he who was with you across the Jordan, to whom you bore witness—look, he is baptizing, and all are going to him" (John 3:26). But John doesn't see failure. He sees Jesus. He hears the true leader singing, so he explains to his dwindling crowd of disciples: "The friend of the bridegroom, who stands and hears him, rejoices greatly at the bridegroom's voice. Therefore this joy of mine is now complete. He must increase, but I must decrease" (John 3:29–30).

Like the stand-in, John rejoices that Jesus is increasing and he is decreasing. Those two dynamics are inseparable. Jesus can only increase if we decrease.

We come alive when the Spirit of Jesus is the center of the church. Prayer makes space for the Spirit of Jesus at the center. He delights in our worship and preaching, but he also wants to run the place. He makes the "magic."

In part 3, we look more closely at how the Spirit works.

PART 3

———

HOW THE SPIRIT RESHAPES A PRAYING COMMUNITY

10

How the Spirit Works

HOW DO OUR PRAYERS INTERFACE with what the Spirit does? How does the Spirit of Jesus reshape a praying community?

Thinking of the power train *prayer → Spirit → Jesus → power*, we can easily envision *prayer*, we know who *Jesus* is, and we understand *power*; but the *Spirit* is fuzzy. He just floats. Unbelief, then, works backward through Paul's cascade: we doubt that the *Spirit* does anything substantial, so we don't bother with *prayer*.

The Spirit's seeming elusiveness, which is anathema to management rationalism, contributes to the weakness of prayer in the modern church. In the parable of the missing CEO, the leaders are flummoxed by the CEO's hiddenness. Secularism already tells us that we live in the spiritless world, so we don't have much sense of how to connect with a mysterious boss.

A Depersonalized Spirit

One reason we miss seeing the Spirit and how he works is that he's actually missing from our Bibles. Twenty-five times Paul uses the word *Spiritual.* All but one of those times, Paul means capital *S,*

Spiritual, referring to the Spirit.[1] Our translations obscure that by translating the word as "spiritual."

Deepak Chopra and Gandhi are "spiritual," but they are not *Spiritual* people whose lives, like Jesus's resurrected life, are sustained by the Holy Spirit. The Spirit possesses us in the same way he possesses Jesus. A Spiritual person is in step with the Spirit and led by the Spirit. The Spirit carries the mind of Jesus into our lives, allowing Jesus's fruit to become our fruit (Gal. 5:22–23).

Here are three passages where the Spirit's presence is commonly obscured: Paul tells the Romans, "I long to see you, that I may impart to you some [S]piritual gift to strengthen you" (1:11). If Paul means spiritual, then he wants to give them some kind of weird, ethereal gift. What exactly is a spiritual gift? Is it like a Hallmark card greeting? A poem? But a *Spiritual* gift means that Paul wants to give something from the Spirit himself, a gift customized to the church's peculiar needs by the third person of the Trinity. It's a personal gift from a personal God.

Likewise, to the Colossians, Paul writes, "We have not ceased to pray for you, asking that you may be filled with the knowledge of his will in all [S]piritual wisdom" (1:9). I pray this daily for our leadership team. They don't need any old wisdom. They need wisdom from the Spirit himself, customized to their particular needs. Each of them faces multiple decisions. They are wise people, but they still need individual attention that only the Spirit can give them.

To the Corinthians, Paul writes about the believer's body: "It is sown a natural body; it is raised a [S]piritual body. If there is a natural body, there is also a [S]piritual body" (1 Cor. 15:44). Christian leaders lament that Christians view heaven as floating on clouds. This verse might be where Christians get that idea. A "spiritual body" has no substance, but a *Spiritual* body is identical to Jesus's substantial and fully touchable body. Jesus's body isn't ether; it's continuously made alive by the Spirit himself. It could not be more personal.

In all three of these examples, the Spirit is managing the church. He gives gifts, wisdom, and everlasting life. He's not floating. He's working.

Jesus gives us a simple but vivid image to explain *how* the Spirit works.

The Wind of the Spirit

Jesus describes how the Spirit interfaces with us: "The wind blows where it [*wills*], and you hear its sound, but you do not know where it comes from or where it goes" (John 3:8).[2] Let me expand on Jesus's words to Nicodemus:

> The wind blows where it [*wills*] [you aren't in control of your plans and dreams—the Spirit is], and you hear its sound [if you make prayer a priority, you'll see the amazing way the Spirit works], but you do not know where it comes from or where it goes [but you can't predict the means, timing, or character of the Spirit's work. You won't see a connection between prayer and the resulting wonder. It's not irrational, it is suprarational, above and outside your view].

So the first step in understanding *how* the Spirit works is surrendering our *demand* to know how. Clearly, the Spirit of Jesus is not our assistant. He's not here to bless our plans. He's the free Spirit of Jesus with his own plans and design. We don't control the Spirit's timing, method, or result. I've tried. It doesn't work. The surprising ways that prayers are answered in the Jesus communities I'm part of are a function of the Spirit's freedom. He's the boss.

And yet, the wind has distinctive patterns. Prevailing winds blow steadily from one direction, day in and day out. My grandfather Lorenz, who left for sea at the age of fifteen to be a cabin boy, told me the story of sailing into the prevailing winds at the southern tip of Chile. For forty days, they struggled to sail into the fifty-to-seventy-five-miles-per-hour winds. On the fortieth day, the discouraged captain contemplated turning around and sailing east via the Indian Ocean and across the Pacific to California. My grandfather suggested he give it seven more days. The next day, the winds shifted, allowing them to circumvent Cape Horn and sail up to California.[3] Clearly, we don't control the wind, but knowing the prevailing winds allow us to be Spiritual weather forecasters.

I opened this book by offering a peek into my morning prayer time with Kim. Below is the story behind that prayer time. It may give you a feel for how the wind of the Spirit works.[4]

Kim and I Learn to Pray Together

Kim, with her autism, had developed a bad habit of pacing upstairs in the very early morning. Jill and I would take turns telling her very loudly (we yelled!) to get back in bed. Early one morning, I decided to go pray with her. As I was getting out of bed, Jill asked me, "What are you going to do, go yell at Kim?" I said, "That hasn't worked for ten years so I thought I'd try praying." Jill laughed and said: "What do you mean? It's been twenty years."

When I got upstairs, I put my hands on Kim and prayed that God would quiet her spirit. As soon as I started praying, I was struck with a new thought: *I have been underestimating Kim's ability to grow Spiritually and control her behavior.* There was no voice;

it was just an unusual thought. About once a week for the next three months, I'd slip upstairs and pray with Kim. Then in mid-March 2008, Kim's pacing stopped overnight. Why? We moved. Unknown to us, the trucks from the meat factory across the street had been waking her up.

I couldn't shake the Spirit's prompting, though, so I decided to have morning devotions with Kim. We'd read a Bible story; then she'd pray as I cleaned up the dishes. Her prayers were brief, just a couple of sentences. That summer I kept feeling that I should sit down with Kim to honor her prayers, but it was just one more thing to do. Sometime that fall, I stopped multitasking, sat next to her, and listened to her pray. Immediately, her prayers blossomed; they lengthened and deepened. I was particularly surprised how thankful she was.

The following year she started telling people, "I'm praying for you." She'd even put her hands on people when she is praying. With her own struggles with anger, she started praying for other people who struggled with anger. Later that year, we lost a grandson, Ben. It deeply affected all of us, but Kim remembered him frequently as she prayed.

Kim has none of our inhibitions with prayer, so when she stops in our office for lunch, if she hears a need, she prays on the spot. She will go where the rest of us are hesitant to go. Especially since the Lord took our daughter Ashley home in 2018, Kim will pray, remembering Ashley, and in her own way lament that she's gone ahead of us.

Lately, Kim and I have closed our prayer time praying for patience for one another. For several years, I just had Kim pray for patience, but then I realized that I needed her to pray for my impatience.

In this story, how do our prayers interface with the Spirit? Let me mention seven ways.

1. Surprise. At almost every step, I have been surprised by the Spirit's work, beginning with the prompting when I first went to pray over Kim. It was totally unexpected and yet thoroughly biblical. And as a parent of a child with disabilities, you are so busy just keeping body and soul together that you don't have the energy or even imagination to think someone with Kim's level of disability could grow Spiritually. The Spirit works in the box, he works outside the box, and he blows up the box. Knowing this encourages us to look for and expect wonder.

2. Imagination explosion. What the Spirit does, as we devote ourselves to prayer, is always wider and deeper than we've imagined. Paul captures the idea this way: "Now to him who is able to do far more abundantly than all that we ask or think" (Eph. 3:20). I went upstairs to pray for Kim not imagining that this would lead to Kim and me having a morning prayer time together or that Kim's prayers would touch other people's lives. I was convicted enough by the Spirit's gentle nudge (about how I'd underestimated Kim), that I stopped teaching adult Sunday school and found an empty room next to the furnace in the church basement, where I began to teach the Bible to Kim and another friend affected by disability. Jill eventually took over the class and began to write an entire Sunday school curriculum for adults affected by intellectual disability. Now seeJesus publishes it as our Bethesda study. Hundreds of churches have begun to use it to actually disciple people with intellectual disabilities. And it all began with a gentle nudge. Knowing that the Spirit creates an imagination explosion pulls us out of our ruts and opens us up to new directions, not just as individuals but as a praying community.

3. Repentance. This story would have been frozen at the level of a good idea if I hadn't repented. That is, I wasn't just convicted of a sin; I turned away from it. Notice the number of times I repented: I went from yelling to praying, from underestimating Kim to praying with her, from multitasking to being attentive. At each point conviction was followed by good old-fashioned obedience. The Spirit shapes us into the image of Jesus. Knowing this encourages us to not push away the good but hard work of repentance and obedience.

4. Dying and rising. When the Spirit brings Jesus, he brings us the life of Jesus. He writes the story of Jesus, of his dying and rising, on our lives. I'll talk more about this in the next chapter, but at each point in this story, I had to enter *mini-deaths*, where I had to put to death a pattern in me: yelling, multitasking, and so on. And now I have a *mini-resurrection* every day as Kim and I pray through our problems and joys. This morning, Kim thanked God for her upcoming Disney trip in September! Sometimes when Kim has a particularly delightful prayer on her speech computer, I'll take a photo of her screen and text it out to the person she's prayed for.

Look how this ties in with number 2, "imagination explosion." The constriction of love is the Spirit's launching pad for the expansion of his resurrection power. Jesus's pattern is our pattern.

Knowing this keeps us from pushing away the dying of love and encourages us to wait and pray for the rising.

5. Hiddenness. The Spirit of Jesus is hidden in the story itself. That is, only as we watch the story do we begin to see his patterns. If you look at praying together through a depersonalized lens, as if God were an answer machine, then you'll miss how the Spirit of Jesus stands at the edges of our stories, orchestrating them. Likewise, my persistent love for Kim, with all my weaknesses, is hidden.

6. *Mystery.* It's easy to miss the simplicity of prayer: God answered my prayer for Kim to stop pacing. But if you try to figure out how prayer works, you will lose the Spirit. You see, our moving date in March was already set when I began praying with Kim the previous December. If you say that Kim's pacing would have stopped anyway, then you quench the Spirit with your unbelief. If we try to *reverse engineer* prayer, if we try to figure out the Spirit's methods, we put God in a box. He's box resistant.

7. *The least of these.* Prior to praying with Kim, I had depersonalized her. Yelling at her was an obvious problem, but less obvious was my underestimating her, and later my multitasking with her. When the Spirit of Jesus slipped in through the window of prayer, I began to treat Kim with more dignity, not as a function of her disability. Praying together started a cascade that re-personalized Kim. Our friendship deepened to the extent that now my kids joke about it. If you miss the Spirit, you miss the person next to you.

The Spirit's Patterns

These same patterns rippled through the two praying churches Jill and I were part of. Mechanicsville Chapel was a small rural church populated by farmers and small-business owners. New Life Church was a suburban congregation populated by Westminster Seminary students and professors. In the early years, we used to joke that only one elder had a real job!

A spirit of prayer permeated both churches. That is, people were quick to pray in either formal or informal settings. For Mechanicsville, it was the traditional Wednesday prayer meeting. For New Life it was a prayer meeting that Dad started in his home, which birthed the church. The following story captures the Spirit's work.

In 1973, Dad spoke at a local church and said, "The gospel can change anyone." After a psychiatrist challenged him, Dad went home wondering, "Do I really believe the gospel can change anyone?" He decided to find the toughest people in Philadelphia to see if the gospel could change them. He knew that a motorcycle gang hung out at a local ice-cream stand, so he went there, got an ice-cream cone, and walked over to a group of rowdy teenagers who regularly gathered there to drink and share drugs. With ice cream dripping down his hand, Dad gave one of his memorable opening lines: "I'm Rev. Miller. Are there any Warlocks here?" When they started taunting him, Dad only made it worse by saying, "Actually, I'm Dr. Miller." Just as the mocking was worsening, a tough-looking redhead—himself a thief, drug addict, and alcoholic—walked up: "Shut up. I know this guy. He picked me up hitchhiking. We should listen to him." The redhead's name was Bob Heppe. Over the next six months, Dad befriended Bob, even listening to his drunken calls in the middle of the night. Dad patiently loved Bob and eventually won him to Christ.

Notice the patterns in Bob's story that are similar to those in Kim's.

1. Surprise. Who would have guessed that God would use Dad's random picking up a hitchhiker and sharing the gospel with him to prepare the way for Bob's coming to Dad's rescue and helping a whole group of tough guys to hear the gospel?

2. Imagination explosion. The psychiatrist's challenge opened Dad's imagination to think outside the box and do something daring. Instead of merely disagreeing with the psychiatrist, Dad let his integrity be challenged. When imagination takes off, that opens the door to adventure and boldness, two marks of the early church in Acts. Bob went on to become a church elder and eventually a missionary to South Asians in London, where he now leads a church-planting movement.

3. Repentance. Dad took the challenge from the psychiatrist seriously, letting his words speak to his own heart and behavior. That led Dad into some daring love.

4. Dying and rising. Dad's obedience to the prompting of the Spirit led him into an awkward situation, a kind of death to pride where he was being mocked by a bunch of guys. The rising came when Bob rescued him. That pattern continued as Dad responded to Bob's drunken calls in the middle of the night.

5. Hiddenness. The Spirit's work is hidden in the story itself. Only as Dad moved out in obedience, risking failure, did the Spirit's work come alive. We discover the Spirit's rich work not by hunting for experiences with the Spirit but by a life of love. Every time I saw or was part of a movement of the Spirit, it bubbled up quietly from below. Dad's picking up hitchhikers like Bob was the hidden work of love.

6. Mystery. The pieces of the story were designed by the Spirit. Dad "just happened" to pick up Bob hitchhiking and share the gospel with him. Dad "just happened" to be at an ice-cream stand, seemingly making a fool of himself, as Bob walked up. The timing was exquisite.

7. The least of these. Previously, Bob had been kicked out of his township because of his record as a petty criminal. He was one of the "tax collectors and sinners" Jesus would have dined with. Dad's dripping ice-cream cone was his dining with sinners.

Kim's and Bob's stories are quite different, yet their Spiritual patterns are similar. With Kim, the Spirit wove a mundane work of love. With Bob, the Spirit shaped a dramatic work of faith. In both stories, saints are in motion. I say this because it's easy to neglect the mundane stories of love. Someone enduring patiently with a difficult parent is every bit as filled with the Spirit as the powerful preacher. Notice also that to explain the richness of the Spirit's work, I told you a story. Churches weak in prayer are also weak in stories.

The Spirit's power is present in both stories, but the conduits to his power are integrity, obedience, repentance, and love. He is the *Holy* Spirit. At the same time, you see a real presence of the Spirit shaping events, creating surprises, and sparking our imaginations. You sense Paul's summary of the Spirit's work: he does beyond all that we can ask or think (Eph. 3:20).

I say this because I believe, when it comes to the Spirit, there is an *unexplored middle.* On the one hand, my Reformed world is concerned that a misguided emphasis on the Spirit can detract from the authority of God's word and good old-fashioned holiness. We've seen people do destructive or unwise things based on hunches and claims such as "The Spirit led me."[5] On the other hand, the charismatic world is concerned that neglecting prayer and the Spirit opens the door to rationalism and powerlessness. If the Reformed world is the car's brakes, the charismatic world is the gas. Is there a not-too-messy middle between these two worlds? That's what we've begun to probe here in this chapter and will continue to do in the rest of part 3.

11

The Spirit's Path

THE SPIRIT'S MOST DISTINCTIVE PATTERN is Jesus's dying and rising, what I call the *J-Curve*®.[1] Like the letter *J*, Jesus's life goes down into death and up into resurrection. If the Spirit is united with Christ, it makes sense that the pattern of Jesus's life would become ours by the same Spirit. When the Spirit brings us the person of Jesus, he also brings the story of Jesus. Try to tell someone about Jesus without telling his story. You can't. You are left with platitudes. His person and his story are inseparable.

If I had to pick the most significant misunderstanding of what happens when we pray, I'd say it's missing the J-curve. We rightly expect God to answer our prayers, but he answers them in the shape of the story of his Son. The Spirit doesn't bring the power of Jesus separately from the path of Jesus.

Without the "map" of the J-curve, you'll be tempted to give up on prayer, and, like my grandfather's captain, sail the wrong way. If we miss the J-curve, we drop Jesus out of the drivetrain, like this: *prayer → Spirit → power.* Jesus isn't spiritual window dressing. He's really quite serious about imprinting us with his path. As my coworker Jon Hori put it, "The Spirit funnels his power through a cross-shaped lens."[2] So where are we going? Into Jesus. What's our path? His path.

Let's explore three different ways Jesus's path impacts our praying.

Dying and Rising Open Us Up to Prayer

First, as a community begins to devote itself to prayer, its members often find themselves drawn into the dying and rising pattern of Jesus's life, which in turn deepens prayer.

Behind the stories I've told of my dad, you can see this pattern of dying and rising. After witnessing the praying community at L'Abri in 1968, Dad began to pray at the Wednesday night prayer meeting. As he put energy into prayer, he began to enter the story of Jesus. The power train kicked in. By the spring of 1970, he was depressed about seminary and even himself. He resigned and then later withdrew his resignation from Westminster. A major evangelism effort of his failed that year. So he went to Spain in June 1970, humbled. The dying to self of his pride opened the door for the Spirit to work in his heart, and that spilled over into his ministry. The Spirit worked this way: *prayer* (Wednesday night) → *dying* (humbling failure) → *rising* (discoveries in Spain).

This pattern continued in Dad's life. During the '70s, God blessed his ministry at New Life Church and overseas, in Ireland and Uganda, where he did missions work. But by the early '80s, my mom was concerned that church was consuming Dad. That's when she wrote the letter to Dad about his "disordered loves" (see p. 63). Mom was inviting Dad to put to death a destructive pattern in his life. Her litmus test for Dad's weakness was his struggle to be attentive to her. It is a familiar problem: the blessing of resurrection can open the door to the idol of ministry.

Mom told me later that while Dad wasn't resistant to her letter, he did not take it to heart. Then she connected the dots for me: two months later, in June 1983, Dad had a heart attack in Uganda. He would never return to Uganda. The wind blows where it wills.[3]

That fall, Dad started a five-hour prayer meeting on Thursday mornings, from seven till noon. He regularly invited anyone to show up, and we'd pray for them. He said, "Just drop in." There was no demand to pray at length, just a warm invitation to join him in prayer. When new guests arrived, he'd make a pot of tea, serve them, and listen to their stories, and then we'd pray together. It was relaxed, yet serious. During a typical morning, we prayed for about half the time. I joined the prayer time in 1985, when I began to work full-time with our new mission. More than any other place, that Thursday morning gathering was where I learned to value and enjoy corporate prayer.

As a result of that meeting, I saw God "do far more abundantly than all that we ask or think, according to the power at work within us" (Eph. 3:20). Over the next ten years we saw our church, New Life, expand and grow, spawning multiple daughter churches. We saw World Harvest Mission (now Serge) grow and expand, and today it has over three hundred missionaries. We saw our Sonship Course take form and transform thousands of lives. Tim Keller (later an influential pastor in New York City) was part of our church and was impacted by my dad's emphasis on the gospel, which in turn affected Keller's preaching. I don't think it is an overstatement to say that our Thursday morning prayer meeting influenced how the evangelical church viewed the gospel, that the gospel was not just for non-Christians but for Christians as well.

If you look at prayer divorced from how the Spirit draws us into the story of Jesus, you miss the central structure of how God answers prayer. You miss how Mom's dying (her honesty to Dad) was answered by God weakening Dad in Uganda. You miss how God drew him down into a death that slowed him and helped him to return to the priority of praying. You miss the multiple wonders that emerged from that praying community. Here's the pattern in this story: *dying* (Mom's honesty) → *more dying* (Dad's heart attack) → *rising* (Thursday prayer) → *more rising* (ministry explosion). Figure 11.1 shows what this looks like.

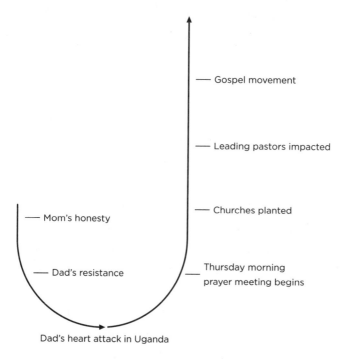

— Gospel movement

— Leading pastors impacted

— Churches planted

— Mom's honesty

— Thursday morning
prayer meeting begins

— Dad's resistance

Dad's heart attack in Uganda

Figure 11.1. Dad's J-curve: dying and then rising

The J-curve helps us link the pieces of the story together. Otherwise, we'll assume that prayer functions to make our world pain free, which leaves us confused, even cynical or bitter, because God has let us down. But if you take prayer seriously, you invite the Spirit's disruptive power, which draws you into the story of Jesus.

Paul speaks of the Spirit's killing function in Romans 8:13, "For if you live according to the flesh you will die, but if by the Spirit you put to death the deeds of the body, you will live," and in Colossians 3:5, "Put to death therefore what is earthly in you." We saw the killing function of the Spirit in Dad's life. First, the Spirit went after Dad's pride, then later after his ministry idolatry. Each time that opened the door to remarkable resurrections. You can see why *Holy* is so frequently attached to the Spirit. This keeps us from equating "filled with the Spirit" with merely human victory or feeling good about yourself. Minutes after Stephen is full of the Spirit, they stone him to death (Acts 7:54–60). Where's Stephen's victory? In his transfigured face as he glows with love for his Savior.

Jesus is on record as having cleaned out his Father's house with a whip. This keeps us from thinking that prayer is a kind of pagan magic that makes our life pain free. In fact, pain *increases* in a praying life, but so do power, love, and hope. That's because dying and rising are the new norm.

Praying Itself Is Dying and Rising

Second, sometimes, the wind just doesn't blow. My grandfather told me how their sailing ship was becalmed for days in the doldrums off the coast of Brazil. Many Christians expect that good praying should have a spiritual "high" to it, a sense that you've connected with God. But the actual experience of prayer can be tedious. The combination of expecting great feelings and encountering boredom is dislocating. It's one of the reasons we distance ourselves from praying together.

But what if prayer itself is shaped like Jesus's dying and rising? The act of praying itself is a kind of dying, where you give up your self-will to "make things happen" and go to God with a collective "Help us." The initial *feeling* of prayer is dying to self, because praying is an act of the will, a decision to shut down your activity and open the door to God's activity.

It may help to spell out the forms of dying we feel when praying with others: Some people pray too long. Some never pray. Others meander, following all kinds of rabbit trails. Some are not attentive to the theme of the prayer conversation, so praying together feels jerky. The time commitment alone is a kind of dying. Corporate pray feels like a waste of time, like you are violating an unspoken management law.

Christian leaders unschooled in the art of prayer can, at times, talk too much when leading a prayer time; they are uncomfortable with silence. Or their prayers are overly eloquent, mini-sermons.

Whom you pray with can also be a challenge. Often the folks who come out to an initial call to prayer aren't movers and shakers. They appear to prefer thrift stores for their shopping. Praying down low, with the hidden people of the church, is a particularly good death, because pretense and pride keep us from valuing seemingly simpler people.

Social media is instant and visual. Prayer is slow and mysterious, which involves a kind of dying. The apostle is correct: "We see through a glass, darkly" (1 Cor. 13:12 KJV). And yet, that darkness incubates the power of God. Paul was so aware of this that he deliberately weakened his communication style with the Corinthians. "I was with you in weakness and in fear and much trembling, and my speech and my message were not in plausible words of wisdom, but in demonstration of the Spirit and of power, so that your faith might not rest in the wisdom of men but in the power of God" (1 Cor. 2:3–5).

By itself, dying does nothing. So how do we link Christ with our dying? Keep showing up. Don't quit. Pray when you are bored. Pray when you are weary. Pray when others are boring. Don't run from Gethsemane. Pray in Gethsemane!

Answered Prayer Takes the Shape of Dying and Rising

Finally, the shape of our prayers and God's answers follows the contours of the cross. Like the seed that dies, prayer disappears into the ground, out of our control, then it bursts out of the soil as a small green leaf.

> The kingdom of God is as if a man should scatter seed on the ground. He sleeps and rises night and day, and the seed sprouts and grows; he knows not how. The earth produces by itself, first the blade, then the ear, then the full grain in the ear. But when the grain is ripe, at once he puts in the sickle, because the harvest has come. (Mark 4:26–29)

The time sequence can be seen in figure 11.2, where there is a long period of praying and then *Spirit → Jesus → life*.

Figure 11.2. Praying at length before a harvest of life

Jesus's description of the farmer's ignorance of how the seed grows ("he knows not how"—Mark 4:27) is identical to his description of how the Spirit works ("the wind blows where it wishes"—John 3:8). God breaks our will by not disclosing what happens when we pray. Then he breaks it further by waiting so long that we become convinced only God can fix this mess. This is familiar territory for Jesus: he describes himself as the seed that dies (John 12:24). When we understand that prayer follows the same path as Jesus, it prepares us for how God answers.

The J-curve illuminates even further the importance of *Jesus* in the church's power train: *prayer → Spirit → Jesus → power*. We've not invited a feel-good Jesus into our community; we've submitted ourselves to the rule of a battle-hardened warrior-king, the Lion-Lamb who's come to deal with evil. He's not here to make our plans work. He's here to draw us into his Father's mission. A praying community continuously invites his disruptive rule. He still calms storms, rebukes demons, and flips tables!

For sure, praying together isn't like pagan magic—it's not a way of getting what you want; it's a way of entering the story of Jesus. We don't know *how* the Spirit works, but we do know *where* he works. He works down low, in humility. We don't learn the Spirit abstractly, separate from the person of Jesus. The Spirit of Jesus loves hidden places where he isn't turned into a show. He loves to work in broken people, people who realize that they can't do life on their own.

As we enter a life of prayer together, we invite the Spirit to reshape our lives around the story of Jesus. So get ready for dying and rising to accelerate in your life!

12

Management by Prayer

IN A RECENT PASTORS' COHORT, I asked everyone to draw up a plan for creating a praying church. The resulting plans had multiple good ideas (e.g., start an elders' prayer meeting, be more thoughtful about the pastoral prayer), but something was missing. I told the pastors: "Guys, none of you put down the strategy of praying for your plan. No one was asking God any questions." One of the pastors said, "How incredible that all eight of us would try to build a praying church without thinking that prayer might be part of the strategy!"

Why the miss? After all, we were in a pastors' prayer cohort focused on a praying church. All the pastors had read *A Praying Life* and attended the Praying Life seminar. Yet instinctively they put planning and prayer in separate buckets. This is a near-perfect example of secularism that relegates prayer to the *not-real* world of fairies and astrology. That is, when we get serious and plan, praying isn't part of the plan. When that happens, the gospel is sitting on the surface of a church, teetering over an essentially pagan power grid. Planning by prayer alters that power grid.

At our next meeting, I showed the pastors the "beating heart" of my planning: multiple prayer cards filled with questions I ask God. Prayer saturates my planning. Everything I do as a leader of a Jesus community begins with prayer. Why? That's how a Jesus follower in a Jesus community does life, whether you are a single woman, a wealthy business person, or a pastor. And quite frankly, prayerless planning is incredibly ineffective. It reverses the J-curve: it begins with life and ends in death.

A spirit of expectant waiting, where you *don't yet plan*—except to pray—is a critical ingredient to a praying church. The author of 1 Samuel is at pains to contrast the impatient spirit of Saul, who can't wait, with the praying spirit of David, who is constantly consulting God.

We saw earlier that Acts opens with a ten-day prayer meeting: "All these with one accord were devoting themselves to prayer" (1:14). They were simply following Jesus's plan: "Wait for the promise of the Father" (1:4). What does that mean? This really drives some management consultants berserk: You don't know. You don't know when or even how. We don't control the Spirit. We wait and pray.

A watchful, prayerful waiting should be the first part of any plan in a Jesus community. For example, at seeJesus we had outlined our marketing strategies. They were good summaries of how we did our work, but something was missing. They didn't capture what drove our growth, so we added this: "Waiting: We prayerfully and actively wait on the Spirit to bring resurrection in the deaths God permits." Waiting in prayer for the Spirit is the most important thing we do.

We tend to think of prayer as mainly *asking*. That's true, but as we saw in the last chapter, its far broader and richer than that.

A praying community reorients how it does life, which includes work and management.

Let's take a look at how Jesus and the early church practiced management by prayer, and then examine a modern-day example.

A Case Study of Jesus's Management by Prayer

Most leaders are quick to acknowledge that recruiting good staff is challenging, so let's watch Jesus do HR (Human Resources) work.

Before Jesus selected his disciples, "all night he continued in prayer to God" (Luke 6:12). Joseph Ratzinger rightly observes, "The calling of the disciples is a prayer event; it is as if they were begotten in prayer, in intimacy with the Father. . . . Their calling emerges from the Son's dialogue with the Father and is anchored there."[1]

Jesus is making one of the most important decisions of his earthly life: selecting the church's DNA. As the world's most God-dependent human being, he can't pick disciples on his own, so he prays. He manages by prayer. In contrast, most churches go into a management mode where prayer functions like a formality.

What emerges from Jesus's prayer vigil is shocking: he selects twelve blue-collar laborers. Instead of Harvard, Jesus goes to the Home Depot. At least seven of the twelve, and clearly the leaders (Peter, Andrew, and John), are tradesman. Matthew, as tax collector, is a cross between a sleazy used-car salesman and an entrepreneur. No priests, scholars, or elites. Jesus follows his own advice to "pray earnestly to the Lord of the harvest to send out *laborers* into his harvest" (Luke 10:2). He picks *laborers*, not leaders.[2] Surprise is one of the Spirit's signature moves.

Why does Jesus bypass elites in favor of peasants? He is creating something entirely new, from the ground up. He needs new

DNA. Earlier he said, "No one puts new wine into old wineskins" (Luke 5:37).

Who would have thought that a group of fishermen would be Jesus's first-round draft picks? And yet, the church's amazing resilience to the onslaughts of unbelief in the last two hundred years is largely a reflection of the blue-collar bent of the church. Peasants are notoriously stubborn, quick with an opinion, and often pithy in their speech.

My wife is a peasant. Growing up on the streets of Philly, Jill got used to the tough side of life. She taught me the skill of walking in a rough neighborhood: be aware of your environment, but keep your head down, don't make eye contact, and keep a good pace. Like Sam the gardener in *The Lord of the Rings*, she's not easily snookered. Popular opinion rarely sways her.

Elites can easily despise or dismiss peasants. This theme echoes all through the Gospels. When the Sadducees order the temple police to arrest Jesus, they return empty-handed and tell their bosses: "'No one ever spoke like this man!' The Pharisees answered them, 'Have you also been deceived? Have any of the authorities or the Pharisees believed in him? *But this crowd that does not know the law is accursed*'" (John 7:46–49). You can feel the elites' utter disdain for the peasants.

Practically, what are the implications for selecting leaders? For starters, I know a lot of churches who *wish* they'd spent a night in prayer before they selected their current leaders. Maybe this is one of those times where WWJD (What Would Jesus Do?) should be something we actually do. My suggestion: stop hunting for leaders. Instead, pray regularly for God to raise up *laborers* for your church. Then hunt for laborers, faithful men and women who show up and do their work well, with humility. Your leaders will naturally emerge out of your laborers.

A Case Study of Management by Prayer in Acts

As we saw, Acts opens with a ten-day prayer meeting. During this time, the apostles make their first HR decision. So when they select Judas's replacement, "they prayed and said, 'You, Lord, who know the hearts of all, show which one of these two you have chosen'" (1:24).

Likewise, when the church sends out the first missionaries, this commission emerges out of a prayer time. "While they were worshiping the Lord and fasting [*prayer*], the Holy Spirit said, 'Set apart for me Barnabas and Saul for the work to which I have called them [*Spirit*].' Then after fasting and praying they laid their hands on them and sent them off [*to proclaim Jesus*]" (13:2–3). Notice the Spirit's power train at work. Prayer isn't window dressing; it's where the Spirit works.

My dad used to ask pastors, "Who selected Barnabas and Paul for their first missionary journey?" Pastors typically would say, "The church in Antioch." Then he would show them this passage. The church affirmed the Spirit's call and sent them off, but the Spirit called them. The Spirit is a real, deciding, thinking person running the show.

How does the Holy Spirit work? Luke doesn't tell us, but I know that when I slow down, especially during my weekly two-hour prayer time on Friday, stuff happens; unexpected thoughts come. In fact, most of our breakthroughs happen during those quiet times of prayer.

Notice the Spirit's signature move: surprise. Just before this, Luke mentions the five key leaders of the church at Antioch. Two of the five (Barnabas and Paul, likely the most gifted of the five) are selected by the Spirit. What church in its right mind sends off its senior pastor and executive pastor into missions? Missionaries disappear! When I worked for ten years in urban Philly, it was like

I was off the grid. And yet, isn't that just what the Father did with his Son?

The Spirit pulls apart this highly successful, multiethnic leadership team, thus seemingly weakening the church in Antioch in order to grow the church in the wider Roman Empire. Imagine how a congregation's vision of missions would change if the senior pastor left for Africa? But pushing out two gifted leaders opens up room for younger leaders to emerge at Antioch. Typically, stronger leaders are reluctant to let go of control, thus stifling younger leaders.

Don't misunderstand. The Spirit isn't opposed to good management. Over the next ten years the apostle Paul wisely pivots between the two key centers of the Greek world—Ephesus and Corinth. But the Spirit can't breathe if management takes center stage. The philosopher Alasdair MacIntyre points out that management has no end goal other than order and efficiency. It's focused on process. It has no *telos*.[3] Only the Spirit of Jesus can lead us into impossible tasks that we never dreamed about.

A Modern-Day Case Study of Recruiting by Prayer

When seeJesus started in 1999, the Spirit had been weakening me for almost a decade in multilayered dying. It's hard to describe how low the Lord had taken me. Work and writing that I had done was credited to other people. I was literally down to one close friend. So when I started seeJesus, I was the only employee. I wasn't sure I could raise enough money to cover my salary. The immensity of shame and loss I felt constantly drew me into a fellowship of Jesus's suffering.

If you've been shunned or slandered, you lack *weight*, in the Hebrew sense of the word translated "glory." When you lack weight in this way, it's hard to get people to return phone calls or to take you seriously. The gift of this lengthy death created new contours in my soul. I became so aware of what it's like to be "outside the camp and bear the reproach [Jesus] endured" (Heb. 13:13) that now I try to be quick to return emails and phone calls.

I was in an unusual place: the Lord Jesus had given me an immense vision of preparing the bride for suffering, but he'd stripped me of all human power to implement that vision. So I had to do everything by prayer. In one of the many twists of the Spirit, what Jesus had taught me about prayer during some of my worst suffering I wrote into the book *A Praying Life*.

But the problem of weightlessness still haunted me. When I tried to recruit a director of ministry for seeJesus in 2010, I had a string of recruiting failures. I was discouraged. With thirteen direct reports, I had little time to write. Finally, during one of my Friday prayer times in 2018, I did two relatively obvious things: I prayed, "Jesus, would you run this thing?" And I decided to recruit only by prayer.

Within months, unusual things began to happen. I'd been convinced that we didn't have anyone inside our work to manage it. We had some "Home Depot" workers (including me), but we needed "Harvard" grads. Then, a surprising thought formed in my mind: *You have the people within your work to lead it.* I treat promptings like this cautiously, since this could just be human intuition. So, like Mary, I hide it in my heart. I've noticed though, that promptings from God have "markers"—they tend to be unusual, outside the box, and yet thoroughly biblical. I was aware of my weightlessness and how it limited my work, but I'd not pushed it away or opened the door to bitterness. I'd received the dying, and I knew that dying well was the launching pad for resurrection. So, like the captain of my granddad's ship, I kept a weather eye out for a wind change.

A few months later, I got another prompting during my Friday prayer time: *Bob Loker could be your director of ministry.* As our board chair, Bob loved and valued our ministry. We'd grown even closer when his wife Becky passed away from cancer, but Bob was a few weeks shy of eighty years old! Yet it struck a chord with me. I called our management consultant, who knew Bob well; the consultant had the same positive response, as did Bob when asked about the position. Bob is vibrant for his age—he bikes an hour a day.

The Spirit's help that spring was remarkable. In addition to Bob joining staff, I promoted three more staff, and our consultant suggested we form a leadership team, something I'd been praying for, for ten years. Then I sought our consultant's help with a management system, and he introduced us to Entrepreneurial Operating System, which has helped us immensely. We are still "Home Depot," but we are *something the Lord made: a cathedral not made with hands.*

I say this because *management* and *the Spirit's work* aren't opposed to one another. The Spirit helps us manage better. You just don't want *management* in the driver's seat. If you put it there, you kill imagination, because the manager can only see what is, but the praying leader sees what isn't. Recall that the Ephesians power train ends in "now to him who is able to do far more abundantly than all that we ask or think" (3:20).

The Bob Loker story is quite ordinary, yet it feels spectacular to me, because I can still feel how weak and overwhelmed I was. I'm acutely aware of this story only because it emerged out of prayer, and I've continued to be attentive to its unfolding. I've *watched and prayed.* So, to the weary saints out there, don't despise the lowliness of your stories. Don't worry that others might not be able to value your stories the way you do. They are his gifts to you. Enjoy them.

A Word to Pastors

Imagine a church consulting firm or a pastors' conference whose selling point is that they will teach you and your staff to go low, to descend into the hidden room of prayer, to slow down your entire ministry and learn how to pray together. It's a bit scary when God's normal sounds odd.

Into the vacuum left by our inattentiveness to the Spirit comes *the manager*, whether it be the pastor, an elder, or an outside consultant. The good manager sees the facts, the processes, and the people that the church needs. The gift of administration blesses the church, but it can easily miss the central fact in any church: the Spirit's resurrection of Jesus from the dead, and the ensuing life and power that come from their union. That blinding light shapes all other wisdom.

The pastor-as-manager can appear to work fairly well in a stable, Christianized culture, but when all hell is breaking loose, you need to put management in the back seat where it belongs and put the Spirit in the driver's seat. Then get ready for the drive of your life!

13

Becoming a
Praying Leader

A PRAYING COMMUNITY IS MULTILAYERED, with both praying leaders and a praying congregation. You need this dual focus to sustain a culture of prayer in a church. A praying leader without a praying church will see some amazing things happen through that leader, but the congregation will tend to live vicariously off their pastor's faith, a problem that is exposed when that person is no longer present. I saw that happen at New Life Church over time. We had a praying leader, but we didn't have structures of prayer (like prayer meetings) to sustain a culture of prayer over the long haul. Likewise, a praying church is difficult to create without a praying leader. Prayer retreats into the lives of a few devout prayers, like Simeon and Anna in the temple. Paul's exhortation still rings true: "*Let the entire church* keep alert with all perseverance, making supplication for all the saints, praying at all times in the Spirit, with all prayer and supplication" (Eph. 6:18 AT).

What better model than Jesus of Nazareth?

An Inside Look at Jesus's Prayer Life

Mark 1 describes the day when Jesus first goes public with his miracles. The day begins with him casting out a demon in the Capernaum synagogue; this is followed by the healing of Peter's mother-in-law from a fever. That evening "the whole city was gathered together at the door" (v. 33). Jesus heals far into the night. The next day, "rising very early in the morning, while it was still dark, he departed and went out to a desolate place, and there he prayed" (v. 35). He prays long enough that the crowd regathers, prompting his disciples to search for him. When they finally find him, instead of healing more people, Jesus announces they are going on a preaching tour of Galilee.

The day is perfectly balanced between public ministry and private prayer. Jesus walks away from an incredibly successful ministry to be with his Father. Notice, Jesus does not multitask. He hunts for a "desolate place" where he can't be interrupted by the noise. Jesus, the perfect God-man, refuses to live outside of fellowship with his heavenly Father.

The Gospels offer two visions of Jesus's prayer life. Luke gives us an exterior vision, which we saw in chapter 4, that focuses on his prayer life and the Spirit. John gives us an interior vision. In John, Jesus repeatedly says things like "I can do nothing on my own; I can only do what I see my Father doing" (see 5:19).

Jesus's prayer life is driven by his experience of sonship. As a son, he can do nothing on his own. He is the most dependent human being who ever lived.[1] All too often Christians see prayer through the lens of discipline, as in, "If I were more disciplined, I'd pray more." But dependence, not discipline, drives Jesus's prayer life.

A praying leader needs the complementary visions of Luke and John. Evangelicals emphasize prayer for mission (Luke), while more contemplative traditions stress Jesus's communion with his Father as a way of nurturing your soul (John). Luke's emphasis, by itself, can depersonalize prayer and lead to legalism. John's emphasis, by itself, can become self-preoccupied and feed our modern obsession with self.

Luke's emphasis on Jesus's exterior prayer life, combined with John's focus on Jesus's interior dependence on his Father, gives us a remarkably coherent picture of what it is to be human. The praying Jesus of Luke is the dependent Jesus of John. Both writers look at exactly the same phenomenon: the first fully God-dependent person, who expresses his dependence in a praying life that waits on the Spirit. Figure 13.1 illustrates this combination.

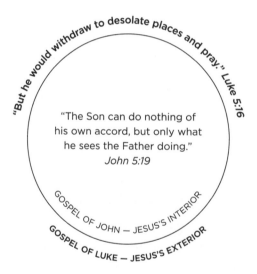

Figure 13.1. Luke's and John's complementary visions of Jesus's prayer life

A Glimpse of John Stott, Praying Leader

Richard Trist, an Australian pastor, described his first encounter with John Stott, one of the world's leading theologians and pastors.[2] Trist had just flown in from Australia to be the preaching pastor under Stott at All Souls Church, in London. As he and his family were unpacking, the phone rang: "It's John Stott here. I just wanted to welcome you to London and let you know I have been praying for you. How are you and Glenda, and the children Luke, Sophie, Lily and Grace?" Trist was struck not only by an invitation to tea but also by the fact that Stott had *already* been praying for him *and* his family by name. Trist soon discovered Stott's personal habits of prayer. As soon as John got up in the morning, he sat on the edge of his bed and prayed:

> Good morning heavenly Father, good morning Lord Jesus, good morning Holy Spirit. Heavenly Father, I pray that I may live this day in your presence and please you more and more. Lord Jesus, I pray that this day I may take up my cross and follow you. Holy Spirit, I pray that this day you will fill me with yourself and cause your fruit to ripen in my life: Love, Joy, Peace, Patience, Kindness, Goodness, Faithfulness, Gentleness, and Self-Control. Holy, blessed, and glorious Trinity, three persons in one God, have mercy to me.

Stott's "prayer system" consisted of an old leather-bound book stuffed with papers containing hundreds of names of people he had met in his travels. After reading the Bible, he opened his prayer book and went to work.

Stott's private prayer life was balanced by a commitment to corporate prayer. When he first became pastor at All Souls, he challenged the congregation not to make prayer an "optional extra." "About 450 come to the church on Sundays to worship; about 25 come to the church house on Thursday to pray. We have begun a new chapter in our church's history. . . . We must pray if we are to succeed."[3] On the second Tuesday evening of the month, hundreds of people would come to pray together at All Souls. Trist says that he'd been in a lot of prayer meetings, but he'd never seen anything like this one. They prayed for everything: the preaching, the small groups, the missionaries, and the wider culture. Whenever Stott was in London, he was at this prayer meeting, taking his seat along with everyone else.

Stott was burdened by the lack of corporate prayer in the church. He wrote:

> I sometimes wonder if the slow progress towards world peace and world evangelisation is due to the prayerlessness of the people of God. We should take the task of public intercession more seriously than we commonly do. If local churches were to bow down before God every Sunday for ten or twenty or even thirty minutes, what might God be free to do.[4]

Now that we've overviewed a prominent leader's prayer life, let me zoom in on a story from my life to see what the Luke-John prayer dynamic looks like.

An Inside Look at Another Praying Leader

In May 1995, the Foundation for New Era Philanthropy collapsed. The mission I worked for at the time and 180 evangelical nonprofits lost millions. We launched a campaign to raise funds, but by late July, I was troubled. The campaign lacked energy. I'd just started taking Fridays to fast and pray. One Friday, I came into my prayer time restless. My "desolate place" was a Sunday school room in the basement of a local church.

I knew something was wrong, but I couldn't put my finger on it. When I feel that way, I'm quiet before God, and I pour my heart into my prayer journal. This sounds like a bad joke, but I've learned you can't rush slowing down and waiting. I have to give space for the Spirit to speak and for my spirit to stop speaking. Neither happens quickly. My planning and problem-solving need to "stand down" to make room for the Spirit.

I don't sit around waiting to hear a voice—I have that already in God's word, so I pray slowly through Scripture. And in this particular struggle, I knew the heart of wisdom was knowing that I didn't have wisdom, so I prayed through Proverbs. As I read and prayed, the theme that jumped out at me was this: "In an abundance of counselors there is safety" (11:14). It hit me: *we weren't getting good counsel.* Then I remembered a meeting the year before with a development consultant. So when I got home, I called him and shared our predicament. We spent an hour on the phone. He was filled with practical wisdom—just what we needed. The following week, on his way to vacation in Maine, he stopped off in Philadelphia and spent a day with us. He transformed our campaign. He helped us raise almost eight hundred thousand dollars, but even better, it led to a ten-year mentoring relationship where he taught me in the area of development.[5]

I prayed because *I could do nothing on my own*; and only then did the Spirit give me wisdom. The process followed the pattern of the J-curve. Realizing I was in a kind of death opened the door to prayer and wisdom from the Spirit. The Spirit is at his best when we are at our weakest.

The Spirit's leading that day was unexpected, "outside the box." As with all the stories he weaves, God was doing something even bigger than I imagined. When I called the consultant, I didn't know that four years later I'd need his skills and wisdom to launch a new mission, seeJesus. I was scared to death of asking people for money, but I needed to learn this new way of loving people. God was preparing "a table before me in the presence of my enemies" (Ps. 23:5), and I didn't even know it. And now, twenty-five years later, the consultant's son continues to mentor me and our staff. The apostle Paul is quite serious when he says that God is "able to do far more abundantly than all that we ask or think" (Eph. 3:20).

Creating Personal Liturgies

In Acts, we see *both* corporate prayer and private praying by leaders. Corporate prayer and private prayer complement each other. As an example of private prayer, "Peter went up on the housetop about the sixth hour to pray" (10:9). That's noon, likely reflecting the Jewish pattern of praying three times a day: morning, noon, and night. I've singled out a leader's private prayer, but the need for regular times of prayer applies to all the saints. When the saints have systematic prayer lives, it enriches corporate prayer.

To be consistent with prayer, you need a system. That's what the medieval church did when it created liturgies. They systematized prayer through what they called divine reading by prayerfully reading Scripture. A typical monastery would pray through all 150 psalms every week. After a psalm was read, the monks might prostrate themselves, praying silently for a minute or so. In the Benedictine Rule the monks prayed, worshiped, and read Scripture at least four hours a day, and more on Sabbaths and feast days.

It dawned on me recently that I'd created a personal liturgy around my family and my work that I pray through every day. It takes me about thirty minutes in the morning. I use prayer cards (three-by-five-inch index cards) that are jammed mainly with Scripture. Below is a glimpse of my daily prayer liturgy. Samples drawn from prayer cards are shown in italics, with Scripture in quotation marks. Every card has a story behind it.

Personal Requests for Myself (Sixteen Cards)

> *"In everything by prayer . . . with thanksgiving let your requests be made known to God. And the peace of God . . . will guard your hearts and your minds in Christ Jesus." (Phil. 4:6–7)*

I begin with this fifteen-year-old prayer card that I started when I noticed cynicism weakening my prayer life. This prompts me to think back to the previous day and look for how my Father helped me.

———

> *"Surely, when the mighty waters rise, they will not reach you. You are my hiding place; you will protect me from trouble and surround me with songs of deliverance." (Ps. 32:6–7 AT)*

I've had this card for twenty-five years. I moved it from my monthly prayers to my daily prayers about seven years ago when I sensed a rising tide of evil.

———

> *"Finally, be strong in the Lord and in the strength of his might. Put on the whole armor of God." (Eph. 6:10)*

I created this card seven years ago, when I felt the growing evil in our day. I use this to prompt me to pray for a piece of Christian armor. Today was "the shield of faith" (Eph. 6:16).

———

"Let no corrupting talk come out of your mouths." (Eph. 4:29)

I struggle with prudence.

———

"Quick to hear, slow to speak, slow to anger." (James 1:19)

I struggle with listening. (Our lovable dog Tully ate a corner out of this prayer card, perhaps testing my obedience to this prayer.)

———

"I, when I am lifted up . . . , will draw all people to myself." (John 12:32)

This is an eleven-year-old prayer that I shifted to daily use about four years ago when I felt completely stymied with trying to get the church to pay closer attention to the person of Jesus.

———

Help me to see women "as sisters" and daughters, and if I can't, help me look away. Help me to "gaze upon the beauty of the Lord." (Ps. 27:4; 1 Tim. 5:2)

Every day I pray for sexual purity.

Prayers for My Family (Forty-One Cards—We Have a Big Family!)

> *"Let your adorning be the hidden person of the heart with the imperishable beauty of a gentle and quiet spirit."*
> *(1 Pet. 3:4)*

I pray this for my granddaughter Jami to be beautiful in and out.

———

> *"Do you love me more than these?" "Yes, Lord . . ." (John 21:15)*

I use Jesus's question to Peter to pray that a love for Jesus would grow in my grandson Zach's life. It has.

Prayers for Work (Twenty-Six Cards)

> *"It is my prayer that your love may abound more and more, with knowledge and all discernment, so that you may approve what is excellent." (Phil. 1:9–10)*

I pray this for our leadership team.

———

> *"[See] if I will not open the windows of heaven for you and pour down for you a blessing until there is no more need." (Mal. 3:10)*

I pray this for our annual fund.

———

"God is able to make all grace abound to you, so that having all sufficiency in all things at all times, you may abound in every good work." (2 Cor. 9:8)

I pray this for our finance and administration team.

———

"I will pour my Spirit upon your offspring, and my blessing on your descendants." (Isa. 44:3)

I pray this for our Arab work.

Miscellaneous Prayers (Ten Cards)

"The Spirit of the sovereign Lord is on me, because the Lord has anointed me . . . to comfort all who mourn, . . . to bestow on them . . . a garment of praise instead of a spirit of despair." (Isa. 61:1–3 NIV)

I pray this for people who are suffering.

A Lovely Cadence

Regardless of whether or not you are a leader, there's a lovely cadence between a life of private prayer and corporate prayer. The one form of prayer strengthens the other. Over many years of private prayer, my faith has grown steadily to a quiet confidence that God will *hear me when I cry.* That faith spills over into the prayer meetings I'm part of. My confidence in God encourages others to be confident in God. It's not so much that I say I have faith, but they feel it with how seriously I take our praying together. Then as their faith grows, that helps them take private prayer seriously. Faith begets faith. In turn, their faith encourages my faith.

Also, I do my best "prayer thinking" in private prayer. For example, writing out and updating my prayer cards helps me to think through "prayer targeting." That is, what exactly do I want? What are the barriers here? Which of my weaknesses do I need to pray for daily? I bring those insights and desires into the prayer meetings I'm part of, which helps others think through their praying.

Here's an example of how private and corporate prayer work together. You saw, above, some of my prayer cards on my besetting sin of overtalking. In prayer meetings, my faith can bubble over and become unchecked, resulting in me talking too much. I'm so aware of my tendency to speak too much, and thus limit the Spirit's role in people's lives, that when I lead a prayer time, I try to limit myself to one three-minute insight per prayer meeting. Mindful of the danger of taking center stage, I frequently do a "cold stop." I can sense the Spirit tugging me to be quiet, and I'll literally stop mid-sentence and say, "I've said enough." I don't even try to land the plane; I just parachute out. If I try to land, I'll find more things to share.

As a leader of a Jesus community, I'm potentially Jesus's biggest competitor. But if I realize, like Jesus, that *I can't even do prayer meetings on my own*, that encourages me, by the Spirit, to put to death my tendency to overtalk. That allows all of us to see Jesus better.

14

Praying Big

WE ARE FOCUSING ON PRAYING BIG, because that's what happens at the end of the power train, when our Father does "far more abundantly than all that we ask or think" (Eph. 3:20). In a book that rarely uses hyperbole (the Bible), Paul is at the edge of human language describing the immensity of the explosion of life, glory, and power that comes from the Spirit of Jesus. Here are several other translations of Ephesians 3:20, all of them groping to communicate the immensity of the Spirit's work:

> Now all glory to God, who is able, through his mighty power at work within us, to accomplish infinitely more than we might ask or think. (NLT)

> Now to him who is able to do immeasurably more than all we ask or imagine, according to his power that is at work within us. (NIV)

> God can do anything, you know—far more than you could ever imagine or guess or request in your wildest dreams! (MSG)

All through Acts you find the explosive power of the Spirit working beyond all that we can ask or imagine. It's God's normal. So knowing the *imagination explosion* at the end of the power train shapes the beginning of the power train—how we pray. We pray big because it's the Spirit's normal.

But the Spirit's power funnels his power through a cross-shaped lens.

Praying Big for My Family

In 1990 I took five of our six kids on what became a miserable camping trip. The kids' selfishness combined with my parenting-by-yelling really shook me. We were headed for disaster. As we were drying off in our minivan after enduring a rain-soaked night, I prayed, "Jesus, you have to save our family." Our kids' lack of love for one another showed me their faith was weak.[1]

Figure 14.1 captures the tension between our family's bleak *reality*, and my kingdom *desire* for faith (believing in Jesus) and love (loving like Jesus). That disparity drove my prayer.

Figure 14.1. Praying big

136

My desire reflects some aspect of God's heart. That is, God didn't want our family to be half-saved. He wanted us to be completely saved, filled with faith and love, and thus to look like Jesus. So I prayed big. Absent a clear kingdom goal, prayer easily becomes therapeutic, formless, and just boring. It can drift into asking for some version of a pain-free world.

John Newton knew how to pray big.

Thou art coming to a king,
Large petitions with thee bring;
For His grace and power are such,
None can ever ask too much.[2]

Jesus encourages us to pray big. If you strip "your kingdom come, / your will be done, / on earth as it is in heaven" from the Lord's Prayer (Matt. 6:9–13), then you let the air out of the prayer, and it turns inward. Jill and I had little interest in our kids excelling in anything but faith and love. Of course, we encouraged them to do well in school and sports, and we enjoyed them when they did their best—but that was secondary to our prayer that they would become Jesus followers.

I still remember the quiet in our minivan—the kids had fallen asleep, exhausted—and then the quiet in my heart after I prayed. I knew God would save my family. I'd heard God's still small voice.

So, what did God do with my minivan prayer? Almost immediately, he began drawing me into a fellowship of Christ's suffering. A kingdom goal draws us into the King's journey. A week before his death, Jesus tells his disciples that his path is our path: "Unless a grain of wheat falls into the earth and dies, it remains alone; but if it dies, it bears much fruit" (John 12:24).

I began to experience suffering, and at the end of that year, burnout. I wanted God to work on our family. God wanted to work on me. Down low, at the bottom of the J-curve, I learned to pray. Over the next twenty years God did wonder after wonder in our children, then in their spouses, and now we're praying for our grandkids. The key was continually facing the tension between our family's *reality* and my *desire*.

The Apostle Paul Prays Big

Praying big emerges out of big dying. My big prayers all emerge from camping trips gone bad. Down low, in the dying, we see more clearly both our neediness and God's desire. It's a remarkably consistent biblical pattern: God's vision to Moses when he's tending sheep (Ex. 3), God's promise to Jacob when he's running for his life (Gen. 28), Daniel's visions in captivity (Dan. 7), and John's vision while exiled on Patmos (Rev. 1).

Likewise, Paul's grandest prayers emerge during his long imprisonment. He lets the Colossians know how his team prays for them. This isn't Paul's prayer; it's *his team's prayer*. It's one Jesus community praying for another. Notice the italics:

> And so, from the day *we heard, we have not ceased to pray for you*, asking that you may be filled with the knowledge of his will in all [S]piritual wisdom and understanding, so as to walk in a manner worthy of the **Lord**, fully pleasing to him: bearing fruit in every good work and increasing in the knowledge of God; being strengthened with all **power**, according to his glorious might, for all endurance and patience with joy. (1:9–11)[3]

Notice, too, the familiar pattern of the church's power train (in bold): *prayer → Spirit → Jesus → power*. Paul's team prays for the

Spirit to give customized wisdom (1:9) so that the Colossians reflect Jesus (1:10). To do this, they pray for the resurrection power of the Spirit to produce in them "all endurance and patience with joy" (1:11).

This prayer is the Spiritual equivalent of "go big or go home." Paul's praying team doesn't pray that they will *try* to bear fruit *as best they can* but that they will "bear fruit in every good work." There's no "give it your best shot" or "I know life is tough." Their prayer glows with exuberance and hope, fully expectant that the resurrection power of the Spirit is available to bring the beauty of Jesus into his body, the church. Big faith drives big prayers.

This prayer is strikingly different from the content of many prayer meetings, which tend to drift downward into the immediate and the tactical. Typically, we can see individual trees but miss the grandeur of the forest. Prayers meander from arthritic hips to wayward children to broken cars. Without a larger kingdom vision, repetitive and unwieldly problems feel heavy and depressing. A Jesus vision, in tension with our current situations, energizes our prayers. It's quite simple: when the body of Christ prays the passions of Christ, we come alive. We were made to dream his dreams.

James O. Fraser Prays Big

James O. Fraser, a missionary to the Lisu people in southwestern China, taught me the twin vision of big praying and facing reality. Fraser began his work among the Lisu in 1911. He loved the colorful Lisu and their mountain villages. For five years he labored among them, preaching the gospel first through translators and then eventually in Lisu. Many professed belief, but all except a handful soon drifted back into idolatry and demon worship. Fraser learned that unless whole families came to Christ, the clan and the power of the demons would overwhelm the individual believer. The break with demons and idolatry had to be complete: the clan had to burn all their idols.

Confronted with the enormity of the opposition, Fraser responded with a campaign of long-distance, corporate prayer. He cultivated a prayer team back in England and fed their prayers with frequent letters about the Lisu, their villages, and their customs. In one letter he described their annual Sword Ladder Festival, when a shaman placated the demons by climbing a ladder of upturned swords. He asked his pray-ers to "target" specific villages and valleys, and even witch doctors, who were particularly hostile to faith. Fraser knew that the spiritual forces he faced could be defeated only through united prayer.

Sitting on the mud floor of a Lisu hut in a remote mountain region, Fraser penned a long letter to his prayer team on "the prayer of faith." He was deeply affected by how tightly Jesus linked prayer with faith.

Jesus answered them, "Truly, I say to you, if you have faith and do not doubt, you will not only do what has been done to the fig tree, but even if you say to this mountain, 'Be taken up and thrown into the sea,' it will happen. And whatever you ask in prayer, you will receive, if you have faith." (Matt. 21:21–22)

Fraser explained the link between prayer and faith by comparing it to the nineteenth-century Canadian farmer whose government promised the deed to 160 acres of land if he farmed it for ten years. Fraser likened the farmer's diligence to the prayer of faith. Fraser wanted thousands of Lisu families to come to know Christ, but he had faith that two hundred families would. He prayed big, but he didn't overstretch his faith. Then, like the farmer, he "worked the land" by tirelessly preaching the gospel among the Lisu and sending a torrent of letters to his home prayer team.

Fraser asked his friends to form a virtual praying community and join him in his prayer of faith to break through the spiritual barriers that gripped the Lisu.

I should value highly the prayer-cooperation of any that felt led to join me in it [for the turning to God of several hundred Lisu families]. What I want is not just an occasional mention of my work and its needs before the Lord during the morning or evening devotions, but a definite time (say half an hour or so?) set apart for the purpose every day, either during the day time or in the evening. Can you give me that time to me—or rather to the Lord?

Fraser's *desire* for two hundred Lisu families to convert shaped his work; yet, after five years with only a handful of converts, he faced *reality* by deciding to write to the director of China Inland Mission, offering to be reassigned. Fraser's desire remained undimmed. He wasn't sure how two hundred families would come to Christ, but he believed God would do it. Faith brought desire and reality together.

The faith that Fraser felt on the floor of the mud hut, and that I felt in our minivan, was a gift. Neither of us sought it. I can't stress this enough. If you seek the experience of faith, you hunt for some mix of euphoria, confidence, and excitement. By shifting the focus from Jesus to the experience of Jesus, you are just hunting for a feeling. That's idolatry, and it quenches the Spirit.

But before Fraser sent the letter asking to be reassigned, he decided to take one last trip among the Lisu. Leaving in October 1916, he preached the gospel in the first village, "careful to avoid any appearance of urgency in giving the message so near his heart." As he was preparing to leave the next morning, his Lisu companion rushed in: "Teacher, wait a little, this family wants to turn Christian, if you will help them." Fraser was cautious. "He had learned that anything short of the complete destruction of all implements used in spirit-worship" would not make room for Christ.[4] Yet, within a few days, seven families had burned all their idols. In village after village, families burned their idols and turned to Christ. Within two months 129 families, totaling six hundred Lisu, had become believers.

God would go on to answer Fraser's prayers beyond all that he could ask or imagine. And yet, that was inseparable from Fraser embodying the dying of Christ with the Lisu. Fraser was very conscious of what I've been calling "the J-curve." Out among the Lisu in 1918 he wrote: "The cross is going to hurt—let it hurt! I am going to work hard and pray hard, by God's grace. . . . As soon as we cease to bleed we cease to bless. . . . St. Catharine's prayers were red with sacrifice, and she felt the touch of the pierced hands."[5]

The dying that Fraser experienced was principally dying to self, where you suffer on the inside as you continuously say no to your desires: "It was drifting that Fraser dreaded most of all—slackness in spirit, sloth, prayerlessness, leading to defeat under trial."[6] He tirelessly served the Lisu, first on his knees and then by his endless treks through their mountains, preaching the gospel, sleeping on dirt floors. Then he labored to disciple them, giving them the tools of the gospel by first creating their alphabet and then translating the New Testament into Lisu—the crowning joy of his life.

Fraser finally gave his utmost when he passed away at age fifty-two from cerebral malaria, leaving behind his pregnant wife and two children. He'd written in his journal in 1918, "We must bleed, if we would be ministers of the saving blood." Now, a century later, out of 1.5 million Lisu, about 1.3 million are believers. One young Lisu, when interrogated by the Communists, said, "Christianity has already penetrated into our flesh and blood and it will not be easy to tear it away from us."[7] Fraser's big desire led to big praying followed by much fruit. In fact, to say that God "is able to do far more abundantly than all we can ask or think" feels like an understatement.

In Fraser's life we can see the importance of a clear goal (the Lisu coming to faith), how he got to the destination (faith and big praying), and what his journey looked like (the J-curve). As soon as we get our destination, our method, and our journey clear, it shapes *how* we pray—which we've begun to explore in this chapter and will continue in the next.

But don't miss the heart of what's going on. Don't be bashful about fighting in prayer for the souls of your children or friends. Join James Fraser on the mud floor of a Lisu hut and his virtual prayer team as he fought against the Sword Ladder Festival. Your family is your Lisu tribe. You have to fight against sports, the phones, and Instagram. You must begin the serious and steady work of praying daily for them and drawing others into prayer for them. It's some of the hardest work you'll ever do, which is why we need to do it together.

15

The Prayer Triangle

I WANT TO PAUSE AND SHOW YOU how to integrate praying big into corporate prayer. Every human enterprise has vision, strategy, and tactics. Vision answers *why* we do things. Strategy is *how* we go about doing them, and tactics are *what* we do today. Figure 15.1 illustrates these three ways of praying.

Figure 15.1. The prayer triangle

Vision is at the top; it shapes what comes below. So James Fraser's vision, what I've been calling "praying big," was for two hundred Lisu families to convert.

The next layer is strategy, which makes the vision possible. For Fraser, that meant mobilizing a prayer team back in England that he would feed with frequent, targeted prayer requests, such as praying against the demonic powers in the Sword Ladder Festival.

Finally, the bottom layer is tactics. These are the specific activities that we do to make the strategy happen. For Fraser, that meant targeting specific villages for prayer, such as Six Family Hollow, where Mother Tsai lived with her family. Mother Tsai was a shining light in her village for Jesus.

Praying up and down the prayer triangle keeps your prayers from getting stuck in the doldrums. Prayer meetings typically get stuck at the bottom of the prayer triangle. They tend to miss strategy and vision. And yet, vision is why we do life. Our vision for our grandchildren is enjoying them and seeing them grow in faith and love. Our strategy is frequent visits or family get-togethers. Our tactics are what we actually do when we are together. Vision is the key—without it, tactics become burdensome. Most of Jill's and my prayers for our grandchildren are vision and strategy prayers. We pray for specific needs that come up, but we are far more concerned for their hearts, that they would walk with Jesus.

Here's how to move up the prayer triangle, from tactics to vision praying. During the COVID pandemic, when praying for someone sick with COVID (tactics), we moved up the triangle and prayed for doctors and researchers who were working on the vaccine (strategy), and then we prayed for an end to the pandemic (strategy), but also asked, "God, what are you doing?" (vision). Then six months into the pandemic, it was obvious that God was pruning his church, drawing us into a kind of corporate death. So I began to pray that God would do what he was already doing—that he would prune his church. It was an easy shift to pray this way because I regularly prayed that for myself. I just enlarged a personal prayer. Good praying is like body surfing. You ride the waves; you don't fight them.

The shape of the triangle gives you a feel for the overall balance of big-vision prayers and smaller tactical prayers. Big-vision prayers are like spice. You don't need a lot to flavor the whole. Tactical praying will usually form the bulk of our praying. I must confess, though, the older I get, the bigger I pray! And then, like Fraser, you go to work, trampling among "your Lisu," being like Jesus and sharing Jesus.

Praying big expands our prayer repertoire. We aren't praying off the same old sheet of music. It also grows our imagination. We begin to think, *Why not?* Below are several case studies from my work of how the prayer triangle helps shape our praying together.

Praying for Prayer

Figure 15.2 shows a prayer card that I wrote in March 2007 as I started to write *A Praying Life*. It is a prayer for prayer.[1]

The card is mainly tactics and strategy prayers, but at the bottom is a vision prayer. I remember writing out the card and reflecting: *What do I want? What do I want God to do?* I didn't want to just write a book; I wanted God to create a *movement of prayer that teaches the church to pray.*

A Praying Life   3/07

Partners: Col. 4:2, "Devote yourselves to prayer, being watchful and thankful."

Bob Allums: 2 Tim. 1:7, "For God did not give us a Spirit of timidity, but a Spirit of power, of love, and of self-discipline."

A Praying Life Book: simple elegance, easy to read, well edited, teach people to pray.

Seminars: hundreds of them.

Movement of Prayer that teaches the church to pray.

Figure 15.2. Prayer card for *A Praying Life*

I wrote this card when I was at the bottom of a J-curve, weakened by multiple outward circumstances. Our ministry was unknown and without any human traction. I didn't even worry whether I had faith to pray this. I just prayed it. (It's toxic to look at your faith. Faith, by definition, looks outside itself to God.) There's a refreshing clarity about weakness that makes prayer completely natural. The veil to heaven thins. God loves weakening us so he can display his power in us. So I prayed big.

I was also attentive to the story God was weaving. I'd tried for several years to recruit Bob Allums to pioneer A Praying Life Ministry, but he'd been hesitant—wisely so. Bob would have had to take a significant pay cut and raise his own support to start a new enterprise that had no precedent (training badly praying Christians to pray). And if it failed, neither of us had the financial resources to rescue him. Plus, he had two kids in college. So this card represented a shift in strategy: I decided to stop recruiting Bob and just pray my vision.

I also prayed that God would give Bob a Spirit of power, of love, and of self-discipline. That's a prayer for the Spirit's power train. I was praying not for a *feeling* of power but for *Spiritual power*. Bob and I both needed that.

So what did the Spirit do? Things got worse. Three months later *A Praying Life* was rejected by a major publisher. And yet God used that weakness to give Bob a desire to join us full-time. Bob called me in July; he wanted to launch. I was so surprised, I questioned him carefully. Yes, he was serious. He explained to me: "I was on the road on a sales trip, driving through the Pennsylvania countryside and it hit me, 'Now is the time.' I won't say the Lord spoke to me, but I believe he did. That's when I called you and diverted my trip to come see you at that restaurant. This decision was the best I've ever made."

We never looked back. God has blessed A Praying Life Ministry beyond all that I can ask or imagine.

How does praying big translate to our prayer meetings? When others are praying tactical and strategic prayers, it's relatively easy to simply expand everyone's vision by praying: "God would you create a movement of prayer that teaches the church to prayer? Would you help church leaders to see that, like Jesus, *they can't do anything on their own?*"

Praying big frees our prayers, and thus our spirits, from the daily grind. Without direction, we miss the forest for the trees. We get "stuck in the weeds." But with direction, no matter how thick the weeds, we have hope and purpose.

But what if you've been praying big for thirty years and the needle has hardly moved? That's the next story.

A Passion for the Person of Jesus

I have a largely unanswered vision prayer. It's actually tough to explain, so bear with me. It's a passion God burned on my heart nine months after that miserable camping trip. During a sabbatical in 1991 when I studied the Gospels, I was stunned by the *person* of Jesus. I was riveted by his compassion, his honesty, his dependence on his Father. The person of Jesus so captured my heart that when we started seeJesus in 1999, our first vision statement was "helping people see the beauty of Jesus." We soon dropped the slogan because no one knew what we meant: Were we a beauty parlor? A worship ministry? An art studio?

I want the church to see how vibrant and alive Jesus is in the Gospels, to begin to love like him, and to enter into his path. I've felt a quiet assurance that God will do it, although I'm not sure he will do it in my lifetime. I'm hovering between hope and reality, very aware that my vision has not happened and yet praying every day.

I wrote the prayer card shown in figure 15.3 in 2006. Notice, that was fifteen years from the time God first put this burden on my heart. It took me that long to say, "I need to be specific about what I want God to do." It's a relatively unusual prayer, because I'm asking specifically for God to help people see the *person* of Jesus. Notice also the prayer for the church to *become like the gospel*, to enter the story of Jesus, the J-curve.

Not quite ten years later, by 2015, I'd had so many failures in trying to help the church to see the person of Jesus that I finally faced reality: I stopped working on any new strategic initiatives related to the person of Jesus. I did make a small tactical decision: I began to pray this card daily. I've noticed a peculiar power about daily prayer as opposed to weekly prayer. Within a year, things began to happen. An Arab Christian joined our staff, and I discovered a pastor in Chattanooga whose heart was stirred with the person of Jesus.

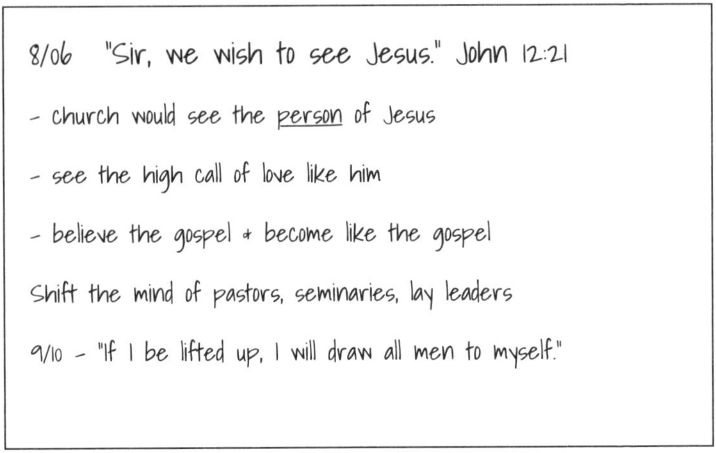

8/06 "Sir, we wish to see Jesus." John 12:21

- church would see the <u>person</u> of Jesus

- see the high call of love like him

- believe the gospel + become like the gospel

Shift the mind of pastors, seminaries, lay leaders

9/10 - "If I be lifted up, I will draw all men to myself."

Figure 15.3. Prayer card "to see Jesus"

Praying big is quite freeing, because it allows you to sustain a life of prayer when you are faced with repeated failure. When Fraser decided to write a letter offering to resign, that was a strategic decision. He hadn't given up on his vision; he was just facing reality.

If you pray big enough and long enough, God begins to do what you want entirely outside of your world. Recently, I showed this prayer card at our staff prayer meeting and encouraged our staff to see the new Jesus film series called *The Chosen.* I believe that series is an answer to this prayer (and others' prayers) for the church to see the person of Jesus. God answers our prayers outside of our circles to protect us from institutional idolatry and preserve his glory.

Notice how, in both of these stories (about Bob Allums and the person of Jesus), the Spirit led me into the path of Jesus, which *reduced* human effort and *increased* prayer. It was actually quite relaxing to *do less* and *pray more.*

All of my ministry prayers are pieces of a single vision that God etched on my heart the year after the minivan prayer: *prepare the bride.* Or more specifically, *prepare the bride for suffering, which will purify the bride and result in the coming of her husband, Jesus Christ.* Very simply, I pray every day in multiple ways that the church would come to look like Jesus.

One Barrier to Praying Big: Human Confidence

A pastor who now leads a prayer ministry told me that he'd been part of a denominational planning team that came up with a plan to double the size of his denomination. He predicted: "It will fail. It did not emerge out of prayer, but of our own self-confidence." He was right. It failed.

It's common for churches or groups to labor over a vision or mission statement, only to have it sit on the shelf or feel dull and lifeless. Even worse, you hear it endlessly recited from the front. It wasn't formed out of waiting on God in prayer, nor was it animated by the Spirit of Jesus. It was just the flesh, and "the flesh is no help at all" (John 6:63).

Big dreaming that is disconnected from a praying community and a praying leader just doesn't work. Luke is at pains to show how all the great works of the Spirit emerge out of prayer: the praying Israelites in the temple led to Zechariah's vision; at his baptism, Jesus was praying as the heavens opened; and at the Mount of Transfiguration, Jesus had been praying. The power train of *prayer → Spirit → Jesus → power* tries to capture that dynamic.

We don't discover our kingdom mission by forming a mission and vision team. What might work in the world of business does not in the kingdom work of Jesus. After all, he is a King who does his will, not ours. All the visions that I saw in my dad's life and my own life and that the Spirit used for good were visions God gave. They grew over time. The visions emerged as we prayed and loved, just as Fraser's vision for the Lisu took shape as he prayed and loved.

A Second Barrier to Praying Big: Weak Faith

But what if your faith is weak? I'd noticed that our staff struggled to pray big. When I asked them about this, Kellie, one of our trainers, said: "It feels inauthentic, as in, it's so big, it's not real. Or it can come across like a cop-out, as in 'God bless the whole world.'"

Kellie was feeling her weak faith muscle. When a weak muscle lifts something heavy, it feels impossible. We can easily read our weak faith into others, thinking, *It can't be real.* When Fraser prayed for two hundred Lisu families, he'd already spent time working out at a Spiritual gym, reflecting on the state of his faith muscle. He could lift two hundred Lisu, but no more. Even that was impossible for him alone, so he enlisted others to help him pray. Together, Fraser and his virtual prayer team back in England could lift this enormous weight.

Kellie went on to wonder out loud: "Do I really care? Do I have a big desire to bring to God?" I love her insightful question, because Kellie realized that we grow faith by loving. Big faith emerges out of big love. My love for my family fueled my minivan prayer. Fraser's love for the Lisu grew his praying. Only as we launch into the deep, only as we begin to love, do we feel the gap between desire and reality. If you are floating through life searching for likes on social media, you will never develop any passions larger than yourself.

Finally, Kellie caught herself mid-sentence. She remembered praying a year ago that the truth would come out about a politician in her state. She ended up being directly involved in an answer to that prayer. She had prayed her *desire* because she was upset by the *reality*; then God drew her into the answer to her prayer. She had loved big, prayed big, and seen God help.

So, at first, Kellie recoiled from praying big. It felt cheesy. And yet, when she thought of something concrete, she realized that she does exercise big faith. When Kellie looked at faith directly, she said, in effect, "I could never move that mountain into the sea." That is, when we confuse faith with confidence and then try to measure our level of "faith," we come up empty. Human confidence waxes and wanes. But you don't focus on faith. If you try to work up faith, it feels hollow. Overstretched faith that is confused with human confidence isn't real faith.

Fraser advised his virtual prayer team:

Overstrained faith is not pure faith, there is a mixture of the carnal element in it. I have asked the Lord for 200 families of Lisu believers. There are upwards of 2,000 Lisu families in the district altogether. It might be said, "Why do you not ask for 1,000?" I answer quite frankly, because I have not faith for a 1,000. I accept the limits the Lord has, I believe, given me.[2]

Praying big comes from and reinforces a whole way of looking at the world. Instead of being gripped by pagan fatalism and saying, "It is what it is," you think, *Why not?* Praying big opens the door to dreaming big. Figure 15.4 shows one of my prayer cards from 2007, when our ministry had encountered repeated failure.

"All things are possible for you." Mark 14:36—Jesus at Gethsemane

"With God all things are possible." Matt. 19:26—Jesus to his disciples

"Nothing will be impossible with God." Luke 1:37—angel Gabriel to Mary

"Is anything too difficult for God?" Gen. 18:14—God to Abraham

"Nothing is too difficult for thee." Jer. 32:17—Jeremiah

Figure 15.4. Prayer card for seeing all things as possible with God

So, what happens when you begin to pray this way? Your imagination comes alive. Evil no longer has the last word. You come at life with a new boldness, a new gusto. You pick yourself off the ground, dust yourself off, and have another go at it. You begin to wonder, *Who knows what God might do?* Hope is born.

To summarize our journey thus far: Prayer isn't just another ministry; it is *the* ministry that sparks the rule of the Spirit of Jesus in all ministries. Only as we wait in prayer does the captain direct us. We've got to pay attention to the captain. We can't publicly honor him and then act as if he can't direct us. Nor are we standing still. Our "ship" is on a voyage into Jesus's dying and rising. We aren't a merchant ship—we are a warship, heading into battle. Our captain is on a mission. Big love creates big dreams, which lead to big praying and big doing. The saints are unleashed!

16

Avoiding the Pitfalls of Prayer

AS WE CLOSE PART 3 ON THE INTERFACE of the Spirit and life, we explore some of the pitfalls surrounding Spirit-led praying. There's something about the pursuit of Spiritual power that can bring out the worst in us. The very elusiveness of the Spirit can open the door to our ever-present flesh, our tendency to pride and self-will. Let's look at some of these pitfalls.

The Pitfall of Over-Spiritualizing

Hollywood delights at making fun of how some Christians pray. A tendency toward super-spirituality has been captured in prayer scenes from popular movies. Here are some of our family's favorites.

In *Meet the Parents*, the prospective Jewish son-in-law, Greg (Ben Stiller), is asked by his future father-in-law (Robert De Niro) to "say grace." Greg, who's clearly never prayed, puts together an awkward, pietistic prayer: "We thank you, oh sweet, sweet Lord of hosts, for the smorgasbord that you've so aptly lain at our table this day, and each day, by day." In his groping for words he finds himself reciting the lyrics of "Day by Day," from the musical *Godspell*, after which he tacks on a hasty "Amen."

In *National Lampoon's Christmas Vacation*, the father (Chevy Chase) asks eighty-year-old Aunt Bethany to "say grace." The slightly senile aunt replies, "Didn't Grace die years ago?" Her toupee-decked husband yells at her, "Say the blessing!" Instantly, she bows her head and recites the Pledge of Allegiance. When she says "Amen," only the father realizes how bizarre this is.[1]

That's just the tip of the iceberg. There's Chevy's Chase's prayer over a dead aunt in *National Lampoon's Vacation*, and the incredibly painful prayer to "dear sweet Baby Jesus" in *Talladega Nights*. When we've done our prayer seminar for high school students, we've played these movie clips, to their delight.

These fake, inauthentic prayers use religious language to mimic sincerity and the presence of the Spirit. That's a tendency of pietism, which brought revival into mainstream Christianity by focusing on our personal relationship with God, Bible study, evangelism, and missions. It made Christianity real. Pietism genuinely wants us to have a living experience with God, but it can slip into searching for experiences with God or even putting those experiences on display.

I emphasize pietism because it's one part of the evangelical church still devoted to prayer. In decision-making, the pietist can at times be led by feelings, claiming "God spoke to me," which can lead to ignoring authority, love, commitment, and wise counsel. There is a sense in which God does speak, but we can easily confuse our feelings with God's speaking, thus elevating intuition above Scripture. The very character of biblical love is covenant love, where you make dogged commitments, such as in marriage or work, often despite your feelings.

Hollywood has put its finger on a break in our integrity, and not without reason. It's easy to see that the above "prayers" are disconnected from life, a mere show. But this doesn't just happen in movies. Too often our public prayers are for show and pious effect. They don't come from the heart. That creates cynicism, which mocks the good. The bottom line is that when pietism goes bad, it gets cheesy.

A whole generation of our youth finds syrupy spirituality cringeworthy. Many have embraced secular liberalism. I often hear from distraught parents who look at their lost children through the lens of pietism. Their analysis varies: "He gave his life to Christ when he was little. He just needs to return." Or "She's in rebellion against God." That's true, but a spirituality rooted in experience with God is not robust enough to withstand the multiple experiences offered by secular liberalism—sexual freedom, seeming authenticity, and freedom from authority.

So how do you avoid fake spirituality in prayer? Be real. Be yourself. Be careful of a "prayer language" when talking to God. Let prayer be part of the warp and woof of your life.

At our youth seminars, we show the evening campfire scene from the Civil War movie *Glory*, when the African American Fifty-Fourth Massachusetts Infantry Regiment is about to go into battle. First a private prays: "Tomorrow, we go into battle. So Lordy, let me fight with the rifle in one hand and Good Book in the other. That if I should die at the muzzle of the rifle, die on water or on land, I may know that You, Blessed Jesus Almighty, are with me. And I have no fear. Amen."[2]

Then the sergeant (Morgan Freeman) prays:

Lord, we stand before you this evenin' to say thank you. . . .
Now, I run off and left all my youngins and my kinfolk in

bondage. So I'm standin' here this evenin', Heavenly Father, to ask your blessin'! On all of us! So that if tomorrow is our great gettin' up mornin', if tomorrow we have to meet the Judgment Day, our Heavenly Father we want you to let our folks know that we died facin' the enemy. We want 'em to know that we went down standin' up, amongst those that are fightin' against our oppression. We want 'em to know, Heavenly Father, that we died for freedom. We ask these blessin's in Jesus name.

Then another private (Denzel Washington) says: "I ain't much about no prayin' now. I ain't never had no family and . . . killed off my mama. . . . Ya'lls . . . is the onliest family I got. And I loves the 54th. Ain't much a matter what happen tomorrow. 'Cause we men, ain't we. We men, ain't we."

The difference between the Hollywood prayers quoted above and those of the Fifty-Fourth Regiment is like night and day. It's phony versus real, fake versus authentic. Our kids aren't stupid. They know when something is not authentic. Modeling and teaching our kids to pray about real problems to a real God who hears and acts can make their faith real.

Another pitfall in public prayer is under-spiritualizing, the opposite problem.

The Pitfall of Under-Spiritualizing

My daughter-in-law Pam, along with our son John, joined a small group in their church. During a closing prayer time, people took turns sharing prayer requests. Michael asked for prayer that God would provide a new air conditioner for him and his wife. Their old one had broken. Pam was up next.

"I can't pray for that," she said. The group was so surprised by Pam's response, they all laughed. She explained, "I've tried praying in my mind for what you said, and it just didn't work." It didn't work because Michael's request wasn't a need (he wasn't poor); it was more of a report. He didn't need someone to pray that he would get a new air conditioner; he simply needed to buy one. Michael hadn't put any thought or heart into his prayer request—and Pam reacted to that. She grew up in a home where religious language was absent. She's a bottom-line, successful businesswoman. Things have to work for Pam. They have to be real.

Pam's honesty startled Michael, but it affected him for good. He said, "Let me try again." He thought for a minute about what was really on his heart and mentioned two genuine needs. Pam's honesty moved the group from being religious to being real. The whole group was blessed.

You might call Michael's prayer *non-spiritualizing*. In contrast, the prayers of the Fifty-Fourth Massachusetts were *real*. They weren't merely having a "prayer meeting"; they were talking to the living God about something very important to them. Pam rightly reacted to something that wasn't real. Her reaction forced Michael to take prayer seriously as opposed to taking prayer glibly.

Compare Michael's under-spiritualizing with a request made by my dad, who, at least in this instance, over-spiritualized. At a church prayer meeting, my dad (the senior pastor) asked prayer for a new washing machine. An elder with a business background, not wanting to offend Dad, pulled me aside and said: "Do they lack funds? Is Jack's salary too low? What's going on?" I laughed and said, "No, they have the funds; Dad just loves having God take care of his needs and seeing God provide through others."

Pietism tends to run everything through a "super-spiritual" lens, so every provision has to be by prayer, which is just a bit odd. Paul doesn't say lazy Christians should pray more for God's provision; he says they shouldn't eat (2 Thess. 3:10)! When Jesus prepares for the Last Supper, he doesn't perform a miracle, he tells two of his disciples to go prepare it. When everything has to be a miracle, it cheapens the real miracles. If Pam had been in that prayer meeting, she would have told Dad, "I can't pray for that." That would have blessed Dad.

Notice how important context is. Both Michael and Dad had the money to buy what they asked prayer for. Of course, if they didn't have the money, it would have been appropriate to pray for an air conditioner or a washing machine.

The Pitfall of Boasting

Because the Spirit brings us Jesus, we are confronted with multiple seemingly conflicting ways of doing life. For example, praying and dreaming big (chap. 14) give us the faith-filled heart of Jesus; but without the correction of the path of Jesus (the J-curve in chap. 11), human power can take over and promote the self by putting faith on display. Faith, when intertwined with pride, kills the very thing it is trying to foster—intimacy with God.

In 1983, as he was about to leave for Uganda, Dad announced that he was going to share the gospel with Milton Obote, the president of Uganda. Jill went up to him and said, "How do you know he wants to meet with you?" This honest question was a good ministry to Dad. It would have been better for him to have said, "This is a long shot, but would you pray that God would enable me to share the gospel with President Obote?" What happened? As a rule, it's not a good idea to predict a resurrection. As it turned out, the trip was Dad's hardest ever. The Spirit took him into a fellowship of his suffering by putting him into a Ugandan hospital with a heart attack.

When Pat Robertson claimed that his prayers had turned Hurricane Gloria away from the coast, Dad said half-jokingly, "I thought my prayers turned that hurricane away!" It might have been better to say: "I suspect many Christians were praying that the hurricane would turn away. God really hears our prayers." Or maybe say nothing and thank God for Pat's faith and, at the same time, pray quietly for Pat to learn the wisdom of humility.

Just as an aside, even when boastful, my dad's prayers could be childlike and submissive to how God would answer. When he was alone in a Kampala hospital, he forgot all about Obote and delighted in sharing the gospel with his Ugandan nurses. God would prefer Dad's tendency over the listless apathy of prayerlessness and inaction. Jesus doesn't have much use for people who bury their talents.

A boast ("I am going to share the gospel with President Obote") uses faith to exalt yourself. The apostle Paul is clear: faith, rightly understood, ends boasting. "Then what becomes of our *boasting*? It is excluded. By what kind of law? By a law of works? No, but by the law of *faith*" (Rom. 3:27).

When you combine faith with boasting, it creates confusion. It sends a double message: (1) God answers faith-filled prayer, and (2) I am the one whom God used to offer this prayer (the boast). Over time, 2 (if left unchecked) can choke out 1. Faith and boasting don't mix well because boasting proclaims the self, while faith, like love, kills the self. Double messages cause a break in integrity, which quenches the Spirit.

Usually when we've mixed boasting with prayer and faith, we've separated love from prayer. This is another pitfall to avoid.

The Pitfall of Prayer without Love

Jill has radar for prayer without love. I was on a pastor's panel when a leading pastor shared that he and his wife seldom prayed together. Several other pastors told him it is easy to pray with your wife—just ask her. I thought, *Hmm, they're not married to my sparky wife.* In the past if I asked Jill to pray with me over the phone, it was not uncommon for her to say no. I never pressed her because I knew why it was hard.

When Kim was born, her disabilities created a whirlpool of needs that drained Jill's energy and faith, leaving her with little capacity to hear wordy encouragements. Some well-intentioned leaders were quick to pray but slow to help or even just listen. James describes a prayer that should *not* be prayed, because it is faith without love: "If a brother or sister is poorly clothed and lacking in daily food, and one of you says to them, '*Go in peace, be warmed and filled,*' without giving them the things needed for the body, what good is that? So also faith by itself, if it does not have works, is *dead*" (James 2:15–17). To paraphrase James, "If you aren't loving a person, then don't pray over that person."

It would be easy to react to Jill's no, thinking she was unspiritual, but nothing could be further from the truth. In our community, Jill is known for her faith and love. It pours out of her. Like Jesus and his brother James, she recoils from religious shows that miss love.

When religious words outpace love, it creates a dangerous, hollow space. The problem is significant enough that God devoted an entire commandment to it. The third commandment, "You shall not take the name of the LORD your God in vain" (Ex. 20:7), is directed not so much against swearing but against shallow or manipulative religious words. For example, if you regularly say to people, "I'll be praying for you," but you don't follow through, then you've used religious language to help the other person feel good. That's a form of taking God's name in vain.

Separating prayer from love shuts down the power train; it quenches the Spirit. Peter tells husbands that if they lack tenderness with their wives, their prayers will be hindered. (1 Pet. 3:7).

We can also quench the Spirit by trying to create artificial Spiritual experiences.

The Pitfall of Drama-Filled Prayers

Prayer meetings can be powerful or even dramatic. Following Jonathan Edwards, I believe we should be slow to judge those manifestations. And yet I've seen Christians slip into hunting for or trying to create dramatic experiences. That can make an idol out of experience, which freezes the power train. The Spirit will not let himself be treated as a drug or stimulant, nor will he separate himself from the person of Jesus.

For example, I was part of a community where we used a "prayer chair." A person would sit on the chair and share heartaches, and we'd put our hands on the person and pray for him or her. The "prayer chair" encourages people to share deeper personal needs, but at times people feel pressured to share private concerns that might be better shared with a close circle of friends. You've likely seen a TV talk-show guest share things he or she would never tell a neighbor. The "prayer chair" can divulge too much for the occasion, asking the Spirit to go into areas he's not ready to go. I prefer the steady work of faithful prayer, loads of forbearance, and prudent openness.

The tendency to turn prayer into a show is enough of a problem that Jesus addresses it in the Sermon on the Mount.

> And when you pray, you must not be like the hypocrites. For they love to stand and pray in the synagogues and at the street corners, that they may be seen by others. Truly, I say to you, they have received their reward. But when you pray, go into your room and shut the door and pray to your Father who is in secret. And your Father who sees in secret will reward you. (Matt. 6:5–6)

You can't get much weirder than standing at street corners bellowing out a prayer. So Jesus says, in effect, "Keep your prayers drama free." He says, "And when you pray, do not heap up empty phrases as the Gentiles do, for they think that they will be heard *for their many words.* Do not be like them, for your Father knows what you need before you ask him" (Matt. 6:7–8).

Next, Jesus gives his disciples a prayer with *not many words*—the Lord's Prayer. It's simple, balanced, and to the point, and it only takes fifteen seconds to pray. Jesus shows us how to pray drama free, with simplicity and faith.

When my dad went through chemo for lymphoma in 1987, I visited him daily in the hospital. Later he reflected on our visits.

> Cancer . . . can strip away pretensions . . . and evoke a deep hunger for honesty. . . . Supported by the love of Paul, I was able to acknowledge the deeper personal distortions that often pass as virtues in a religious community.
>
> . . . So I confessed some ugly inward blots: . . . my astonishing readiness to adopt a superior attitude towards other people, my

tendency to substitute words for reality when talking about my relationship with God, and my quiet, skillful elevation of my personality in conversation. "Words, words, words," I cried, sick of my much talking.[3]

Sometimes it's better simply to be quieter. Jon Hori, on a ministry trip to Haiti, had an opportunity to see what that looks like. Here is his observation of seeing someone quietly praying:

Although we've been in Haiti for a few days, it was our first day of hands-on ministry and everyone was excited. The two teams quickly loaded the yellow school bus, got settled in the dark green bench seats and waited for the bus to start . . . and waited . . . and waited. We were ready, but the bus was not.

While waiting for a mechanical miracle, I noticed Bob Allums quietly walking away while texting on his phone. I jokingly asked, "Calling your local mechanic to come and fix the bus?" He replied he was texting his prayer supporters back in the States to pray that the bus would start. I am ashamed to say that we could have waited there all morning and that thought probably would have never crossed my mind. I sheepishly reached into my pocket and pulled out my phone and said, "Um, yeah, me too." Less than five minutes after Bob's texts went out, the bus started. He looked at me, gave me knuckles, and said, "Isn't our God awesome?" Some may call it coincidence. I call it God's answer to the prayerful texts of a righteous man.

In short, public prayer opens the door to drama, pride, and hypocrisy in ways that private prayer does not. In fact, Jesus tells the guy praying on the street corner to stop his theatrics and go into his closet. If you pray better in public than you do in your closet, it might be wise to pray less in public and more in your closet.

If a praying church is like a warm, glowing campfire, we first need to value the campfire and then to learn how to start and maintain one. But occasionally, the fire gets out of control and damages the surrounding forest. Sometimes we need to contain the fire by throwing water on it to bring down the heat. Humility creates a barrier around the fire. Silence brings the heat down. The goal isn't a huge fire but a steady one. And having sat around hundreds of campfires, I've noticed that a good campfire is something everyone attends to. That's the subject of part 4, on the art of praying together.

PART 4

THE ART OF PRAYING
TOGETHER

17

Beginning Low and Slow

I SUSPECT MANY OF YOU are in a relatively prayerless church. How do you even start to help your church value praying together? How do you sustain your own new hunger for prayer? The answer is simple: you begin the way Anna did—by praying.

> And there was a prophetess, Anna, the daughter of Phanuel, of the tribe of Asher. She was advanced in years, having lived with her husband seven years from when she was a virgin, and then as a widow until she was eighty-four. She did not depart from the temple, worshiping with fasting and prayer night and day. And coming up at that very hour she began to give thanks to God and to speak of him to all who were waiting for the redemption of Jerusalem. (Luke 2:36–38)

Where did the gift of Jesus, which led to the destruction of all evil and to a new heaven and earth, begin? With Anna in the temple praying. Of course, it began from all eternity, and yet it needed a human instrument, a conduit. Anna's praying was one of the sparks of the power train: *Anna praying in the temple* (Luke 2:37) → *the "Spirit will come upon you"* (Luke 1:35) → *Jesus's birth* → *power*. Anna was like a janitor, completely hidden from the elites of the day. Mary met Anna after Jesus was born, so Mary saw the power train at work only in retrospect. Hidden warriors like Anna are usually discovered only in retrospect. When you meet a young convert from a non-Christian background, it's not uncommon to discover a praying grandmother behind the scenes.

All great movements of the kingdom begin low and slow, with hidden pray-ers who keep showing up to pray. Who pray when they don't feel like it. Who pray when there is no change. Who pray when they are discouraged. They are *continual in prayer*, and then they slowly attract others pray-ers to join them.

Maresa and Mary understood this.

Modern-Day Annas

When Maresa started attending Church at LifePark, near Charleston, South Carolina, in 2011, she came with an Anna-like burden to pray and to see her church becoming a praying community. She mentioned this to the senior pastor, and he connected her with Mary. In 2011 Maresa and Mary began to pray together weekly on Mondays. Gradually, a few others joined until, in 2013, they numbered about a half dozen praying Annas. They all came with the same burden—that their church would become a praying church. They started praying that God would expand their prayer group to include men and other ethnic groups. God made their prayer group more diverse, but still there was no breakthrough.

Then, in 2018, an elder at their church challenged his fellow elders and pastors to not just give lip service to prayer but work toward becoming "a praying church." Chad, the senior pastor, bristled slightly at this challenge, but God began to work in him and others. At a discipleship seminar in Nashville, he was convicted by a presenter who said he'd been "a praying man" but had become a "man of prayer." That is, he prayed before and after meetings, but prayer didn't saturate his life. Not long after this, Chad asked the elders to put together a prayer team to explore how to become a praying church. The team visited the Brooklyn Tabernacle in New York City. While meeting with one of the pastors there, the team asked, "What's the one thing we are missing to become a praying church?" The pastor said immediately, "Your senior pastor needs to catch a vision for prayer." Chad and Maresa looked at one another; the Spirit had struck a chord. Later that evening, at the prayer service, Chad went forward to ask prayer for a loved one. There he was very moved by the presence of God—God met him. He now knew, beyond a shadow of a doubt, that he wanted LifePark to become a praying church.

Over the next several years LifePark started a Thursday evening prayer service, a weekly noontime prayer meeting, and a prayer team. Maresa is now full-time with the church as a prayer director. She's thrilled to watch the Lord stir more hearts to pray as they continue to explore what it means to be a praying church.

The pattern of living in Jesus's dying and rising permeates Maresa's story. She was drawn to prayer by an ache in her heart stemming from her life circumstances. Aches are transferable. That is, if God has given you something in your life that breaks your heart, and the only thing you can do is pray, that weakness and the prayer it fosters are transferable to every other part of your life. Similarly, Mary's personal ache drew her to prayer, which eventually began to reshape her church. Luke tells us that a personal ache drew Anna as well. After she was married for just seven years—young and vibrant with her whole life ahead of her—her husband died, likely leaving her a lifelong widow and childless (2:36). Nothing could be harder. Like Hannah, she turned to the house of prayer and found a home there. She prayed the Messiah in.

Maresa and Mary also experienced the dying side of prayer when they prayed for seven years with no major breakthroughs. Maresa said they were able to persevere because God kept answering their small prayers: for example, that God would bring men to pray with them, and for greater ethnic diversity. That encouraged them to be patient with their bigger, unanswered prayers. During those years, God taught them to wait on him. They learned that in everything Jesus is Lord of the harvest. They also regularly encouraged one another's faith by taking time to celebrate answers to prayer. It kept the Spirit's resurrection power fresh and alive for them all.

Maresa and Mary's experience is not uncommon. Prayer often bubbles up from down low, from people like Anna. Maresa said that their biggest challenge was simply the church's success. It was growing by leaps and bounds. When answers to their prayers came, they came sideways, as is so typical of the Spirit's working. Who would have guessed that an elder would admonish his fellow elders for their weakness in prayer? Who would have guessed that Chad would be drawn, seemingly out of the blue, to become a "man of prayer"? Or that a pastor in New York would challenge him directly? Or that the Spirit would meet Chad as he was praying down front? "The wind blows where it wills" is the fundamental dynamic of the Spirit.

I encourage "janitors" not to be discouraged in their hidden work. Be content that the "bathrooms" sparkle. Ole Hallesby, in his classic book *Prayer*, compares the work of revival to mining. It might take a week to bore a long hole in a mining shaft.

After the hole is drilled, it's packed with dynamite, a charge is set, and in an instant tons of rock break loose. Everyone's attention is focused on the excitement of the explosion, but the real work is the tedious boring. In a revival, the speaker who electrifies the audience and leads many to Christ is the person who sets off the charge. The person boring the hole is the praying janitor, who made it all happen. God has designed his church to look like his Son, who spent most of his life hidden. Thus, the most important people in the church, the Annas, are often invisible. It's his way.

Maresa did not respond to her church's weakness with a spirit of criticism. She didn't become a critical version of Anna. On the scale of irritation, a prayer Pharisee ranks fairly high. When we become our church's critics, we are no longer hidden saints, but we've joined the growing ranks of *prickly* saints.

I've started challenging Christians who are overly critical of the church, "I guess you wouldn't have liked Jesus very much when he was on earth." That upsets them, but I push back: "Well, Jesus's body was broken then, and it is now. If you don't like his broken body now, you wouldn't have liked his broken body then."

One of the delights of a hidden ministry of prayer is that you can do exactly what you want your community to do—pray. You get to prayer by prayer. And Jesus's promise still stands: "For where two or three are gathered in my name, there am I among them" (Matt. 18:20). So finding a prayer partner, like Maresa did, is a wonderful way to begin.

Practice Anticipating

What sustains people like Anna to keep praying? A sense of anticipation of what God might do though prayer. A pastor in a prayer cohort I had led wrote to me six months later and described it this way:

> Something changed in me during or through that cohort. Something clicked in a new way with prayer. I know the focus was on the church, but God did something in me that I don't know how to explain. I get excited about the "boringness" of praying for the same things again and again (low-level, no thrills farming work) to a God-who-hears—and then who does move the prayer stories forward. *It's like a surprise Christmas morning, getting to unwrap a forgotten present when he answers!*

What "clicked" for this pastor was *faith.* He saw how life worked. That sparked *hope*, which spilled over into the work of *love* (prayer). When faith is weak, you are gripped by some combination of cynicism or lethargy—the kissing cousins of unbelief. Not surprisingly, Anna and Simeon (Luke 2:25–35) are both older—they understand life's deep structures, that the good things in life are gifts, and prayer lies at the heart of God's gift giving.

Megan Hill describes this same faith in her excellent book *Praying Together*:

> Earlier this week, I met with two older women in my church. We discussed a few matters for prayer—a gospel podcast for Arab-speaking millennials, a paralyzed Christian sister, the labors of our pastor—and then we sat quietly. After a moment one of the women said, with a sparkle in her eyes, "Sisters, are you ready?" Her enthusiasm stirred my heart. And, as if embarking on an epic adventure, we all smiled, straightened our shoulders, and began to pray together.[1]

The pastor's comparison of prayer with the delight of receiving a forgotten Christmas present is apt in another sense, because Advent involves waiting for the Christ-child. That's the feeling of prayer. It's not passive waiting, as in hoping that my wife forgets about her job list for me, but *anticipatory waiting*.

That's why Paul and Silas pray and sing in prison. They are anticipating that the Spirit will again reenact the resurrection of Jesus and deliver them. The Spirit works through the earthquake, overturning the false narrative that Paul and Silas are troublemakers. Their two-person praying team first transforms the prison, then the jailor, then his family and beyond (Acts 16:12, 16–40). When they are powerless, they don't just survive—they thrive. Instead of being overcome by evil, they overcome evil with good.

A Word to Pastors

Many of you are "Annas in the temple." You long for your churches to be praying churches, but the resistance or inertia leaves you stymied. Why not seek out the "Annas" in your church and ask them to pray that your church would become a house of prayer? I encourage you to be attentive to these Annas in the same way you might be quietly attentive to your wealthy families. To be genuinely thankful for their generosity is not just wise but good. Without these heavy givers, you couldn't pay the bills. Why not also be attentive to the heavy pray-ers? They are your church's hidden wealth. God *honored* Anna and Simeon by telling their stories. The "Annas" and "Simeons" of your church are the nuclear power plant that fuels so many of the good things we can too easily credit to good planning or talent.

18

Forming a Divine Community

JESUS'S HIGH PRIESTLY PRAYER focuses on the creation of a divine community between us and the Trinity. Jesus prays "that they may all be one, just as you, Father, are in me, and I in you, that they also may be in us" (John 17:21). That's prayer's "end game," becoming one with God. Let's see how to get there.

Start with a Structured Time of Concentrated Prayer

Our ministry, seeJesus, orbits around our three weekly prayer times. About thirty of us gather for prayer at ten in the morning for almost an hour Monday, Wednesday, and Thursday. On Friday, we devote two hours to personal prayer time. In total, we spend four to five hours a week in prayer, a tithe of our time, half in corporate prayer and half in private prayer.

Our prayer meetings are the "grandchildren" of the Thursday morning prayer meeting my dad started in his living room in 1984. It eventually moved from the living room to Serge (where it continues) and to seeJesus in 1999. I've been a part of this regular prayer meeting now for almost forty years.

We didn't set out to tithe our time; it just ended up that way. Until you've actually tithed your money, you don't know either the cost or the blessing of tithing. Tithing doesn't just take 10 percent of your money; it changes how you spend the other 90 percent. You must be more thoughtful about your money because you start off with less. A prayer tithe does the same thing. You *have to* pray because when you take four to five hours out of every workweek, you have less time to get your other work done! And like tithing, you need to give it up front. If you wait to the end, nothing will be left. You have to defend the time.

A Jesus community, whether a church, a mission, or a family, must have structured times of prayer. It's not uncommon at our prayer seminars for people to say they don't need structured prayer times because they pray continually, "on the fly." I commend their spirit of prayer, but I'm skeptical about whether they've genuinely entered what Ole Hallesby calls the work of prayer. If I'm discussing this with a married man, I'll ask, "So do you have a time during the day when you sit and listen to your wife, over dinner, or do you just connect 'on the fly'?" You can't develop intimacy while multitasking. You must have regular times of undivided attentiveness. Jesus did. And because business meetings, like the skinny cows of Pharaoh's dream, tend to eat up the fat cows of prayer, I encourage people not to combine a prayer meeting with a business meeting. The church in Acts, as we've seen, frequently and regularly paused for prayer-only meetings.

And they devoted themselves to the apostles' teaching . . . and *the prayers*. (2:42)

[Peter] went to the house of Mary . . . where many were *gathered together and were praying*. (12:12)

Notice the phrase "the prayers" (2:42). It refers to set times of prayer, which in the Jewish culture of Jesus's day had become a threefold pattern of morning, noon, and evening prayers. We see the same pattern in Paul as he talks about his and the church's prayer habits.

> Without ceasing I mention you always in *my prayers*. (Rom. 1:9–10)

> I do not cease to give thanks for you, remembering you in *my prayers*. (Eph. 1:16)

> We give thanks to God always for all of you, constantly mentioning you in *our prayers*. (1 Thess. 1:2)

> I remember you constantly in *my prayers* night and day. (2 Tim. 1:3)

Paul's team and other churches join him in this work.

> Epaphroditus . . . always struggling on your behalf in *his prayers*. (Col. 4:12)

> I appeal to you, brothers, . . . to strive together with me in *your prayers*. (Rom. 15:30)

> For I know that through *your prayers* . . . this will turn out for my deliverance. (Phil. 1:19)

The phrases "my prayers," "our prayers," "his prayers," and "your prayers" suggest dedicated times devoted to the work of prayer.

There's no one way to structure prayer in a Jesus community. The International Justice Mission, Washington, DC, has a daily thirty-minute personal prayer time at nine in the morning, followed by thirty minutes of corporate prayer at eleven. The mission supplements that with quarterly retreats. The Brooklyn Tabernacle Church has a ninety-minute prayer meeting on Tuesday night, led by Jim Cymbala.

Both of these Jesus communities *devote* themselves to prayer. It takes a chunk of their time, where prayer functions like a load-bearing wall. It's not a window treatment or paint color—it carries weight. The Spirit's power train operates at the heart of their corporate life.

It can be a shock to our new staff to spend this much time in prayer. Listen to the comments of two staff, both pastors, on what it was like to enter our praying community:

Within the first 6 months of prayer meetings with seeJesus, I had spent more time in prayer than in all my 20 years of pastoral ministry. In pastoral ministry it wasn't a priority for me and seemed unproductive. The majority of leadership I served under would pray before and after meetings but very little time just in prayer. The pressure of producing a product on Sundays or in programs pushed prayer aside. It's relentless; it just never lets up. When prayer meetings did occur, they were unbalanced—20 minutes of sharing and 5 minutes praying. Silence was uncomfortable and not "allowed."

When I first came on staff, the thought of three weekly prayer meetings seemed overwhelming. I thought it would take away time from work. In other words, I thought I'd be more stressed trying to make up for lost time in prayer meetings. It took at least 6 months before my heart's pace slowed to appreciate the prayer meetings. Two things about the prayer meetings made a difference: (1) they were set regularly and non-negotiable and (2) they were led differently. In time, I realized 3 hours a week was hardly anything. I can waste 3 hours doing far less important things. Now, personal and corporate prayer has become an integrated way to do life and ministry. I manage, dream, plan, and ponder through prayer. Much of my greatest tangible ministry has been initiated and accomplished and answered through prayer.

Take Prayer Seriously

My presence at prayer meetings is crucial to our community taking prayer seriously. Once a leader of a major ministry asked me if our mission could run their prayer ministry. I demurred and afterward thought, *You can't delegate prayer any more than you can delegate intimacy!* Imagine a husband who tells his distraught wife: "I know you are going through a rough time, so I've asked my assistant to take you to lunch and really listen to your heart, and then give me a report. I want to care for you, and this is the most efficient way to do that." That would be ridiculous.

Jim Cymbala, founding pastor of the Brooklyn Tabernacle Church, makes their Tuesday prayer meeting his most important meeting of the week. He accepts a speaking engagement only if he can be home on Tuesday. When you attend their Tuesday prayer meeting, you can see why. Jim doesn't just lead the prayer time; he comes to pray. His praying life leads the congregation into prayer.

At seeJesus, we require attendance at our prayer meetings. New staff sometimes think that attendance is optional—after all, it's just a prayer meeting. So at 10:02 they might get a text: "Prayer time now." Or later I might remind them, "Try to avoid scheduling appointments during our prayer times." We seldom need to remind people now; everyone wants to come—it's a joy to gather.

Make Space for Love and Faith

We begin our Monday and Wednesday prayer times with about twenty-five minutes of "open-mic" time, which gives space for the Spirit to enable anyone to share. It creates a level playing field where accounting clerks and ministry directors have equal and ample access. We laugh together, hear stories, share prayer requests, and give ministry updates. As one staff member has said about our prayer times: "It is a family where we are loved unconditionally. Praying together is the strongest of glue. God is our fortress, but our prayer times provide strong walls of love, care & integrity."

Notice the close connection between love and prayer. By opening up to each other, we're not just loving the people we are praying for; we're also loving the people we are praying with.

Praying together opens the door to love, where one person's burdens become everyone's burdens. If someone is struggling, we slow down to give that person time to share. If someone is doing well, we rejoice with him or her. We are attentive to one another, first in conversation and then in prayer. We don't pray together in order to create community; praying together is just a gift of the Spirit to make Jesus present. One person commented, "If you miss a prayer meeting, you miss having your faith encouraged, your hope renewed, and your love deepened."

To "spark" opening up, I'll call on people who have concerns in their lives or ministries. Once people realize that prayer and love are linked, they draw one another out. I'll get a text reminding me to ask someone to share. As staff members draw each other out, stories begin to develop, and people ask for updates. Like Jesus in the Gospel of Luke, we *look*, *feel compassion*, and then *act* in prayer.

Our open-mic times leave space for the Spirit to speak through people, prompting them with wisdom, hope, or Scripture. The Lord, in his wisdom, kept me low for many years, where I had no voice, giving me an awareness that the Spirit lives down low (Isa. 57:15).

Love shapes the boundaries of our prayers. Occasionally we will pray for distant cousins with knee surgery, but in general I shy away from that, because these people aren't part of the community. Nor am I a fan of widely posted prayer lists. They are lifeless, disconnected from the person and the story God is weaving. I've seen prayer lists overwhelm people's fragile faith. With a list, you don't get a sense of the person who is in need, nor do you see any unfolding story. A praying community isn't a factory where you input needs and output answers. I'd much rather people gather to pray, though it is helpful to update one another after gathering. We do that with a "prayer channel" in Slack. Others do it with an email or text thread.

If the saints genuinely see themselves as the front lines of the kingdom, then being alert to the variety of their saint stories and praying for them enrich the prayer meeting. If I had to summarize in one word what happens when a Jesus community begins to pray, I'd say *surprise*. Unexpected things happen. Celebrating surprise, the unexpected activity of the Spirit, encourages everyone's faith that the Spirit is at work.

Here's a snapshot of a recent staff prayer meeting: Six days before the last American soldiers were pulled out of Afghanistan in 2021, many Americans and Afghan coworkers were still stranded. A friend of one of our trainers runs a school for girls that is now in

Taliban territory. Our trainer had lost touch with her. Another staff member mentioned he'd been up at night praying for the situation in Afghanistan. So we went right to prayer. People on our staff have different political views, so I "fenced" in our prayer time by suggesting that we focus on the refugee crisis. I could feel people's anxiety, so I prayed using Psalm 46, which pictures a collapsing world and yet the safety and serenity of the city of God. Then we closed by reading the first paragraph of Revelation 8, where our prayers return to earth with incredible power. The result? We did some good work. Plus, people's faith was built. We weren't overcome by evil, but we overcame evil with good.

Listen Attentively to One Another

Praying together has some complexity to it. If I'm praying alone, I only need to be attentive to God and my heart. But a praying community is a triangle: I need to be attentive to God, myself, and you—the person praying with me. It's *you* who make things complicated.

Learning to be attentive to one another as we pray takes some work. Imagine listening to this conversation about Philadelphia sports:

> JACK: I can't get over how steady Nick Foles was at the Super Bowl when the Eagles beat the Patriots.
> MAX: My son plays ice hockey for a travel team.
> LAYNE: Have you seen the Phillies' new pitching rotation?

What's wrong with this conversation? Everything. No one is listening to anyone else. The first person is talking about football, the second about ice hockey, and the third about baseball. No theme connects the conversation. No thread holds these things together. Here's another disjointed conversation:

ELANOR: Did you hear that Jill was in an accident?
CLAIRE: Last night, we went to see that new *Star Wars* movie.
MARGARET: I have just been overwhelmed with the kids.

Same thing here. No one's paying attention to what the others are saying. We know how to talk sports or life together, but we don't know how to pray together. But it isn't that different. It takes time to learn how to pay attention to one another, to listen for themes, and to contribute based on what you are hearing.

Especially at first, people naturally just pray for what's on their hearts, completely ignoring what others are praying. They miss the thread of the conversation, which creates a jerky prayer meeting. When a prayer time has become jerky, I wait until our next prayer time to remind people to be attentive to one another and the prayer theme. When they are attentive, I'll commend them, even interrupting the prayer time to tell them how well they've listened to one another. It's taken time for us to not have a jumble of prayer requests but to listen to one another as we pray and build on each other's prayers—almost like a conversation.

No matter what, some still miss the thread, much as they would in conversation as well. We just accept these folks as they are. We don't want a perfect prayer meeting; we want our love to be perfect.

A similar problem is overtalking. At least initially, people prefer talking to praying. So in two of our prayer meetings, we have a "cold stop" after thirty minutes of open-mic time. Anything left unsaid can just be woven into their prayers as "pray announcements." In general, it's best to not let the talking time exceed the prayer time.

Leading a prayer meeting is like coaching a football team or conducting an orchestra. Doing it well is enormously complex. A football coach needs to know each player's strengths and weaknesses, the game plan, formations, plays, the opposing team, and so on. An orchestra conductor needs to know each instrument, each player, and each detail of the score almost by heart. A prayer leader has a lot to learn too. It takes practice and experience to lead well.

I have a strong bias for the prayer meeting itself (as opposed to more formal prayer services or orchestrated prayer times), because it intertwines prayer, community, and love. Increasingly I'm seeing churches create effective evening prayer services. This is a huge improvement over a prayerless church, but at times I wonder if some churches are creating *prayer machines*. Prayer requests are anonymous slips of paper; we don't know the backstories or the people behind the requests. If we aren't engaged in people's stories, it weakens our ability to endure—the secret sauce of prayer.

Becoming a Divine Community

Eventually, as we spend time together in concentrated prayer, a *divine community* emerges. Everyone becomes aware that the Spirit is active, bringing life to our work, shaping our plans, and leading us. We hear comments like these:

> Prayer meetings function like mini-Sabbaths during the week. We cease our work (which doesn't come naturally) for a few minutes to remember our dependence on the Father, give thanks for all He is doing, enjoy his presence, and ask for his leadership and help. When we do this together, my enjoyment of what God's doing throughout the whole team increases, and my perspectives are renewed about what drives our work and who's at the center.

Our prayer times remind us to actually come before the Father. Just like this morning, I was reminded to pray about a busted radiator as soon as it busts. Though there are deep theological waters behind that, it doesn't feel like theology. It feels like a living connection to God. It keeps us glimpsing the breadth of God's kingdom.

Praying in community is a kind of ancient stumbling stone, a test from God. Do we really care? Do we really love? My passion is to create a praying community where God, not prayer, is the center. That's what I pray for and work at with all the energy the Spirit has given me.

A Word to Pastors: Tips for Preparing for a Prayer Meeting

Every pastor I know prepares sermons. An ill-prepared sermon is a weak sermon. Why would the prayer meeting be any different? Here are some tips for preparing for prayer:

- You don't prepare for a prayer meeting the way you prepare for a sermon. If you do, you'll kill the prayer meeting by overtalking. Limit any teaching to three minutes. You must leave space for people to pray, even to pray badly. You must leave space for the Spirit.
- Prepare for the prayer meeting by developing a rich, comprehensive life of *personal* prayer. Your sermons get better the more you preach, and prayer meetings get better the more you pray. To put it simply, you prepare a prayer meeting by preparing your heart. Maybe the best analogy for preparing your heart is dieting. If your doctor told you to go on a weight-loss diet, you wouldn't start your diet the

day before your follow-up visit. Dieting must become a lifestyle over many months.

- The most important thing that needs to grow in you in order to lead a prayer group well is faith. Your faith, not theirs. If you believe, they will in time believe. If you are quietly cynical, doubting that "God hears me when I cry," then they will be quietly cynical. Your childlike confidence is their door to childlike confidence. You can't fake that.
- The second most important thing is love. If you love them, then your prayers for them will be human and thoughtful, as opposed to preachy and formal. If you love God, then God's heart will shape your heart. So you'll enjoy the saints' struggles but gently, in time, connect their struggles to a larger vision of God's heart.
- A third tip is feeding and growing hope in your life. That means looking at your life and then their lives through a resurrection lens. You pray for resurrection, look for it, and then celebrate it when it comes. That means that when hope is weak, you don't fake hope with pastor-speak. You learn to die well, in a fellowship of Jesus's suffering, which will help you to be attentive to the saints' dying, giving them space for lament.
- Finally, do not *preach* faith, hope, and love in a prayer meeting, even in tiny sermonettes. Instead, *be* faith, hope, and love. That is, let the saints pick it up; let it be an ache on your heart. They will learn simply by praying with you.

19

Restoring Prayer to
Sunday Morning

I STILL REMEMBER THE TEN-MINUTE pastoral prayers (when I was four) in the Christian Reformed Church in Ripon, California. Actually, I mainly remember my mom, with four little kids squirming in the pew, complaining about their length! And yet, those prayers preserved an ancient tradition of the church where prayer had *pride of place* on Sunday morning.

In some churches, the pastoral prayer is still offered with depth and sincerity, but in general the death of Wednesday prayer meeting has been accompanied by a weakening of Sunday morning prayer as well. In order to form a praying church, we need to take back Sunday morning for prayer.

No one did Sunday morning prayer better than the post–New Testament early church. Their habits don't carry the weight of Scripture, but they do preserve some of the passions and practices of the apostles, particularly in the primacy of corporate prayer.

The Early Church: Prayer at the Center of Worship

Corporate prayer was at the heart of early church worship. In fact, the expression *the prayer meeting* was nonexistent in the early church, because it implies you could have a meeting without prayer. One scholar describes the Sunday morning service: "Christians—in a manner unparalleled among pagans—prayed together. Their place of worship was a place of corporate prayer, with many people praying, standing near each other . . . 'before the face of God.'"[1]

Their service began with readings from the Bible, then a fifteen-minute sermon, followed by a longer worship time with corporate prayer as the centerpiece. Worship ended with the kiss of peace and Communion.[2] Notice the lovely emotional cadence: they engaged the mind (the word and sermon) and then the heart (praying and worship) and finally the body (the kiss of peace and Communion). The modern church reverses that by beginning with the emotions (singing) as a warm-up for the real meat, the sermon. But for the early church, the meat of the sermon paved the way for an encounter with God in worship, prayer, and Communion.

The importance of this communal prayer time is underscored by the fact that the writings of the early church fathers "gave exceptional attention to prayer, vastly more than to the sermon."[3] They even gave detailed instructions on how to pray: standing with arms raised.

The early church believed that corporate prayer joined them to divine power. Because they didn't want unbelievers messing up the power center, they eventually asked seekers to leave after the sermon. Nor did the church fathers want broken relationships to weaken their prayers—praying while angry disrupted the power center. They took seriously Jesus's exhortation that if anger separates you from a brother, you should leave your gift at the altar (Matt. 5:22–24). They interpreted leaving your gift at the altar as corporate prayer, since prayer was their "rich and better sacrifice."[4]

When Sunday morning includes time for extended prayer, it fosters a culture of prayer. Augustine tells us that when early Christians parted, they said "remember me"—short for "remember me in your prayers."[5] Their sense of a vast community of praying Christians made its way into the Apostles' Creed in the phrase "I believe in . . . the communion of saints." *Living saints* joined with *departed saints* in a timeless prayer communion. It's a vision of prayer consistent with the ministry of prayer that Jesus and the Spirit have now.[6]

Rethinking Sunday Morning

Let me offer five suggestions for how churches can restore corporate prayer to Sunday morning. This doesn't just apply to pastors—if the saints are expecting to meet God in worship, in the preaching, *and also in prayer*, that will eventually affect church leadership as well. It's not uncommon for the saints to pray for the preaching. Why not also pray for the praying?

Unleash the Saints

What about ten minutes of open mic for praying saints? The early church's open time of prayer reflects what we know from both Acts and especially 1 Corinthians 11:4–5, where Paul implies that there was an open time of prayer including both men and women.

In 1982 the Lausanne Committee for World Evangelization issued this appeal:

> We resolve ourselves, and call upon our churches, to take much more seriously the period of intercession in public worship; to

think in terms of 10 or 15 minutes rather than five; to invite lay people to share in leading, since they often have deep insight into the world's needs; and to focus our prayers both on the evangelization of the world . . . and on the quest for peace and justice in the world. . . . We long to see every Christian congregation bowing down in humble and expectant faith before our Sovereign Lord.[7]

It's a joy to hear what the saints have on their hearts, what they are thankful for, and what they are worried about. The saints are bubbling over with desire and passion—give that space!

Giving the saints some space makes room for the Spirit of Jesus. If the entire worship service is orchestrated, how would the Spirit break in? We rightly give the pastor space in his preaching to explain and apply the word. At times, the pastor is particularly "anointed." That is, the Spirit empowers his preaching in a special way. That's good. Can that also happen to the saints in prayer?

Jesus frequently leaves space for people. He creates space by being silent, asking questions, or just waiting. For example, when Jesus meets Mary Magdalene after his resurrection (John 20:11–18), instead of revealing himself, he stands quietly as she questions the angels, and he speaks only when she turns and makes eye contact with him. Even then, he asks her two questions, drawing her out. In the space Jesus creates, Mary emerges as a person—we see her take-charge personality and her passionate devotion.

What if someone messes up the open prayer time? That's part of the beauty of the body of Christ. We attended a church for many years with an open prayer time on Sunday that was stopped when a prickly saint had a mini-rant. The leaders just needed to talk to him. Perfection isn't in the performance but in the body of Christ praying from their hearts to God through Christ's perfect intercession. Like much of life, praying together can get messy.

Any time Kim senses an open mic for prayer, she jumps in with her own prayer. She interrupts because at home we've labored to give her a "voice" during prayer times. Her prayers are delightful since we have no idea what she will say and whether or not it is connected with the occasion. When Kim starts praying, Jill tightens up (like the pastor who told me he was terrified of an open mic) and everyone else starts smiling! Kim's prayers are sincere, from the heart. She will often break the ice in ways that the rest of us would not. So at her fortieth birthday party in front of a hundred people, just after she blew out her candles, she "interrupted" the schedule with her own prayer remembering her beloved sister Ashley, who passed into glory three years earlier. A hush settled over the crowd. It was a sacred moment. Kim's mini-lament brought Jesus into her party.

I've been particularly moved in prayer times with adults affected by disability. There is no pretense, no posturing; it's just saints unleashed. It never fails to bless me. As Paul says, "On the contrary, the parts of the body that seem to be weaker are indispensable" (1 Cor. 12:22).

Restore Public Laments

Public laments were at the heart of ancient Israelite worship, making up about one-third of the Psalms. The early church preserved the bold honesty of the Hebrew laments. Tertullian (AD 200) describes what lament praying was like on a Sunday: "We meet together as an assembly and congregation, that, offering up prayer to God as with united force, we may wrestle with Him in our supplications. This violence God delights in."[8]

Notice the passion and honesty of the early church's prayers. Following the pattern of Hebrew laments, these prayers are in tension with God. Laments are driven by a robust faith that expects God to do something: "we . . . wrestle with Him in our supplications." That makes praying together interesting; it's real. The passion we might feel when watching sports is not out-of-bounds in prayer.[9]

What about an open-mic time so parents can lament over grown children who've walked away from the faith? What about, in a pastoral prayer, praying for someone who's been recently abandoned by his or her spouse? What about praying for young moms who are beyond weary, or for young, single women who long to be married? What about praying for parents who are raising a child with disabilities? Of course, this takes discretion; you might want to ask a person's permission ahead of time, but generally in our churches we don't give the abandoned spouse or the weary parent room to lament. Public laments not only honor the weak but also dignify their suffering by openly acknowledging it. That kills the floating shame that, for example, many abandoned spouses feel.

For example, at New Life Church in the early 1980s, one elder ran off with another elder's wife. Instead of shoving it under the rug, the next Sunday the elders announced this and then prayed for them. It was one of our most powerful worship services. It killed gossip and opened the door for conversation with and compassion for the two abandoned spouses. It made Christianity real—and, frankly, interesting.

Flip Prayer and the Sermon

I'm intrigued by the early church's pattern of beginning a service with Scripture reading and a sermon, then moving to a lengthy time of worship that includes singing and an open prayer time, and finally Communion. Worship and prayer weren't the warm-up for the sermon but the climax. The sermon is *about* God, and singing and prayer are *to* God. It's a natural progression from *building* faith to *expressing* faith.

This might make the whole service more engaging. Someone told me today, "My husband tunes out the sermon." Practically, in any meeting, the energy ebbs in the latter half. Flipping the sermon and worship brings energy into what is naturally a lower-energy part of Sunday morning and puts the sermon in the higher-energy part of the service. This switch communicates that *knowing* is not just with the mind but with the whole person. Imagine the saints coming to worship expecting not only to be nourished but also to meet with God.

Remember, much of what we do in worship is prayer. Nearly every song is a prayer. When we switch gears from singing to praying, we continue our praying in another mode.[10]

Let the Pastoral Prayer Be Pastoral

A friend wrote me recently: "I find it *very* difficult to sit through a long pastoral prayer being voiced by one person. My mind wanders and I am thinking, 'How long will this go on?' I say this as someone who *loves* to spend an hour praying with another person—which I do twice a week." Pastoral prayers that are real go a long way toward solving this problem. So pray about real problems that the saints are facing.

For example: Tim, a pastor in Boston, begins his prayer on a particular Sunday by worshiping, followed by confession of sin. But instead of a generic repentance, he prays at length against the sin of bitterness. (He picks a different sin each week.) Then he prays through some of the needs of the congregation, naming each person: a coworker with an accident, a husband who just lost his wife, a new baby, several deaths of loved ones. Then he moves outward, praying for one of the ministries the congregation supports—this time, Gordon College. Next he prays for the mayor, his wife, and his children. Then he prays for the president of the United States and especially the crisis in Ukraine, followed by praying for China and the Olympics. He closes with the congregation praying the Lord's Prayer. At each point, Tim prays for each need from several angles. Because the prayer is so connected with reality, it is actually interesting—not because it is eloquent but because it is real. You barely notice that Tim prays for nine minutes. He loves his congregation, his community, and his country through his prayer.[11]

When Jim Cymbala of the Brooklyn Tabernacle leads their Tuesday evening prayer service, he isn't just leading a prayer meeting with a thousand people: he's praying. He has a spirit of prayer about him. After a video presentation, you expect Jim to announce what happens next. Instead, he's quietly praying up front. He's talking to God. That invites the thousand people who are attending into that same spirit of prayer.

But you can't form a spirit of prayer through public praying. The only way a pastor can cultivate a praying spirit is by a rich prayer life, hidden in the closet.

Close with a Blessing

The oldest preserved text of Scripture comes from two silver amulets in a seventh-century BC grave near Jerusalem. Scholars painstakingly unwound the tiny scrolls and discovered a blessing similar to the one that Aaron prayed over the assembly in Numbers 6:24–26, which begins, "The LORD bless you and keep you."[12]

We were made to bless and be blessed. Our culture lacks a uniform way of saying goodbye, yet we instinctively want to bless one another when we say goodbye: "Take care" is a blessing; so is "See you later." The latest secular blessing is "Be safe." I encourage pastors to close a service by blessing the congregation. As the church's Spiritual leaders, they are praying grace into the saints.

In the mid-1990s, a friend of mine visited the First Evangelical Free Church in Fullerton, California, where Chuck Swindoll was the senior pastor. During a worship service attended by over three thousand people, they broke into small groups and prayed. Then the prayer leader encouraged people to shout out prayers for the whole congregation to hear. People stood up and shouted out brief prayers, which were quickly followed by others. The whole prayer time flowed easily—you could tell they'd worked on this over a long period of time. I say this simply to encourage you with patience. Even something as cumbersome as a prayer time with three thousand people can be learned in time.

A Word to Pastors

I hope none of these suggestions comes across glibly, as if I'm saying, "Oh, just do this." It's easy for me to say, "Pray ten minutes," but that ten minutes has to come from somewhere.

My dad, who was a church-planting pastor, told me on several occasions that changing Sunday morning was stepping on sacred ground! So make changes incrementally.

But where do you begin? With prayer. Write down, either in your prayer journal or on a prayer card, what change you'd like to see on Sunday, and then pray that every day. I might pray that for six months to a year before I proposed anything. In my experience, saints love to be involved, to be part of the Spirit's work. So, first ask several mature Christians to pray unscripted prayers; then gradually open this up to anyone.

Here are some cautions about prayer on Sunday. First, I discourage pastors from writing out their prayers. Not only does this take time, but the written pastoral prayers I've heard feel heavy; they get stuck in the dying side of the J-curve and mute resurrection.

Second, be careful of overly sophisticated prayers. They can dampen the saints' desire to pray by creating an unnecessarily high bar that people feel they can't attain. Overly articulate prayers can shut people down who are already fearful of speaking in public. Sometimes polished prayers lean gnostic. Gnosticism was a Greek heresy that created a "spiritual" hierarchy—the higher you went, the more "spiritual" you supposedly became, and the less you were connected to the physical world. That's why being real is so critical.[13]

To be clear, the problem isn't prayers rich with theological truth. Sometimes, though, the complexity of the prayer is driven by an expectation that "the pastor should pray better." I suggest first praying Paul's eloquent prayers in your "closet" and letting those prayers become part of your life: then when you "go public," these prayers are already functioning in your life. That makes them real.

Third, some prayers aren't just prayers but are mini-sermons, like when a closing prayer functions as a sermon recap. Or there's the "cover prayer," which is used as a cover for the band to set up. It saves one minute. I suspect it isn't even a prayer, because I've never seen the band set up while someone is preaching. Are we respectful of preaching but not praying?

20

On a Resurrection Hunt

PRAYERS DEAL WITH PROBLEMS. For example, most psalms are prayers of *asking*, which take a problem to God; or prayers of *thanksgiving*, when God has fixed a problem; or prayers of *lament*, when God hasn't yet fixed a problem. Prayers may flow from request to lament to worship, and then back again. The psalmist writes,

> In my distress I called to the LORD,
>   and he answered me. (Ps. 120:1)

Praying often begins with a problem—the difficult marriage, the wayward child, the challenging job. In fact, every praying person I've met learned to pray because God gave him or her an overwhelming problem.

So, not surprisingly, prayer meetings can easily become problem-centered, with a litany of requests that seldom seem to change anything. Instead of building faith, they weaken faith. You don't see God at work; there is no unfolding story. Consequently, we can get stuck in death, at the bottom of the J-curve. What should be a wellspring of life and faith (the prayer meeting) breeds a creeping unbelief. We become quietly cynical about praying together.

The secular equivalent is looking at too much TV news. We weren't designed to live in a world of evil, so we easily become despondent if that fills our thoughts. In Tolkien's *Lord of the Rings*, evil captures three good rulers simply by their looking at evil: Saruman looks too long into the crystal ball; King Théoden listens to Wormtongue; and Lord Denethor, weary from his battles with the Dark Lord, gives in to despair. In each case, concentrating on evil overwhelms the good. When that happens, we lose hope.

How can we break our fixation with problems when praying together?

Encourage Each Other to Go on a Resurrection Hunt

When I've asked Christians, "What was the apostle Paul's life like?" people gravitate to the negative—lots of suffering, hard, painful. They look at Paul's life through a dark lens. They get stuck in Paul's dying and miss his multiple resurrections. They are surprised when I tell them that Paul would disagree with them. Then I read Paul's description of what happens to a praying community by paraphrasing Ephesians 3:20, as if Paul were speaking about himself:

> God has been doing far more than I could ask or imagine. The power of the Spirit of Jesus permeates everything I do. Yes, I regularly participate in the dying of Jesus, but that suffering opens the door to real-time resurrection. I repeatedly experience the Spirit's power in me and our team. By God's grace, we've launched hundreds of Jesus communities in the Greek world, filled with people whose lives have been transformed by Jesus. I can't imagine a more joyful, productive life!

Paul looks at life through a resurrection lens.[1] We might paraphrase Paul's description of his prison life this way (Phil. 1:12–18):

> I know you've been concerned about my chains, but you'll never believe what has happened: *Because of* my imprisonment, the *entire imperial guard* in Rome has heard the gospel—that's six thousand or more elite soldiers! Seeing this, the church has become bolder in witnessing. Yes, some are trying to get me in trouble by aggressively sharing the gospel, but who cares? More people are hearing about Jesus! So what looks like a terrible injustice has turned into an amazing opportunity! I'm literally bursting with joy!

Paul expects that as we devote ourselves to prayer, the Spirit of Jesus continually will breathe resurrection life into our lives. So he's alert to the Spirit's activity, which colors how he sees life. He encourages the Philippians to also be on a resurrection hunt: "Finally, brothers, whatever is true, whatever is honorable, whatever is just, whatever is pure, whatever is lovely, whatever is commendable, if there is any excellence, if there is anything worthy of praise, think about these things" (Phil. 4:8).

This isn't syrupy optimism—it's what life looks like with our Lord Jesus enthroned in radiant glory. Consequently, when I'm in a prayer meeting, I'm on a resurrection hunt.

My resurrection hunt begins outside the prayer meeting. Just this week Bob Loker showed me a screen shot he'd taken from our online Spanish training. One of the trainers was a distinguished pastor in Chile, while another lived in Guatemala (you could see the tin roof and walls of her house). The photo captured the beauty of Jesus's body, of rich and poor gathered together as equals, learning together. In fact, in this session the Guatemalan woman was training the Chilean pastor. I asked Bob to share the photo on our next staff prayer call. As we prayed, we enjoyed the beauty of the body of Christ. We saw resurrection!

I recently helped my 97-year-old mom look at her week through a resurrection lens: a family member was starting to read the Bible regularly; an Indian woman who'd been through a severe loss had grown in her maturity in Christ; and Spain had relaxed travel restrictions, enabling her to get away. So when Mom and I went to pray, we began by thanking God. We weren't putting on blinders; we were taking off blinders that kept us from seeing the present work of the Spirit, from seeing resurrection.

When I was growing up, our family tuned in to beauty. Every June, we'd drive up the Pacific Coast Highway from San Francisco. Around every bend was a new, breathtaking vista. We were awed by the beauty. Once when we pulled into an overlook, we saw whales playing in the distance. The detour we took added a couple of hours to our drive north, but we enjoyed every minute. We do that in our staff prayer meetings too. We pause for beauty.

One way to help others see beauty is to open a prayer meeting by asking: "How have you seen God at work? What is he doing?" That gives space for stories to bubble, which we can then briefly enjoy and pray for. When we do this, we are putting feet on what Paul tells the Colossians to do: "Continue steadfastly in prayer, being watchful in it with thanksgiving" (Col. 4:2).

When we view life through a resurrection lens, it's contagious. Soon others are on a resurrection hunt. Bob Loker was the one who spotted the beauty of a small Jesus community in Latin America. My mom pointed out to me the change in the Indian woman ten years ago.

At a recent staff prayer meeting, Mafdi, our Arab staff worker, showed us a video of a new Arab believer praying. We were all moved by how honest and faith-filled the man's prayer was. I shared an old prayer card I had for the Arab world (fig. 20.1).

Dream Card—2007

"Sing to the Lord a new song, his praise from the end of the earth, you who go down to the sea, and all that fills it, the coastlands and their inhabitants. Let the desert and its cities lift up their voice, the villages that Kedar inhabits; let the habitants of Sela sing for joy, let them shout from the top of the mountains. Let them give glory to the Lord, and declare his praise in the coastlands." Isa. 42:10-12

Figure 20.1. Prayer card for the Arab world

When I pray this card, I imagine myself standing in Jerusalem with the prophet Isaiah. First, he looks west to the Greeks and says, "You who go down to the sea, and all that fills it, the coastlands," and commands them to "sing to the Lord a new song" (42:10). Then he looks east to the Arab world, to "the villages that Kedar inhabits," calling them to join this universal chorus and "shout from the top of the mountains," and to "declare his praise in the coastlands" in the west (42:11–12). Isaiah's prayer comes full circle.

By sharing this prayer card in our meeting, I highlighted the size of the resurrection we were seeing through Mafdi. When I began praying with this card in 2007, I didn't know a single Arab

Christian. I just prayed a dream. Now God had blessed us with a full-time Arab worker reaching out to Arab seekers.

When we help others see, it encourages their faith. Everyone has old prayers that seem stuck in the mud. Hearing how God *answered* a fifteen-year-old prayer encourages people's faith, which helps them endure in the hidden work of prayer.

Seeing how God can work through problems is one thing. But problems are still problems. And some can seem like tiresome aggravations. How do we pray for them?

How to Pray for Problems

Some prayer habits drain the life out of a resurrection mindset. Aunt Edna's weekly request for her arthritic hip is a case in point. I suspect her hip has slain more prayer meetings than Samson's jawbone of an ass killed Philistines. How does Aunt Edna's hip kill prayer meetings? For starters, it tends not to get better. Nor does her hip stand alone. It reminds Uncle Eddie of his bad ankle and Wilma of her aching shoulder. Hearing a litany of low-level medical problems that don't go away actually breeds doubt about God's ability to answer prayer. (I must confess, though, now that I'm older, I find Edna's requests slightly more interesting. "Oh, really, Edna. What surgeon are you going to? Full or partial replacement?" I'm joking, although I'm aware enough of this problem that when Kim and I have our morning prayer time, I limit myself to praying for only one body part for Jill and one for me. So if I go with my ankle, that leaves the hip for Jill!)

A pastor reflected on this problem, "I grew so weary of prayer request time in the church, I began calling it (to myself) 'Grandma's toe fungus time'—just about every church prayer meeting I was part of revolved around physical needs; seldom did it move beyond that."

So how should we respond to Edna's hip pain?

First, enlarge your heart for Edna. She's a hurting saint. So don't just tolerate Edna; feel for her. By being attentive to Edna's hip, we follow Jesus's pattern of looking, feeling compassion, and acting.[2] Being attentive to these seemingly small needs is a lovely way to bind a community together. In time, others in the prayer meeting share Edna's burdens. Love expressed in prayer binds Jesus communities together.

I do discourage random medical or job requests that come from outside the praying community. We aren't a prayer machine; we are the praying body of Jesus. So we say, "If you have needs for prayer, then come and join us."

Second, enlarge Edna's heart by praying for the *complete Edna.* Ask her how she's doing, who's helping her around the house, and how her spirits are. Pray for her whole life, her soul, her endurance. Hunt for kingdom movement or kingdom barriers in her life, so you're praying beyond her immediate concern.

Third, enlarge Edna's vision to other sufferers. Help Edna and others in the prayer meeting to "lift their eyes up to the harvest" and look beyond themselves. You might pray for the Uyghurs in China, or a friend of a friend who is imprisoned in China for his faith, or children in America who are being sexually mutilated by transgender surgery. That broadens everyone's horizon. If my first move enlarges my love for Edna, my next move broadens Edna's love for the world.

I often do something similar with Kim when her prayers focus just on herself. By pointing her to a broader world, I'm teaching her to love. Along with Kim, I can struggle with a self-focus in my prayers. It's easy for us just to pray for our ministries, our needs, and miss the broader work of what Jesus is doing.

Moving from Self-Focus to Resurrection Focus

The problem behind the problem-centered prayer meeting isn't just a missing resurrection focus; it's a self-centered focus. Consider the apostle Paul's other-centeredness.

At the end of Acts, when Paul is shipwrecked on the Island of Malta, the locals build a bonfire to dry off the survivors. Then it starts to rain, so Paul gathers more fuel.

> When Paul had gathered a bundle of sticks and put them on the fire, a viper came out because of the heat and fastened on his hand. When the native people saw the creature hanging from his hand, they said to one another, "No doubt this man is a murderer. Though he has escaped from the sea, Justice has not allowed him to live." He, however, shook off the creature into the fire and suffered no harm. (28:3–5)

Notice three ways Paul is not self-centered. First, he's not health obsessed. It's normal to shake off a snake that has bitten you; it's not normal to keep working. Paul's reaction to the snake fleshes out his self-reflection "My life is worth nothing to me" (Acts 20:24 NLT). Paul can say that because he has a new resurrection life in Christ.

Second, he's not obsessed with honor. Paul has singlehandedly saved the entire ship. Others should be jumping up to collect sticks in gratitude for Paul's bravery and wisdom, and yet he cares little about how he is regarded. That frees him to take the role of a slave.

Third, he's not obsessed with comfort. He and his shipmates wash up on shore, soaking wet, cold and exhausted, and yet Paul leaves the warmth of the fire to gather sticks for the fire. Like his Lord and Savior, Paul washes feet.

Paul's other-centered self-forgetfulness takes my breath away. This Jesus-obsessed man leads a life of 24-7 love. He never takes a break from love. He is a relentless lover.

When we pray together, we all have the delicate task of caring for people, taking their concerns seriously but simultaneously helping them see through a resurrection lens and moving them into the work of love. Looking at problems through a resurrection lens keeps us from getting stuck in death and injects hope into our prayer times.

A Word to Pastors

A pastor recently shared with me his weariness with prayer. I asked, "Have you asked Jesus to help you with this?" He started laughing. "No."

Tell Jesus you are bored; tell him you can't pray; tell him you don't believe. Then pray that out loud. Disclose to your fellow pray-ers your heart struggles. Don't hide your weakness; display it. As you endure in prayer, you begin to see his patterns. In short, the activity of praying with others has an inescapable dying side that you cannot bypass, one that must be endured.

21

Becoming Real in Prayer

IF CHAPTER 20 EMPHASIZED not fixating on problems when we pray together, this chapter focuses on not failing to share problems, especially big, discouraging ones.

I've seen my mom transform prayer meetings. She comes in weary with life, depressed about the state of her heart, and feeling distant from God. But she doesn't keep it to herself. She begins saying something like this: "I'm overwhelmed with life. I need prayer." Then she describes how and why she's overwhelmed. At one prayer meeting she shared that she lacked a "sincere and pure devotion to Christ" (2 Cor. 11:3). Her honesty instantly changed the atmosphere. When this happens, others feel safe to be real about their struggles. Her weakness energizes the prayer meeting and opens the door for real prayer about real problems.

At first blush, her honesty might seem to inject a note of pessimism and cloud a resurrection lens. It would if a resurrection lens were mere optimism, but a resurrection lens is not optimistic—it's realistic. It sees the great reality in life: the resurrection of Jesus by the power of the Spirit, who continually retells the story of Jesus's dying and rising in his body, the church. That allows us to join people in their deaths, and to pray for and anticipate resurrection.

Why We Hesitate to Get Real

Robert, who trains youth pastors to use our *The Person of Jesus* study, had been quietly sharing with me a series of significant health crises he was battling—heart, kidneys, and stomach. But after six weeks of updates and praying for him, I was puzzled that he'd not mentioned it at our staff prayer meetings. When I asked him why, he said:

> As a pastor, 95 percent of requests I heard over the years were in regards to physical needs. I longed for people to share other kinds of concerns as well: emotional struggles, faith struggles, husband/wife struggles, parenting struggles and financial struggles. Consequently, I became cynical about sharing physical needs.
>
> I am facing a ton of challenges—concerns for my friend's failing marriage, the spiritual condition of my children, issues with my house—but I don't want to dominate a prayer time with my health concerns.
>
> Finally, I don't want it always about me. My tendency is to be an open book, and sometimes I think people grow weary. About three months ago I started a prayer card on James 1:19, "Think before you speak." Perhaps the Spirit is creating a sanctified pause in me.

Robert is rightly reacting to a church culture with narrow bands for prayer. Like a dying restaurant with a heavy carb menu, the prayer meeting can be leaden. Also, he's rightly aware of his own heart—he can focus on himself and his problems too much, so he's on a speaking diet!

Still, I encouraged Robert: "Don't overthink this: you've got serious problems and God can help you, but that can't happen if you don't share. This is a group of praying friends, and these problems are potentially serious." The problem with Edna's hip wasn't her hip but that the prayer meeting was dominated by hip-like problems and never went deeper or wider. That wasn't Robert's problem.

Helping Others Open Up

Later that week, at our Thursday prayer time, I opened the door for Robert to be candid about his health: "It's important for us to share what's troubling us, whether in ministry or our personal life. We need to hear from one another. If we don't' share our heartaches, then the body can't respond well. If we don't hear from one another, it's like a nervous system that can't feel pain. That's what happens in leprosy."

Robert smiled and said, "He's talking about me." He shared his family history of heart problems, and that his heart medicine was affecting his kidneys.

Richard began by praying for long life for Robert. Richard was praying big. His prayer went to the heart of Robert's fear. Then he thanked God for Robert, asking that God would bless his work.

Then Felicia descended into strategy and prayed for his overall health, and then moved quickly into tactics, that he'd have wisdom with all the different messages coming at him from the health community.

Then Donna thanked God that Robert had been attentive to what his body was saying and had not dismissed it. She acknowledged that serious health problems could be scary. Then she shifted from Robert's body to his mind, using Philippians 4 to pray that he'd not get caught up in health issues and would instead focus on "what is right and true." She stayed at tactics, praying that he'd be attentive to his nutritionist.

Next our office assistant prayed for Robert's heart from a variety of angles: that he'd be at peace, filled with hope, and his faith would be built up. She repeatedly circled back to faith and hope, using Romans 8 to pray that he'd see this as "for his good."

Then Jon entered Robert's world by reflecting on how sobering it was to grapple with a body that's getting older. He prayed for a deepening wisdom and assurance for Robert—not only wisdom for medical care and lifestyle changes but also wisdom for the journey.

I closed by reflecting on how crucial Robert's ministry is, as he helps students to see the beauty of Jesus. I prayed, using Ephesians 6, for his protection from an attack from the evil one, who wants to discourage, derail, and ultimately destroy him. I prayed that God would surround him with songs of deliverance. Then I prayed that he'd have the grace to hang in there with the new plant-based diet he was on, that he'd be able to "eat for Jesus."

By inviting Robert to share, I encouraged him, like the apostle Paul, to be "in weakness." We didn't offer "plausible words of wisdom," but we turned to God in prayer, which in time unleashes a "demonstration of the Spirit and of power." Consequently, our faith didn't "rest in the wisdom of men but in the power of God" (1 Cor. 2:3–5).

By listening to Robert and surrounding him with prayer, we loved him. By praying for his heart from multiple directions, we built up his faith. Consequently, Robert left encouraged; he wasn't alone; God was at work. Hope grew.

Of course, all this takes discretion. I've seen people share about their marriage in a way that was potentially destructive, because people sided with the sharing spouse, having heard only one side of a complex situation. In a case like that, it's incumbent on the leader to pull the sharing spouse aside and counsel discretion.

When individuals like my mom and Robert open up their hearts, it blesses the whole prayer gathering. But how does a community as a whole open up when it is suffering?

Opening Up about Corporate Weakness

In 2005 our mission went through a crisis that forced us to shrink to two full-time staff. Our marketing wasn't working; the church had little interest in what we were doing, and we had several budget deficits. I pasted a note on my computer that summarized Jesus's Matthew 13 kingdom parables: "The kingdom is low, slow, and hidden. Be patient." It was our story.

Knowing we were going through a kind of death helped us pray effectively. We prayed for resurrection but lived in the death that God had permitted. We didn't try to be something we weren't. Later, as our mission began to grow again, I regularly encouraged our staff at prayer or whenever they were discouraged, "Remember, the kingdom is low, slow, and hidden." Almost all our staff can recite that little mantra. I wanted them to see and participate in the death we were in and not run from it. That is, it was okay to be weak and forgotten together. I wanted our staff to see that together we were in a Jesus-story. It became our way of boasting "in the cross of our Lord Jesus Christ" (Gal. 6:14). We flipped the narrative.

Since then, God has blessed our work in amazing ways, but we are still underfunded, understaffed, and overwhelmed. Boasting in our weakness allows us to laugh at ourselves. I mean, half our leadership team is on Medicare! Yesterday, we found a fifty-thousand-dollar mistake in our planning, which means postponing our move out of the three bedrooms and one living room we rent for our offices.

In his first letter to the Corinthians, the apostle Paul is frustrated that their quest for a celebrity culture is leading them to hide their weaknesses. He points them to the weakness of the cross (1:18–25), their own weakness (1:26–31), and how he himself was weak with them (2:1–5). Their weakness opens the door for resurrection power. His own weakness led to a "demonstration of the Spirit and power" (2:4). Our weakness leaves space for the Spirit to do his wonders.

Our slogan "low, slow, and hidden" helped our community watch what God was doing by locating where we were in God's story. We weren't trying to be something we weren't, nor were we giving in to despair. It's tempting for leaders to not talk about the elephant in the room—we'd lost money, people, and impact. Our work had become weak. Talking about it openly normalized dying. We didn't pretend everything was okay.

I encouraged the pastor of a large, multisite church (their post-pandemic attendance dropped by 50 percent), to flip the narrative by receiving the death they were in. I encouraged him to tell his congregation that he and other pastors were discouraged. I told him of other megachurches that were running from their death, trying to whip up enthusiasm for the church's vision. It's painful to watch. I know their pastors are discouraged. Why not tell us? Lead us in lament. How much more fruitful it is to openly acknowledge our weakness and follow Jesus into this passion.

My pastor friend said to me: "We are half the size we were. What do we do with our budgets and all the buildings we have to maintain?" I replied: "You are in a death, so live like you are dying. Like Jesus in his passion, be attentive to your people, your budgets, doing layoffs as graciously as you can. During Jesus's passion he washed feet, encouraged his disciples, prayed for them, protected them at Gethsemane, healed a servant's ear, rebuked Peter, offered himself, rebuked the chief priest, cared for Pilate, received a beating, and forgave the soldiers. He was fully alive, active in love, attentive to small things even when he was losing." That's what makes Jesus's passion so stunning. Is there any better work than preparing Jesus's body for burial?

Story tellers *watch* carefully. If you don't watch, you don't have a story. The Jews were gifted at *watching* because they knew that if you prayed and waited, God would eventually show up. All their great stories have watching imbedded in them: Esther, Ruth, and Joseph take us on thrill rides where the hero goes into a death, and then, in time, an amazing resurrection occurs. In some ways, watching the story unfold is the highest art of prayer because it requires watching patterns emerge over a period of many years. Leaders must *look* at what's going on and then lead their community in *watching*. And if you are suffering in any way, it is such a joy to be watching and watched, praying and prayed for. You are no longer alone!

22

The Prayer Menu

CONVERSATION WITH GOOD FRIENDS runs the gamut of human experience: you laugh, you cry, you listen, you lament, you enjoy. It's one of life's greatest delights. Remarkably, you can have this same level of conversation with a two-year-old and an eighty-two-year-old. And yet, when God joins the conversation (prayer), everything stiffens up. It's like your mom has just walked into a sleepover. The giggling stops and everyone gets quiet. Why do we shut down our hearts when we begin to pray together?

This "prayer chill" is made worse because often no conversation thread holds the prayers together: requests multiply and prayers bounce from subject to subject.

So how do we talk to our heavenly Father like we might to good friends? Quite simply, what does it mean to become human again *as a group*? Many people have found their ability to pray together enriched by the "prayer menu" shown in table 22.1. It uses Jesus's three patterns of relating as a model for the richness of human interactions. This prayer menu will help expand your prayers outside their usual ruts.

Every week, I create a "conversation menu" for Kim. Because of her autism, she struggles to vary her conversation, so I write seven conversation starters in her speech computer. I try to capture her "voice" and her interests. We've saved many of them, and she'll often go back and rehearse them. Kim is fully human, of course, but people don't know it until they hear her heart. Think of the prayer menu as a series of conversation starters for our tendency to autistic-like praying. There is some complexity to the prayer menu, so I ask you what I ask Kim: "Be patient as I explain this." It will enrich your prayer life. First, an overview.

An Overview of the Prayer Menu

On the left side of the table, you see three sides to the person of Jesus: his compassion (care for people), his honesty (care for truth), and his dependence (care for his Father).[1] The richness of the person of Jesus offers us a way out of our prayer stiffness. It allows us to become human again.

Across the top of the chart, you see three perspectives: me, my world, and God. That is, What's going on in me? What's going on in my world? What is going on in God's heart? This creates nine boxes or windows, each one a way of being human in prayer. Each invites questions to ask ourselves in order to prompt new ways of praying.

Row 1: Compassion

The first row guides us in caring for the person.

1. Feel? This window prompts us to ask ourselves, *How am I doing?* or *How are we doing?* Devout Christians can be reluctant to ask this, because they are aware of living in a self-obsessed culture, where compassion is directed inward. And yet, if we shut

Table 22.1. Praying according to three patterns of Jesus's interactions

	Prayer Menu*		
FOCUS	MY HEART (IN)	MY WORLD (OUT)	MY GOD (UP)
Goal	Enter my own heart.	Enter the lives of others.	Enter God's heart.
COMPASSION Care for people	1. FEEL? My feelings: Where am I? How am I feeling? Tense? Anxious?	2 . COMPASSION? My feelings for others: How are others around me doing? How are they feeling? How do I incarnate, empathize? What is their world like?	3. ENJOY? My feelings for God: How can I thank, worship, and enjoy God today? How have I seen him at work in my situation and the world around me?
HONESTY Care for truth	4. REPENT? Truth for myself: Do I repent? Do I have hidden sin? What does God's word say to me?	5. HONEST? Truth for others: Do I need to give the gifts of honesty to someone? What concerns me about this person or group?	6. LAMENT? Truth before God: Have I opened up my broken heart to God? "Where are you, God? How long, O Lord?"
DEPENDENCE Care for God's will	7. DESIRE? My desire for myself: What do I want? Does it align with what God wants? Am I willing to wait? Am I wrongly pushing my will?	8. NEED? My desire for others: How do I love those around me in prayer? What do they want? What do I want for them? What good can I do for them and their situation?	9. WATCH? God's desires: What is God doing? What story is he writing? Have I submitted to God's story for me, for our community?

Three Patterns of Jesus (left margin label)

* Copyright © seeJesus 2020, a global discipling mission

down how we are feeling, our feelings will leak anyway or we will withdraw. The psalmist asks himself,

Why are you cast down, O my soul,
  and why are you in turmoil within me? (Ps. 42:5)

When we come to our Father, we need to be ourselves, which includes our feelings. This can be hard in prayer meetings, and yet, sharing your broken heart energizes praying together. The real you needs to meet the real body of Christ.

2. *Compassion?* The most frequently mentioned emotion of Jesus in the Gospels, compassion involves stepping into another person's shoes, but we can jump from need to need and forget to pray about the person who feels that need. The antidote is also asking God to meet people in their fear or anxiety. By slowing down and lingering over a person, prayer becomes a conversation among those who are praying.

3. *Enjoy?* Now we direct our gaze upward to our Father. I call this "Enjoy" because if we don't enjoy the giver, then thanksgiving withers into mere duty. As a child, I memorized in our Westminster Shorter Catechism that our chief end is to glorify and *enjoy* God. So in one prayer meeting we were rejoicing over the baptism of a young Arab man in Europe that Mafdi had been discipling. We enjoyed how God had worked during the crisis in Syria through German chancellor Angela Merkel's welcome of Arab refugees. Her welcome was rooted in her faith and the example of her father, a Lutheran pastor.

If our requests look to the future, enjoyment reaches into the past. When God helps us in our community—as he does continually—we can remember in our prayer time the people who made it happen. This morning we were celebrating our largest See Jesus workshop ever, and I reflected on the work of our trainers. We began by celebrating people. When we do this in prayer together, it makes praying fun, decenters us, and lifts other people up, which makes room for the Spirit of Jesus!

Row 2: Honesty

The second row, which helps us care for truth, is weaker than the other two in community prayer.

4. Repent? This window prompts us to direct truth at ourselves. For example, this morning I asked our staff to pray for me concerning my email habit. I stay on top of hundreds of emails by answering them quickly, but as can happen with all good things, checking email has become an addiction. And last week in my morning prayer time with Jill, I lamented how I'd subtly boasted the previous day. (At least, I thought it was subtle!) I needed Jill's help. As Paul says, "I know that through your prayers and the help of the Spirit of Jesus Christ this will turn out for my deliverance" (Phil. 1:19). That's a help we overlook. We're comfortable with the generic "sinner," but we don't like getting specific. The shame stings. And yet honesty about besetting sin energizes a prayer meeting. It's something we all struggle with. It's real life.

5. Honest? This window directs truth outward. It guides us in praying for justice. I will often pray, especially for political problems, Jesus's promise that what is hidden will be revealed. I pray that because unless we know the truth about something, justice is hindered. Praying for justice and truth also means relinquishing our demand for justice. When we forgive those who sin against us, we acknowledge and then release our demand for justice. Realizing that we ourselves need forgiveness tempers our demand for justice. The result is patience.

6. Lament? This directs our honesty to God. As I mentioned in chapter 19, because of the influence of the gnostic mind on the church, public laments are exceedingly rare in prayer meetings. And yet the Psalms are filled with laments, where the psalmist is in God's face. For example:

How long, O Lord? Will you forget me forever?
　How long will you hide your face from me? (Ps. 13:1)

Jesus laments on the cross, "My God, my God, why have you forsaken me?" (Matt. 27:46). A lament is something that breaks your heart. Laments feel disrespectful of God, and yet they are actually faith-filled because they take God seriously.

Row 3: Dependence

The third row is about our will in relation to God's will.

7. Desire? Much of the substance of a good prayer meeting is giving space to people's desires, what we routinely call prayer requests. Jesus prays in Gethsemane: "Abba, Father, all things are possible for you. Remove this cup from me" (Mark 14:36). In our prayer meeting, I work to stay in touch with people's desires. Usually, our desires are too small. Jesus's repeated command in John 14–16 to ask anything is immensely clarifying. This is where praying big can help our desires to come alive.

8. Need? This window expands our praying beyond ourselves by praying, "Your kingdom come, your will be done" (Matt. 6:10). Jesus's remarkable promise about the power of agreeing in prayer often fuels our faith and encourages us to pray daring prayers: "Again I say to you, if two of you agree on earth about anything they ask, it will be done for them by my Father in heaven" (Matt. 18:19). It is important not to overthink Jesus's words. Just ask.

9. Watch? Now we ask: What is God doing? What is the story? This window integrates all nine windows into a coherent whole. Here, we slow down to see the patterns of God's work and connect the story threads. God is weaving a story—so it is essential to conform our prayers to his will. This is when we pray the second half of Jesus's Gethsemane prayer, "Yet not what I will, but what you will" (Mark 14:36). In dependence on God, our wills come together. But we need to begin with the simplicity of what we want, which, in time, can mature into what God wants.

A Symphony of Prayer

Below is a snippet from a staff prayer meeting. I've interspersed the title of the window that matches each prayer request so you can see how these prompts work to direct our prayers. These prayers are unscripted. Mafdi has just told us about a young Arab seeker who's attending his online *The Person of Jesus* study. The young man is open to the gospel, but he's struggling. Dianne prays first:

> Lord, I thank you for the ministry you've given to Mafdi to hurting people ["Enjoy"], and to people who are seeking you, and for so many opportunities on so many different levels. I thank you for the way that you've made him, for giving him a compassionate heart, for giving him the *Person of Jesus* study to use in his studies ["Compassion"]. I pray for this young man who has been told that he's ugly by his own mother. It's just heartbreaking, and I pray that in time you will work in his heart and show him how precious he is to you, and he is exactly the way you want him to be and look ["Feel"], and he's not ugly. Lord, show him how beautiful he is because he's your precious creation ["Compassion"]. So I pray that this would be a special time in this young man's life and for all the people that Mafdi ministers to ["Need"]. Thank you for opening so many doors and care for Mafdi and his family I pray.

Dianne prays from her heart, so her prayers are mainly from row 1. She begins focusing on God and Mafdi ("Enjoy"), then shifts to window 2, "Compassion," as she prays for this young man, who's been told by his mother that he's ugly. You can sense Dianne's empathy ("Feel").

Robert prays next. But first some context. The pandemic opened up multiple opportunities for our online studies. In June 2019, Mafdi released a one-minute Arabic video about Jesus on Facebook. In two weeks, it had nine thousand views. Forty people signed up for an Arabic study of Jesus, but no one showed up! The response showed an interest in Jesus but also fear. So we prayed that God would break through the fear barrier. We *prayed big*, which allowed us to lament over the fear that gripped this world. Lamenting works best when you look failure in the face and don't window dress it with optimism. In autumn of 2019, God began to open multiple doors. In the following prayer, Robert reflects on the story God was weaving:

> Lord, thank you ["Enjoy"] for the ways in which you're breaking down the walls of fear in the Muslim world ["Needs"]. I think just two months ago Mafdi started this advertisement, and all these people said they were coming and no one showed up ["Watch"], and how we just prayed and asked for fear to be taken away ["Lament"], and now people are starting to feel the freedom to come out of the shadows and not walk in fear. So thank you Lord Jesus ["Enjoy"] for breaking down barriers and for using Mafdi. Thank you for the ways light is breaking into the darkness. It's just a beautiful story of the way you work ["Watch"]. Thank you for letting us be a witness to it.

Jon Hori prays next:

> Father, thank you ["Enjoy"] that naturally people get sick and tired of mean people, and it sounds like the Arab world in the

most honest pockets are tired of the evil that they are facing ["Watch"], and so we pray that might accelerate and there would be a greater freedom and a boldness to be able to not only hunger after you but seek after you, and that you would give Mafdi greater opportunities to be a person of peace and truth and compassion ["Needs"]. As he was describing this community that's developing naturally, as you build it, I couldn't help but think that those are the people that you would have gathered around you at the manger. Those are the people you would have invited ["Compassion"]. And so thank you that you give hope in your person ["Enjoy"] but also through Mafdi ["Compassion"]. So we pray that that might multiply in a great and very powerful way.

Jon's prayer builds on the community of Arab seekers who joined Mafdi's online studies. We've known many of their first names and their stories. We've seen a dozen baptisms online. So Jon's prayer recalls the rough crowd at Jesus's manger. Jon sees the story of Jesus mirrored in Mafdi's online studies.

Dianne, Robert, and Jon bring themselves to their prayers. Dianne leads with her feelings, and Robert and Jon pray with their thinking. That is almost identical to how Jill and I pray together. Dianne prays local (focusing on the young man), and Robert and Jon pray global, remembering our big praying. This creates a symphony of prayer that allows us to become human again.

Problems with Agreeing in Prayer

What if those who have gathered to pray together disagree, especially on cultural and political issues? Scripture is clear: if we can't agree about matters of opinion, we should be silent. Paul tells the Corinthians that sensitivity to a weaker brother or sister who believes we shouldn't eat meat sacrificed to an idol outweighs our desire to get him or her to see the truth in this matter (1 Cor. 8). Consequently, in a Corinthian prayer meeting, Paul would not have prayed that people would be liberated from their fear of eating meat sacrificed to an idol, although he might have prayed that with a smaller group or by himself.

This sensitivity applies to all the windows in the prayer menu, but especially the window "Being Honest," where we are praying for truth and justice. I caution our staff about praying for political issues where we might not agree. During the riots in the summer of 2020, I'd preface a prayer time by saying: "We have divergent political views, so as we pray about our current cultural situation, I'd encourage you to be discreet and pray for areas where we might agree. For example, we can always pray for *shalom*, for peace." That dampens our prayer meetings, but it is the dampening of love.

This brings up a tough question. When is something an *opinion*, as in food sacrificed to idols (1 Cor. 8), and when is something *evil*, as in the man committing incest with his stepmother (1 Cor. 5)? Incorrect opinions need to be treated with respect. Evil needs to be openly rejected. It takes Spirit-guided wisdom, soaked in Scripture, to know what is an opinion and what is evil, what we should be silent about and what we should openly pray against. Last week, after one of our trainers told me of a transgender boss, we prayed for fifteen minutes against the transgender confusion in our culture.

How can you use the prayer menu? If you are leading a prayer meeting—whether with your family, with friends, or in a church setting—you can review the prayer menu before, during, or after prayer. *Before* allows for neglected windows to be entered more intentionally. *During* allows for directed movement with greater self-awareness about topics being prayed. *After* allows for post-diagnostic heart examination in a prayer journal.

A Word to Pastors

The church has been cautious about praying about cultural issues largely because almost anything you pray could offend someone. Silence can be wisdom, but it's left a vacuum. I hear almost no public praying that addresses the seismic cultural shifts we are going through. That's not always been the case. On the morning of Paul Revere's ride in 1775, the militias gathered in their town squares, armed with their muskets, led by their elected captains. Guess what they did first? They consulted their pastors.[2] The militias wondered, *Should we fight the British regulars or stand down?* They turned to their pastors to help them understand an immediate cultural problem. The modern equivalent would be people asking their pastors: "What should we post on Facebook? Are we overly cautious? Have we seceded from the public square?"

When pastors have prayed, at least here in the Northeast, they have tended to pray based on the latest headline, which can easily miss Jesus's command "Judge not" (Matt. 7:1), or Paul's "Do not pronounce judgment before the time" (1 Cor. 4:5). So where do you begin? Like anything, I would pray about what to pray about and how to pray about it. I'd pray with the elders for the Spirit's gift of wisdom.

PART 5

SPECIALIZED PRAYING IN COMMUNITY

23

Constant in Prayer

NOW THAT WE'VE LOOKED at some of the internal balances to keep in prayer, we turn our attention to being constant in prayer in the variety of communities around us. For me, praying at breakfast with grandkids, praying with a friend, praying with Jill, and praying with my mom are all ways of being constant in prayer.

Jill and I were having breakfast out with our son Andrew and his three children. At the end of the meal our waitress surprised the kids with a box of toys. All three chose plastic Slinkys. It took Seth, age four, about a minute to get his Slinky completely tangled. In my fifty-some years of trying to untangle Slinkys, I have never been successful. But hope springs eternal, so I tried once again. No success. I handed the Slinky to his dad, who is quite mechanical, but Dad failed too. I said to Seth, "Let's pray." I prayed that we'd untangle his Slinky. Then a thought popped into my head: *Find the good part of the Slinky, grip a strand of the coil, and slowly turn the slinky and see if it untangles itself.* I couldn't even look down as I turned the coil—I was nervous it wouldn't work. But it did! As I handed the Slinky to Seth, who was now grinning broadly, I said, "Look, God heard our prayer!"

Seth and I were constant in prayer. Prayer flowed naturally out of our encounter with a tangled Slinky. Not only did God help us, but he also built Seth's faith, which in turn protected him ever so slightly from the functional atheism of our age. My only regret was not inviting Seth to pray, instead of me. That would have increased his ownership of the prayer and thus cemented his faith even deeper. We usually think of being constant in prayer as quietly and privately praying throughout the day. That's good, but it also has the wider meaning of being quick to pray with others. Our individualistic culture has internalized Paul's instruction to pray without ceasing. In a group-oriented culture (like the New Testament), believers naturally include others in their praying, since praying is something *we* do, not just something *I* do.[1]

As I was writing this, my son John called. He was excited: A teenage friend of the family had professed faith in Christ just the day before. John invited her over and explained the gospel again to her and encouraged her to pray. She hesitated, "I don't know how to pray." John knew that prayer was like breathing for a Christian, so he said, "It's easy, just tell God what's on your heart." Her prayer was beautiful, from the heart. Then John asked me for advice about a challenging relationship with a Christian leader. As I listened, I said, "John, based on what you've said, I'd back off and just pray instead." I described a similar situation where I'd backed off and been praying daily for some Christian leaders. John agreed with me. We were both constant in prayer.

Jill called next. She described a challenging relationship. After listening, I asked, "Have you been praying with this person?" Jill said, "Yes, several times a week." I replied: "Good. That means the door is open to the Spirit's work of enchantment." As we talked, the Lord gave me a thought, a simple suggestion of something I could do this week to help Jill with this relationship. Though we didn't pray at the moment, we'd been praying every day for this situation. We were constant in prayer.

Notice the multiple variations of being constant in prayer: my praying with Seth over a broken toy, my son John encouraging a teenager to pray, my encouraging John to pull back from a relationship and pray, and finally an ongoing, prayerful concern for Jill's friend. Being constant in prayer makes us God-aware. When we live in steady communication with our Father, the life of Jesus pulsates through his church.

Christians usually run Paul's exhortations to be constant in prayer through our grid of Western individualism and assume that the need for constancy applies to each of us separately. Of course it does apply to me, but Paul uses a plural verb (*proskarterountes*) when he says, "Be constant in prayer" (Rom. 12:12); and three of Paul's four uses of the Greek word *adialeiptōs*, meaning "constantly" or "unceasingly," modify plural verbs for praying or giving thanks to God (1 Thess. 1:2; 2:13; 5:17). The idea is *all of you, together, in your communities, be constant in prayer.*

When a praying community comes alive, prayer emerges spontaneously at multiple levels. Scheduled prayer meetings anchor a community in constant prayer, which, in turn, opens the door to spontaneous praying like what I've just described. Being constant in prayer nourishes a Jesus community like a well-watered garden.

Let's look more closely at how this works in the mini-communities that make up the body of Christ—in friendship, family, and marriage.

Praying with Your Spouse

Praying with your spouse can be extraordinarily challenging. I mentioned earlier about the pastor who shared that he didn't pray with his wife. His actual comment could be echoed by many: "My wife and I do not pray together regularly. . . . I've got this weird block there with my wife. . . . We do have an awesome marriage, but to be honest we don't have a regular prayer and devotion time, not even close."

Praying with your spouse is remarkably intimate. This morning, while we were waiting for an Uber driver to pick me up, Jill and I had five minutes to pray together. At four minutes, I started getting antsy, worried that I'd keep the driver waiting. So I glanced down at my phone. Jill noticed (she always does!) and said, "I can't pray with you checking your phone." End of prayer.

Uber anxiety aside, I think I've discovered the secret of praying with your spouse. In one word: *incarnate*. By that I mean step into his or her shoes 100 percent. So if your wife wants to lead a prayer time, let her lead. If your husband wants to pray for ten minutes, let him pray for ten minutes. If your wife wants to correct you during your prayer time, let her correct you. If she wants to remind you to take out the trash, let her remind you. Praying together is so fragile, the only way you can pull it off is to reduce your will to zero, which includes not checking your phone while your spouse is praying!

So how do you begin? You guessed it—you pray for your praying! I began about five years ago by writing on the edge of a prayer card, "Help us to pray together." I wasn't sure how to pull this off. Soon it occurred to me that I could follow Jill's Bible reading plan. So I began reading the same passage she was reading. That gave us a point of contact. Then I asked whether she would mind if I had devotions in the same room when she had hers. She was okay with that, though she had to adjust, because she loved to pray out loud. Then I suggested that we have a brief prayer time together. She said yes, and now we pray together for ten minutes almost every day.

What are the benefits? First, as I mentioned earlier, Jill prays better than I do. She has a tenacity, a heart that engages God at a deep level. She moves easily into lament. Sometimes I find her passion unnerving, but she helps me pray better. In fact, we both help one another pray better. I bring order and faith; Jill brings passion and honesty.

Second, we have a long list of things we can't do well unless God does them. The biggest is getting inside our grandkids' hearts. We have fourteen living grandchildren, whom we love dearly. It sounds trite, but when we pray, God does things. Praying regularly improves our relational "targeting." That is, we are aware of our grandkids' needs as persons, which in turn leads to new ways of loving them.

Third, praying with Jill cares for her soul in a way that words to her alone could never do. Our souls were meant to be praying together, feeding on Christ, pouring our hearts and desires out instead of bottling them up.

Finally, the only way you can sustain love, especially in close relationships, with all the complexities of your sin and the other person's, is to saturate your relationship in prayer. Constant love requires constant prayer.

Praying with Friends

David Powlison and I enjoyed a close friendship for many years. We prayed for one another regularly, but we didn't pray together. About fifteen years into our friendship, David suggested after lunch that we pray together in one of our cars. It felt strange, like going out on a first date. Of course, it wasn't that way; nothing is more natural than two Christians pausing to pray together. Yet the initial awkwardness I felt was a function of the spirit of our age, which puts prayer into a "pious" bucket. The last thing we want is to look super-spiritual.

Once, after David had heart surgery, he called me from the hospital very depressed. I'd never heard him so low. He described feeling dislocated; he'd even lost his sense of personhood. David later described our phone call this way:

> I phoned a trusted friend and sketched what was going on. To this day, he has not been able to explain exactly why he did what he did next. He did not give me physiological information. He did not say, "Don't worry." He did not ask me questions. He did not try to counsel me. He did not pray for me. Instead he read the Psalms of Ascent, one after another, fifteen straight psalms without pause, without comment, from Psalm 120 through Psalm 134. He cared for me as a person immersed in a very unpleasant experience.[2]

So what was going on in me? As David was sharing, I was praying quietly—his struggles seemed so deep that anything I would say felt either shallow or cheap. Advice was out of the question. Mere praying over the phone seemed so weak compared with the depth of his struggle. James scolds us about cheap prayers. When someone is in deep need, don't pray, "Go in peace, be warmed and filled" (2:16). Then this thought popped into my head: I knew David loved the Psalms. So instead of praying for him, I stepped out of the way and let the Spirit minister directly to him from the

Bible's book of prayers. David relaxed noticeably as the Spirit used the word to rechannel his thoughts.

Notice that hallmark of the Spirit—surprise. Both David and I were surprised by the Spirit's leading. The Spirit led me to *not* pray—at least not as I normally would. Notice, also, the pattern of the J-curve, dying with Christ. To incarnate with Jill is a kind of dying. Likewise, to not pray for David in my own words stopped my natural tendency to give a quick fix. Love reshaped my prayers.

We even nourished one another with our prayer requests. Once when David asked me how he could pray for me, I said, "Ask God to make me *childlike in faith*, and to make what I do and say *helpful to others*." David later wrote an article on that prayer request.[3] Previously, my coworker Bob Allums had encouraged me, as I wrote *A Praying Life*, to make it helpful. I recoiled slightly from Bob's suggestion. I wanted a *life-transforming* book; the Spirit simply wanted *helpful*. So I prayed, as I wrote, that the book would be helpful.

Praying with Mom

My mom, Rose Marie Miller, works in London as a missionary with South Asians. She lives with my sister Keren and her family. Mom is very involved with discipling Asian women, who honor and prize the elderly.

Every Sunday, early in the morning, we talk for about forty minutes and pray for ten. I enjoy hearing about her world. She tells me about the different Indian women she's befriended. Each friendship is a story that develops over time. I'm also a safe place for her to lament about things that aren't working well. She seldom complains about her declining body. My goal is to encourage her faith; my method is love.

233

We don't just "close in prayer." Knowing we are going to pray together shapes our conversation. We started praying together about a dozen years ago after I suggested we pray for any of her twenty-four grandchildren who weren't following Jesus. Occasionally, we pray for some of her fifty-four great-grandchildren as well. We've seen God draw some to Christ, and we've widened our prayers for her missionary team. We've seen some remarkable answers, but it's been a particular joy to see Mom's faith encouraged.

When prayer expands from the scheduled prayer times into the mini-communities, like this one with my mom, it penetrates the warp and woof of the church's culture. The Jesus community is becoming like Jesus, God-aware. It becomes *a praying church*.

24

A Band of Brothers

I WAS THRILLED WHEN, many years ago, my son John and his good friend Tim approached me, asking me to mentor them regarding sexual temptation. As young men, they were full of passion for Jesus but privately trapped by sexual sin. They knew that they weren't changing, that they needed help. Looking back now, John and Tim said to me recently: "Among peers we are open about our failures with sexual temptation, but we hid in public or with mature Christians. We had no problem confessing to one another, but it was the blind leading the blind. Neither of us was going to tell the other person to change. Unless we got help, we'd be the same in another twenty years."

Sexual sin has one significant upside for men: it is so powerful, so gripping, you can break its power only by learning the depths of Christ. That's why I was thrilled—hope was on the horizon.

Learning to Pray: The Heart of Discipleship

When we started meeting together, we had a problem: I saw their situation as desperate, but they didn't. They wanted tools, tips, and accountability. I wanted them to see that such things produced only surface change. They wanted to improve. I wanted them to enter the dying of Jesus. I wanted them to be desperate, to see that they couldn't change themselves, that they needed the Spirit of Jesus like they needed air. So for five years I prayed for them daily: "But as for you, O man of God, flee these things. Pursue righteousness, godliness, faith, love, steadfastness, gentleness" (1 Tim. 6:11).

Notice the breadth of my prayer. John and Tim were focused on just sexual sin, but that was like working out just your right arm at the gym. Sexual sin was the tip of the iceberg of a life of self-indulgence. I knew their life orientation had to change. I told them: "You guys are telling me you want to climb Mount Everest. But you've confused Everest with Mount Pocono (a small mountain near us). Not only that, you are out of shape, overweight, and overconfident."

I was preparing them for a long battle, not a quick fix. If they could see the impossibility of the task and their own weakness, they would pray. More than anything else, they needed to learn a Jesus-like dependence, that *they could do nothing on their own.*

So I began by teaching them to pray *after* they'd messed up. Just a simple prayer of confession, owning up to their sin, and then disowning their sin by claiming the forgiveness of Jesus and remembering that they are sons of God and brothers of Christ. I wanted a simple, clear confession, and then a simple turning to Christ. The confession needed to be made in community, with the three of us, in person or by text.

I didn't want them just moping over their sin, as in "I blew it last night. I can't believe I keep doing this. Man am I a mess." Shame over sin is good, but I didn't want them to get stuck there. I wanted shame to lead to a clear confession. Shame that doesn't come to

God and rest in Christ is penance, where you beat yourself up in your prayers as a way of paying for your sin. This is better: "Father, I sinned against you last night by _____. Thank you for the blood of Jesus that covers my sin. I can't change on my own. Would you help me to hate my sin?" I knew grace came to sinners, but moping and regretting only get you halfway to the cross.

Once they began to regularly confess their sin *after* they sinned, I encouraged them to pray *during* their sinning. This shocked them, but I didn't want any part of their lives to be outside the rule of Jesus. Usually in the act of any sin, you want to shut God out completely, but if you interrupt sin with prayer at sin's most powerful moment, you weaken Satan and make room for the Spirit. Tim later reflected: "When Paul first suggested this, it seemed crazy. *Stop and bring Jesus into the moment?* I'd rather talk to him afterward. Yet if you invite him into the moment, you have to address it. It weakens the power of sin."

But maturity began to build in them only when they prayed and asked for prayer *before* they gave in to temptation. Vulnerability to sexual temptation doesn't come with a warning label; usually you are self-preoccupied, feeling discouraged, depressed, or just desperate for a quick escape. You give yourself a "pass" for a quick sin. So "prayer by text" was crucial for this battle. Here are some of their texts from years ago:

Guys, please pray for me. I'm feeling incredibly weak tonight and full of self-pity. Not a good place!

I had a Victoria's Secret catalog come in the mail. I threw it out quickly, but even the freaking cover is killing me. I've never gotten that in the mail, and this was addressed to me.

Here's a prayer-by-text conversation:

> TIM: Hey guys, my morning is going well. Continue in the battle, thanks for praying for me.
> ME: Thanks for texting, "Father, fill Tim with your Spirit."
> JOHN: So beautiful! Thanks for the text, Tim! Jesus, help all of us to look to you today.

Next day:

> TIM: Jesus, I begin my day with you and ask that your Spirit will guide me as I continue in the battle today.
> JOHN: Amen. Jesus help Tim today to feel your pleasure and victory.

These "text-prayer meetings" might seem trite, but they represent a resounding victory over shame and for biblical manhood. The real man, who is in Christ, can *repeatedly* share his weakness and ask for help. It's one thing to believe Jesus forgives your sin; it's another to believe that after you've done the sin a hundred times. At some point we figure either Jesus or our friends have reached their forgiveness limit. Peter thought the number was seven times. Jesus corrected him using the high number of seventy-seven times (or seventy times seven) (Matt. 18:21–22). Repeated confession breaks the power of shame by shifting the focus of shame from self-loathing to sin-loathing. Confession transforms shame into guilt, which is easily destroyed by the blood of Jesus. Later, John described the value of each layer of prayer with the following health analogies:

- Praying after temptation—like calling 911 or going to the ER.

- Praying during temptation—like going to the doctor and getting a health checkup.
- Praying before temptation—learning how to eat healthy, getting regular exercise.

Almost all failures with sexual temptation have a strong self-pity or suffering-avoidance side to them, even if it is nothing but the suffering of saying no to your own desires. So I often reviewed with John and Tim how receiving suffering drew me into a *fellowship of Jesus's suffering*, which weakened the power of temptation. Slowly by slowly, a small praying community formed, a band of brothers.

Overcoming Barriers of Cynicism

Several years into our discipling, I discovered John and Tim had no pattern of *continual* prayer. Their personal prayer life was almost nonexistent beyond our little band. They were at the first base camp at Everest, but they didn't have the Spiritual strength and stamina to climb to the upper camps and eventually the peak.

When I asked them about their prayerlessness, they half-joked, "Why do we have to pray if you are doing our praying for us?" I tried, "Just five minutes in the morning." That didn't work. So I shortened it to one minute, but still failure. That's when I uncovered that old prayer killer—they were cynical about God hearing and acting for them.

Cynicism looks at good and sees darkness. Before every silver lining is a dark cloud. It kills the childlike simplicity of coming to my heavenly Father and saying: "Help me. I can't do this by myself." Even when a prayer was answered, John and Tim would think, *It would have happened anyway.* Or *Yeah, right.* I could pick up their cynicism because I battled it in my own life. Cynicism is usually masked by hypocrisy, because you keep your cynicism to yourself but openly "amen" the value of prayer. They said: "We'd had so many failures, we were cynical over whether we could change. We were cynical about prayer. We didn't expect God to act. He might act in small ways, but nothing big. We never said this out loud, but it was in our hearts. Deep down we doubted that God could change us."

I pushed hard to get them into the world of prayer. I knew if I could get them talking with their heavenly Father even for just a minute, they would begin to encounter him and discover that he cared for them in the details of their lives. I wanted them to discover that our world, our Father's world, is enchanted.

What finally broke through their cynicism was a remarkable answer to our prayers for purity. After all my work with them, we still weren't much beyond base camp. On their own, they sought out a mutual friend, a gifted counselor who specialized in sexual temptation. He worked closely with them, with the result that there was a dramatic breakthrough in their lives. This wise Christian helped them get into some of the nitty-gritty of their habits in ways that I could not. The change in them both was remarkable.

It had all the hallmarks of my Father's work: (1) God heard our prayers. Tim and John both changed dramatically. They had substantial and lasting victory over their besetting sins. To my everlasting delight, they climbed Everest! (2) It had the Spirit's signature outside-the-box surprise: the person praying (me) wasn't the person who made most of the change happen. God protects us from pride by displaying his glory through multiple saints.

John and Tim were so transformed that they both now have ministries discipling young men who struggle with sexual temptation where prayer is the centerpiece. This is beyond what I would have imagined! They are both praying men who are quick to pray with me. John commented on how important praying together was for his men:

Texting prayers is a huge part of what I do with guys. They hate it initially. But they need to learn that the fight against temptation is communal. It's a group of us learning to pray together. You aren't in this journey alone. You can't do this journey alone. In fact, you aren't allowed to merely pray on you own. You must text a prayer. Reading their texted confession helps me know what they are actually praying. Are they groveling before God? Self-pity? Do I see death without resurrection? Do they come to rest on Jesus and his grace?

When we draw others into a praying community, in some strange mysterious way God's Spirit begins to breathe life into the situation. I've seen Christians fail in ministry or life. They always see other reasons why they failed, but they completely miss their prayerlessness, their inattention to the Spirit of Jesus.

Men's Allergy to Prayer

Men, in general, struggle with praying together. Tim and John told me: "Guys fight prayer. It feels feminine, not action-oriented." And yet, prayer had become woven into both of their lives.

They continued:

Once we began to change, we realized that not only is change not possible without prayer, but prayer keeps the change fresh. Prayer brings all the discipleship tools that we learned to life.

None of this is sustainable without prayer. The only way for us to live as men of God is to be praying with trusted men.

With manhood under assault from our cultural elites, men are clinging to more overt forms of masculinity. For example, most young pastors I know work out regularly. They look buff. Nothing wrong with that. But when I dig into their prayer life, not so much.

Another barrier for men with prayer is "guy humor." Guys love to mock one another. Mocking does have a lovely role in humbling the proud, but when it becomes a steady diet, it leads to a faux intimacy. You feel close, but it's a thin facade. The imagined closeness is just a veneer. I've seen multiple guy cultures ripped apart when things have gotten rough.

Learning to climb this Everest takes weak men and makes them into warriors who know how to bring their weakness to our Lord Jesus in prayer.

A Word to Pastors

When I mentor younger pastors about their prayer lives, I ask them how powerful sexual temptation is for them. For most, it's pretty high. Then I share my particular sexual temptations, how I pray for them, and how God has helped me. I ask, "How do you pray about your sexual temptations?" They are usually quiet.

The pastorate can intensify the struggle with sexual temptation, because you have an identity to protect. The potential shame is magnified. Plus, your instincts tell you that churches often don't know what to do with a pastor who might have a besetting sin.

I also ask pastors about their relationship with strong-willed men and women in their churches. Many pastors struggle, at times, with powerful people in their congregations, who often bring a wealth of practical experience. The pastors, often with less business experience, need the wisdom and generosity of these people, but at times the same people can be critical or controlling. So I ask pastors, "How do you regularly pray for the strong men and women in your congregation?" Again, silence. So in two of the most challenging areas of their ministry, sex and power, many pastors are not participating in a divine community. I encourage them to pray daily, specifically, for what or whom they need help with, and ideally with a band of brothers.

25

Turbocharging Our Prayers

A LARGELY FORGOTTEN PATTERN of praying is fasting. I first encountered fasting thirty years ago when a young couple told me how her father had fasted for three days after they'd approached him about their desire to marry. He came out of his fast at peace with the marriage, having fasted for wisdom over something that was very important to him. At the time, I had no idea why this father fasted, but I knew Scripture mentions it, and almost assumes it when we need a breakthrough of some sort.

I share stories of my own fasting in this chapter not to boast (Matt. 6:16–18) but to give you a track to run on, because fasting is relatively rare now.

Fasting for a Breakthrough

Throughout Scripture we see the theme of fasting for a breakthrough. In Esther, when King Ahasuerus issues a decree that will lead to the murder of all Jews, the whole community begins to fast and lament (4:3). Later, when Esther agrees to approach the king, she asks her fellow Jews to join her in a three-day fast (4:16). The result? The king grants her request, leading to the rescue of the Jewish people.

When Nehemiah hears that Jerusalem's walls are broken down, he immediately begins to fast and pray (Neh. 1:4). Only later do we discover that while he was fasting and praying, a plan emerged in his mind. As Americans, that feels backward. Don't we first plan and then ask God to bless our plans? But *we* are the ones who have it backward.

Prayer and fasting create a foundation for new movements of the Spirit. Luke is particularly sensitive to this theme.

- When Mary and Joseph present the infant Jesus in the temple, Anna, who's been fasting and praying "night and day," immediately recognizes him as sent from God (Luke 2:36–38).
- Jesus begins his public ministry with a forty-day fast. He is *led* by the Spirit to fast, but after fasting he comes out of the desert in the *power* of the Spirit (Luke 4:1–2, 14).
- After Paul encounters Christ on the Damascus road, he fasts for three days (Acts 9:9).
- The decision to send Paul and Barnabas emerges out of prayer and fasting (Acts 13:2–3).

So what makes fasting so effective?

Why Fasting Is Effective

When I began a weekly twenty-four-hour fast on Fridays almost thirty years ago, I soon saw why fasting is so effective: it thins the veil between you and heaven by cutting off your most basic desire—food. Something happens to your spirit in fasting that makes you more aware of the spiritual world. You are more in tune with

God and his ways. Fasting kills our food appetite, and prayer kills our time appetite. One kills our body's desire; the other kills our mind's desire. In fact, I began the weekly fasting because of suffering I was going through, which had already begun to thin the veil.

Fasting works because it draws us into a mini-participation in the dying of Christ. By putting to death one of our most basic needs (food), we enter into what the apostle Paul calls a fellowship of Christ's suffering (Phil. 3:10). It artificially forces us into the dying of self. The temporary killing of something so basic to our flesh results in a filling of the Spirit. That explains why fasting produces multiple evidences of the Spirit's work: surprise, fresh power, and new wisdom.

Food got us into the mess we are in, but it wasn't really the food: Adam and Eve "saw," "took," and "ate" forbidden fruit in an act of rebellion (Gen. 3:6). Fasting reverses that by saying no to desire. The desire for bread is on the crowd's mind the morning after the feeding of the five thousand. They confront Jesus on the beach at Capernaum, wanting another free meal. They realize that Jesus has, like Moses, given them manna in the wilderness—but Jesus refuses their request, pointing them to eternal food (John 6:22–35). Fasting moves you from physical bread to Spiritual bread. It stops Adam's "saw," "took," and "ate" and opens the door to a living communion that Jesus enacts in the Last Supper as he takes the bread, breaks it, and gives it. Cutting off our most basic desire helps us see our true desire.

Also, the longer your fast, the weaker you become physically. David describes the effects of a longer fast:

> My knees are weak through fasting;
>> my body has become gaunt, with no fat. (Ps. 109:24)

That weakness mirrors the state of our souls and makes prayer easy. Any kind of poverty (financial, relational, monetary) opens you up to God. That's why Christians from the developing world are often so robust in faith. Poverty weakens you, leaving you with few options, so you are quick to cry out for grace. Jesus tells Paul, "My power is made perfect in weakness" (2 Cor. 12:9).

Not having to fuss with meals gives you more time to pray, but that's secondary: fasting opens a window to heaven. It answers Jesus's prayer

> Your will be done,
>> on earth as it is in heaven. (Matt. 6:10)

It gives you a box seat in the unseen world.

Fasting for Corporate Repentance

One of the church's neglected J-curves is the dying of repentance. Paul clearly links corporate repentance with Christ's death in Colossians 3 and Romans 8. The Old Testament repeatedly links prayer and fasting with repentance.

- The prophet Joel pleads with Israel to repent by fasting: "'Yet even now,' declares the LORD, / 'return to me with all your heart, / with fasting, with weeping, and with mourning; / and rend your hearts and not your garments'" (Joel 2:12–13).
- When Daniel repents on behalf of Israel for their sins, he seeks God "by prayer and pleas for mercy with fasting" (Dan. 9:3).
- Nehemiah, like Daniel, repents for Israel's corporate sins while fasting (Neh. 1:4–11).

Fasting mirrors what we want to happen in our hearts, humbling and weakening us. David makes the connection between fasting and humility when he laments that his enemies have misinterpreted his fasting.

When I wept and humbled my soul with fasting,
  it became my reproach. (Ps. 69:10)

One reason the church no longer links fasting and repentance is that we think of sins individually, not corporately. Plus, it's extraordinarily difficult to see corporate sins, such as materialism. Corporate sin is shared, so there is little tension in the community. Everyone is doing it, so it feels normal.

The Puritans frequently called for days of fasting and prayer in early America. If the crops failed or there were problems in the church, they'd call for a "Day of Humiliation," when they'd fast from sunup to sundown and gather at the church to hear a sermon on the problem. Then when God helped them, they'd have a day of thanksgiving. Here are a few examples drawn from a Puritan pastor's journal referring to their days of prayer and fasting:[1]

- January 2, 1645—A solemn day of humiliation kept because of "the extremity of the season," and concern for the church and town.
- January 1, 1647—A fast due to "the affliction of sickness and death of some in this town," that God's would stay his hand from "this day hence."
- April 15, 1648—A day of humiliation for a member who had resisted the church's discipline.

- February 28, 1661—A "day of humiliation before the scriptures" to seek reconciliation with everyone in the church.

Like the Hebrew prophets, the Puritans never looked at events abstractly but instead reflected on the state of their own hearts. Following the Puritan pattern, President Lincoln, on three different occasions during the Civil War, called for national days of fasting and prayer.

As you know, sexual sin, especially among men, grips our churches. A leader in a national campus ministry told me that 100 percent of their male applicants and 50 percent of their women struggle with pornography. What about "outing" this silent killer with a day of prayer and fasting for sexual purity?

What to Expect from Community Prayer and Fasting

Fasting was pervasive in the post–New Testament early church. Christ followers took seriously Jesus's words "The days will come when the bridegroom is taken away from them, and then they [the church] will fast" (Matt. 9:15). A copyist in the early church added "and fasting" to Mark 9:29, where Jesus says, "This kind cannot be driven out by anything but prayer."[2] Almost every early church father commends fasting. Here are their insights regarding the effects of fasting:[3]

- Fasting at Lent was a way of drawing you into union with Christ as you "died with him."
- Fasting before baptism prepared your heart.
- Fasting promoted holiness and purity.

More than anything else, expect to be drawn into the dying and rising of Jesus when you fast. Unlike paganism, fasting is not a means to gain power or get God to do our will. That's what the Israelites were trying to do when they complained to God:

> Why have we fasted, and you see it not?
>   Why have we humbled ourselves, and you take no
>   knowledge of it?

God replied:

> Behold, in the day of your fast you seek your own pleasure,
>   and oppress all your workers. (Isa. 58:3)

The year when I began to fast and pray every Friday was the hardest of my life. God gutted me. He reshaped my life's path, pulling me out of one direction and sending me in an entirely new, unexpected one. If you had asked me in the middle of it, "Where's the resurrection?" or "What is God doing?" other than repeatedly humbling me, I would have had no idea. I lost any semblance of control over my life. God was giving me his best gift—drawing me into the dying and rising of his Son. His power is made perfect in weakness.

I wasn't surprised when a pastor friend described how much more difficult life became at his church after he began to fast and pray. He told me: "The tensions within our church leadership kept growing during this past winter. I prayed and fasted so much that my wife strongly encouraged me to stop, as I had lost a good amount of weight and was looking and feeling physically ragged."

The rising that came out of my own difficult period of fasting took multiple forms, but most significantly, four years later we started seeJesus. Only at the last minute did a new ministry emerge as a possibility. That pattern continues: many of this book's stories in which the Lord produced a breakthrough grew out of my weekly day of fasting and prayer.

The leader of an indigenous African mission that reaches out to Muslim imams (spiritual leaders) has all the mission's staff fast the first forty days of the year. They sustain themselves by drinking vegetable juice. As of several years ago, they had led over fifteen hundred imams to Christ. So, if you begin to fast and pray as a community, fasten your seatbelt!

Practical Suggestions for Fasting

Below are a few suggestions from my personal experience, but they may also apply to whole communities. (None of these suggestions are intended to substitute for professional medical advice. Always seek the guidance of your physician.) First, some thoughts on a twenty-four-hour fast:

- Starting with twenty-four hours means skipping two meals. At first, you can get pretty hungry in the afternoon, but you get used to it.
- Consider combining a food fast with a social-media and news fast.
- Drink coffee, tea, and vegetable juice. Stay away from fruit juices, if possible.
- If you have hypoglycemia or anything similar, a partial fast may be an option.
- Keep a normal work and exercise schedule. Try not to tell anyone you are fasting.
- Have a single long period of quiet, prayer, journaling, and reading Scripture.

- Fast weekly, but there is no rule on this.
- If you fast for breakfast and lunch, try not to pig out at dinner. I know from experience that it defeats the purpose!

During hard seasons Jill and I have done three-day fasts, sometimes together, sometimes separately. Our fasts almost always have a specific focus. King David, in a lament over friends who betrayed him, describes how he'd prayed and fasted for these betrayers:

> But I, when they were sick—
>> I wore sackcloth;
>> I afflicted myself with fasting;
> I prayed with head bowed on my chest. (Ps. 35:13)

Here are some thoughts on a seventy-two-hour fast:

- At times, you'll get hungry, but that feeling usually passes after a couple of hours. We must have a hunger memory, because it is usually at meal times that we feel the hungriest.
- I find that this long a fast doesn't impair my work until the third day.
- Do this longer fast with a specific purpose or problem in mind, such as a relationship problem, a health problem, or the need for a breakthrough.
- Since I'm interrupting our family's dinner routine, I tell Jill I'm fasting. She will often say, "Oh good. I don't have to cook," or even join me. Other times, I join her. If I am the only one fasting, I'll just sit with Jill and Kim during dinner and drink coffee or juice.

- Before you decide to fast, look over your schedule. If I have a group lunch meeting or family event coming up, I'll either shorten the fast or do it on different days. If I have a lunch appointment with a friend, I'll explain that I'm fasting and just drink coffee or tea.

We have lost this ancient way of mortifying our flesh and thus turbocharging the church's power train. I wonder how many plagues (cancer, racial unrest, pandemic, tribalism, youth deserting the church, etc.) God needs to send us before he gets our attention and we remember the benefits of fasting and prayer.

A Word to Pastors

Calling for a day of fasting and prayer is an effective way of integrating everyone's daily life with the news and with the wider world. When you do that, the saints are no longer passively watching the news, letting their faith be drained away, but you are putting them on the front lines against evil, both in the culture and in their own hearts. Almost everyone I know says they are too busy to do this. But what a wonderful way to minister to your church's *souls* by helping them to slow down and pray together.

Conclusion

WHEN I WAS TEN YEARS OLD living in Redwood City, California, I had an allergic reaction to poison oak that covered my body. I was almost out of my mind with itching and pain. My face ballooned to twice its size. Even my vision had flipped. Later, one of my sisters said I looked like a pumpkin!

After two weeks of this, I crawled into my parents' bed and my dad prayed Psalm 23 over me. By the end of his prayer, I felt the pain drain away from my body and, for the first time in two weeks, I fell fast asleep. When I woke the next morning, the itching had dissipated. I'd been healed. God had answered our prayers.

Isaiah sums up the very essence of prayer:

> From of old no one has heard
> or perceived by the ear,
> no eye has seen a God besides you,
> who acts for those who wait for him. (Isa. 64:4)

That was the experience of a Viking raiding band that became stranded on an island in the Black Sea. Facing starvation, they said, "The God of the Christians frequently helps those who cry to him.

. . . Let us enquire whether he will be on our side."[1] These violent men, medieval terrorists, prayed to this new Christian God, and he acted for those who waited for him.

That was the experience of the Massachusetts militia when Paul Revere alerted them to the approaching redcoats. "Many companies gathered at their meetinghouses, and did not march until they had united in prayer. The militia from Dedham center heard a prayer from their clergyman as they stood in front of the meetinghouse. Then they all marched off together."[2]

Since many of us have lost touch with praying in community, I've gone back to the basics in this book: *Why pray? What is the church? How does the Spirit work?* and *How do we pray together?* But with all that, it's easy to lose the simplicity of prayer—prayer is children asking their Father for help. The abbot of an Egyptian monastery in the late Roman era put it so well:

> When you make high festival and when you rejoice, *cry Jesus.* When anxious and in pain, *cry Jesus.* When little boys and girls are laughing, let them *cry Jesus.* And those who flee before barbarians, *cry Jesus.* And those who go down to the Nile, *cry Jesus.* . . . And those whose trial has been corrupted and who receive injustice, let them *cry the Name of Jesus.*[3]

A pastor emailed me recently, "At our family prayer time this morning, my five-year-old son was excited to pray for one of our family friends. In his excitement he announced, 'Everybody stand back—I'm getting ready to pray!'"

Everybody stand back—the church is getting ready to pray!

Acknowledgments

I'M GREATLY INDEBTED TO MY DAD (Jack Miller) and to Richard Gaffin for their insights on the Spirit, which they both initially gleaned from Geerhardus Vos. What Dad developed practically, Gaffin did in Pauline studies. The combination was revolutionary for me.

My editor, Liz Heaney, has helped me enormously to make this a clearer book. This is our fifth book together, and I don't know what I'd do without her! I'm also thankful for the multiple readers whose feedback improved this book. Particularly helpful were Pastors Jimmy Agan, Lyle Caswell, Paul Reader, and Steve Estes. I'm also indebted to seeJesus staff and friends who helped me "think the book": Jon Hori, Liz Voboril, Bob Allums, Timo Strawbridge, and Colin Millar, along with Maggie Snyder, Katie Sullivan, Gretchen Barry, Julie Courtney, Shontel Vander Lugt, Laura McCaulley, and Jill Miller. Each of the following readers had good insights as well: Matt Lucas, Gena Cobb, John Miller, Geoff Smith, and Maresa DePuy.

Crossway's staff have assisted me enormously at so many levels: Justin Taylor, for encouraging this book; Claire Cook, for her hand in the cover design process; and the sales and marketing team, for all their hard work. Thom Notaro, one of Crossway's editors, has been a big help in cleaning up the book.

These seeJesus staff have also given valuable aid: Donna Herr, my assistant, with my frequent questions about Microsoft Word; Michele Walton, with marketing; and Liz Voboril, with writing the discussion guide, which will be available at seeJesus.net/aprayingchurch.

I dedicate this book to Bob Allums. Bob had set up about thirty chairs in the Bethkes' basement in Elgin, Illinois, in January 2000 for what was my second A Praying Life seminar. God had brought me so low, so many times, I was thankful the chairs were half-filled. Bob's heart was captured. He immersed himself in the seminar, and the following year he began to do our seminars part-time.

Eight years later, Bob took a large pay cut to join seeJesus and launch our A Praying Life Ministry. Since then, Bob has traveled the world, leading hundreds of seminars in over thirty countries. He's created a multinational team of leaders who are teaching the church to pray through seminars and cohorts.

Bob is a Barnabas, an encourager of the church, whose infectious joy and faith permeate all he does. It is a delight for me to dedicate this book to Bob Allums, my friend and partner in the gospel!

I also dedicate this book to my dear and faithful friends in Polk County, Florida, whose generosity made this book possible: Keith and Payton Albritton, Robert and Helen Allums, David and Elizabeth Boulware, Jamie and Creigh Brown, Christ Community Presbyterian Church, Dax and Michelle Gibson, Jack and Tina Harrell, Shawn and Kelly Jones, Scott and Julie McBride, Adam and Melinda Parker, Dane and Tracy Parker, Redeemer Winter Haven, Todd and Theresa Riggs, Jason and Cara Roland, Brian

Seeley, Dwight and Jayna Smith, Don and Ann Spooner, Timothy and Tina Strawbridge, Strong Tower Church, Gretchen Sweet, Trinity Presbyterian Church, Jim and Christy Valenti, Justin and Jen Wilson, and Steve and Kinsey Young.

Notes

Chapter 1: A Glimpse of a Praying Community

1. Kenneth Scott Latourette, *A History of the Expansion of Christianity*, vol. 7, *Advance through Storm: A.D. 1914 and After, with Concluding Generalizations* (New York: Harper and Row, 1971), 445–62.
2. James K. A. Smith, *You Are What You Love: The Spiritual Power of Habit* (Grand Rapids, MI: Brazos, 2016), 3.

Chapter 2: Who Killed the Prayer Meeting?

1. Ben Patterson, "Vectoring Prayer," *Christianity Today* (online), June 2, 2004, https://www.christianitytoday.com/pastors.
2. "Silent and Solo: How Americans Pray," Barna, August 15, 2017, https://www.barna.com.
3. Immanuel Kant, *Religion within the Boundaries of Mere Reason and Other Writings*, trans. and ed. Allen Wood and George di Giovanni, Cambridge Texts in the History of Philosophy (New York: Cambridge University Press, 1998), 186.
4. Throughout this book I'll use the word *Spiritual* to refer to things related to the Holy Spirit and his work in our lives, and the word *spiritual* to refer to things related to the real-but-invisible aspects of our world. Multiple Reformed scholars have said that *Spiritual* should be capitalized in the apostle Paul: Geerhardus Vos, *The Pauline Eschatology* (Grand Rapids, MI: Eerdmans, 1961; repr., Phillipsburg, NJ: P&R, 1994), 164–67; Richard B. Gaffin Jr., *Resurrection and Redemption: A Study in Paul's Soteriology* (Phillipsburg, NJ: P&R, 1987), 80–92; Anthony Thiselton, *The First Epistle to the Corinthians: A Commentary on the Greek Text* (Grand Rapids, MI: Eerdmans, 2000), 1258, 1283–85; and Sinclair B. Ferguson, *The Holy Spirit* (Downers Grove, IL: InterVarsity Press, 1996), 54.
5. Thank you, Gretchen Barry, for this insight!

6. Edith Schaeffer, *Common Sense Christian Living* (Nashville: Thomas Nelson, 1983), 205.

Chapter 3: The Missing Spirit of Jesus

1. Geerhardus Vos, *The Pauline Eschatology* (Grand Rapids, MI: Eerdmans, 1961; repr., Phillipsburg, NJ: P&R, 1994), was the source of my dad's new understanding of the Spirit.
2. Both Dad and Gaffin developed Geerhardus Vos's insights on the Spirit. Dad concentrated on prayer and the Spirit in Luke, Acts, and John, while Gaffin focused on Pauline studies. See Richard B. Gaffin Jr., *Resurrection and Redemption: A Study in Paul's Soteriology* (Phillipsburg, NJ: P&R, 1987), 78–92; and Vos, *Pauline Eschatology*, 136–71.
3. Gaffin, commenting on 1 Cor. 15:45, wrote, "Christ (as incarnate) experiences a spiritual qualification and transformation so thorough and an endowment with the Spirit so complete that as a result they can now be equated. This unprecedented possession of the Spirit and the accompanying change in Christ result in a unity so close that not only can it be said simply that the Spirit makes alive, but also that Christ as Spirit makes alive. Specifically, this identity is economic or functional, in terms of their activity." Gaffin, *Resurrection and Redemption*, 87.
4. C. D. "Jimmy" Agan, in personal correspondence with me during February 2022, said this: "One of the key points in the verse is a contrast between Adam as one who has life in him as a gift from God and Christ as one who has a quality of life in himself that allows him to give life to others. Adam is 'living' (*zōsan*), but Christ is more: he is 'life-giving' or 'life-making' (*zōopoioun*; the verb *poieō* means 'make, do, create'). In the context Paul contrasts *psychikos* [related to *psyche*, meaning "soul, self, person"], that having to do with the ordinary or natural life of a living being, and *pneumatikos*, that having to do with the supernatural life given and empowered by the Holy Spirit. Adam has the first kind of life: he is really alive, but his is the kind of life that can be diminished spiritually, physically, relationally, emotionally. Christ has the second kind of life, which is resurrection life: his is the kind of life that cannot be diminished in any way, because it comes from the Spirit; and so Christ can give Spirit-life to us, causing us to come alive in our souls (the new birth of regeneration) and, one day, in our bodies (resurrection). Christ has so much life through the Spirit that he can give and give to others *and yet have no less life in himself than he had before*. All of this is implied in the contrast between Adam as a "living being" (*psychēn zōsan*) and Christ as "life-giving Spirit" (*pneuma zōopoioun*)."

5. Richard B. Gaffin Jr., *By Faith, Not by Sight: Paul and the Order of Salvation*, 2nd ed. (Phillipsburg, NJ: P&R, 2013), 75.

6. Mysteriously, Jesus, as the Son of God, fills the universe, but he can reach a fallen world only through the Spirit. Gaffin writes: "The life-giving activity predicated of the resurrected Christ is not predicated directly; the Spirit is an absolutely indispensable factor. Only by virtue of the functional identity of the Spirit and Christ, effected redemptive-historically in his resurrection, is Christ the communicator of life." Gaffin, *Resurrection and Redemption*, 89.

7. This is how Vos put it: "The Spirit is not only the author of the resurrection-act, but likewise the permanent substratum of the [our] resurrection-life." Vos, *Pauline Eschatology*, 165.

8. To Gaffin's *glory, power,* and *life,* I've added *wisdom* and *love.* Gaffin, *Resurrection and Redemption*, 69.

Chapter 4: A Short History of the Praying Church

1. Matthew highlights Jesus's preaching with five sermons, recalling the five books of Moses: Matt. 5–7, 10, 13, 18, and 24–25.

2. By saying that Jesus failed to start a prayer meeting, I'm simply describing that Jesus, the incarnate Son of God, asked his disciples repeatedly to pray, and they failed to do so. It's no different from Jesus's inability to do miracles in Nazareth because of the people's unbelief.

3. I added the word "together" because "pray" is plural in the Greek.

4. As Jimmy Agan shared with me in personal correspondence (February 2022), "Acts 1:1 hints at this: if Luke's 'first book' included 'all that Jesus began to do and teach,' then the second book—Acts—records what Jesus *continued to do and teach through the agency and power of the Spirit.*"

Chapter 5: Saints in Motion

1. These opening sentences are from Liz Voboril. She and Jon Hori, my podcast partners, especially helped me articulate this chapter.

2. I thank Jimmy Agan for the following reflections (personal correspondence, February 2022): "To the pastor who might feel like he's being loaded up with bricks: Paul's model of the church in Ephesians invites us to rest in a ministry priority that is close to our Father's heart! I'm not suggesting 'you should do more of this in addition to everything you are already doing, without changing a thing.' Remember how sweet it was the last time this happened naturally, organically, as a gift from the Spirit? Now, what small change could you make, with the help and support of others, to create opportunities to enjoy that sweetness more

frequently, and more intentionally? What if you did less of everything else to make that a priority?"

3. In the Jerusalem temple, the monolithic 570-ton Western Stone, possibly the cornerstone itself, can be seen only by descending in an underground tunnel.

4. I realize the situation is more complex than my three-part summary. Some say worship is the most important part of the church. Others prioritize mission or serving on a team that regularly engages needy neighbors or non-Christians. Others may emphasize small group, where they can be vulnerable and push past Christian platitudes. But, still, these can all be equally prayer-resistant. (Thanks to Jimmy Agan for these reflections.)

5. "Church Priorities for 2005 Vary Considerably," Barna, February 14, 2005. https://www.barna.com.

Chapter 6: Feeding the Saints

1. The problem of feeding people church rather than Christ tends to be worse among larger churches. I see less of that in active smaller churches or in self-consciously disciple-making churches.

2. Of course, I don't mean magic in the pagan sense, where we try to control God; it's just a fresh way of describing the wonders that come when a Jesus community becomes a praying community.

3. Here's the full text of Paul's blessing in Eph. 1:4–14; *italics* indicate union with Christ, and <u>underlined pronouns</u> show Paul's identification of himself as one of the saints:

> In love he predestined <u>us</u> for adoption to himself as sons *through Jesus Christ*, according to the purpose of his will, to the praise of his glorious grace, with which he has blessed <u>us</u> *in the Beloved. In him <u>we</u>* have redemption through his blood, the forgiveness of <u>our</u> trespasses, according to the riches of his grace, which he lavished upon <u>us</u>, in all wisdom and insight making known to <u>us</u> the mystery of his will, according to his purpose, which he set forth *in Christ* as a plan for the fullness of time, to unite all things *in him*, things in heaven and things on earth.
>
> *In him <u>we</u>* have obtained an inheritance, having been predestined according to the purpose of him who works all things according to the counsel of his will, so that <u>we</u> who were the first to hope *in Christ* might be to the praise of his glory. *In him* you also, when you heard the word of truth, the gospel of your salvation, and believed *in him*, were sealed with the promised Holy Spirit, who is the guarantee of <u>our</u> inheritance until <u>we</u> acquire possession of it, to the praise of his glory.

Chapter 7: Are Saints Real?

1. Richard B. Gaffin Jr., *By Faith, Not by Sight: Paul and the Order of Salvation*, 2nd ed. (Phillipsburg, NJ: P&R, 2013), 76. All of chap. 3 (61–89) builds to this climax. In pp. 85–89, Gaffin critiques this weakness in our Reformation heritage. Gaffin is building on John Murray's insights in Murray's essay "Definitive Sanctification," *Calvin Theological Journal* 2, no. 1 (1967): 5–21; also in *Collected Writings of John Murray*, vol. 2, *Select Lectures in Systematic Theology* (Carlisle, PA: Banner of Truth, 1977), 277–84.

2. I treat this extensively in Paul E. Miller, *J-Curve: Dying and Rising with Jesus in Everyday Life* (Wheaton, IL: Crossway, 2019), pt. 3.

3. My coworker Jon Hori put it so well: "At the heart of the miss for most churches/pastors is a failure not only to see the church/saints correctly but also to see love as the center of mission/ministry correctly. We miss the importance, challenge, and even glory of loving like Jesus."

4. I agree with McFadden on Eph. 1:1, that "faithful" is a weaker translation than "believers." Kevin W. McFadden, *Faith in the Son of God: The Place of Christ-Oriented Faith within Pauline Theology* (Wheaton, IL: Crossway, 2021), 256n57.

5. A new vision of saints helps us be patient with the prickly ones. Even the prickly ones are often able and willing to go places where more mature saints struggle. I had an encounter recently with an angry saint. I couldn't get a sentence out without him cutting me off, and yet this man has a faithful ministry that has touched many lives. Eph. 4:2 tells us how to live with prickly saints: "Be completely humble and gentle; be patient, bearing with one another in love" (NIV). That gave me the permission to let his anger roll off me like water off a duck's back.

6. Thank you, Dane Ortlund, for this insight!

7. Martin Luther, *Lectures on Galatians*, vol. 26 of *Luther's Works* American Edition, ed. Jaroslav Pelikan and Helmut T. Lehmann (Philadelphia: Fortress), 232. Luther almost exclusively preached sin (law) then forgiveness (gospel). As good as this is, by itself it can pull the gospel in a purely negative direction. See Carl Trueman, *Luther on the Christian Life: Cross and Freedom* (Wheaton, IL: Crossway, 2015), 61–66, 95–97, 173–74. See also, Gaffin, *By Faith, Not by Sight*, 85–89, and Gaffin, *Resurrection and Redemption: A Study in Paul's Soteriology* (Phillipsburg, NJ: P&R, 1987), 14–15.

8. David Powlison referred to this "one string guitar" in private conversation with me. For a fuller treatment of this problem, see Powlison, *How Does Sanctification Work?* (Wheaton, IL: Crossway, 2017), 53–60. Jimmy Agan has pointed out (personal correspondence, February 2022): "The

'just muddle through' attitude is often rooted in (1) reading Romans 7 as Paul's description of his life as a Christian, with the implication that 'if a great Apostle could only hope to muddle through, why should I expect anything different?'; and (2) assuming that the Flesh-Spirit warfare described in the NT is a stalemate. Neither of those is the intended reading of the relevant NT texts."

Chapter 8: Saints Unleashed

1. J. R. R. Tolkien, *The Fellowship of the Ring: Being the First Part of The Lord of the Rings* (1954; repr., New York: Ballantine, 1994), 370.
2. In this passage there are four plural pronouns and fourteen plural verbs. We miss the *you* plural because our English *you* sounds singular. Some regions in America have created their own plural *you*: for example, the South, with *y'all* and *all y'all*; Philadelphia, with *youse* or *youse guys*; the Ohio River Valley, with *you-uns*; and Pittsburgh, with *yinz*.
3. Carl von Clausewitz, *On War* (New York: Penguin, 1968), 189.
4. Steven Zaloga, *Smashing Hitler's Panzers: The Defeat of the Hitler Youth Panzer Division in the Battle of the Bulge* (Lanham, MD: Stackpole, 2019), 74–75, 78, 205–6, 250.

Chapter 9: The Parable of the Missing CEO

1. This parable, like many of Jesus's parables, has obviously fictional elements. For one other example, in Jesus's parable of the rich man and Lazarus, the rich man has a conversation with Abraham between heaven and hell.
2. To see the video on YouTube, search "'From Now On' with Hugh Jackman." I'm indebted to our trainer and my friend Timo Strawbridge for this insight.

Chapter 10: How the Spirit Works

1. The exception is Eph. 6:12. See notes 2, 3, and 5 in chap. 3.
2. I've substituted "wills" for "wishes" because "wills" links to the theme of Jesus's will in John. Prayer is an act of the will that always involves surrendering my will.
3. Lorenz Carlsen wrote his sailing memoirs in the unpublished "The Sad Tale of the Gallant Ship Octavia and Her Master," 13–17.
4. I've told this story first in Paul E. Miller, *A Praying Life: Connecting with God in a Distracting World* (Colorado Springs: NavPress, 2009), chap. 6, and then, updated, in Miller, *J-Curve: Dying and Rising with Jesus in Everyday Life* (Wheaton, IL: Crossway, 2019), chap. 21.
5. I explore this in depth in *A Praying Life*, chap. 31, "Listening to God."

Chapter 11: The Spirit's Path

1. Paul E. Miller, *J-Curve: Dying and Rising with Jesus in Everyday Life* (Wheaton, IL: Crossway, 2019).
2. See also Richard B. Gaffin Jr.: "The resurrection is a conforming energy, an energy that produces conformity to Christ's death. The impact, the impress of the resurrection in Paul's existence is the cross." Gaffin, "The Usefulness of the Cross," *Westminster Theological Journal* 41, no. 2 (1979): 234.
3. After Dad passed in 1996, Mom told me on several occasions that she felt God had permitted Dad's heart attack to deal with his struggle with idolatry. I had not made the connection until she told me that. In no way did she wish the heart attack on Dad.

Chapter 12: Management by Prayer

1. By quoting Ratzinger, I'm not endorsing other aspects of his philosophy. He continues: "We cannot simply pick the laborer in God's harvest in the same way that an employer seeks his employees. God must always be asked for them and he himself must choose them for this service. This . . . is reinforced by Mark's phrase: 'Jesus called to him those whom he desired.' You cannot make yourself a disciple—it is an event of election, a free decision of the Lord's will, which in its turn is anchored in his communion of will with the Father." Joseph Ratzinger, Pope Benedict XVI, *Jesus of Nazareth: From the Baptism in the Jordan to the Transfiguration*, trans. Adrian Walker (San Francisco: Ignatius, 2007), 170.
2. It's clear from Matthew's use of the word "laborer" in the parable of the laborers in the vineyard (20:1–16) that Jesus means blue-collar workers, just like his fisherman-disciples.
3. Alasdair MacIntyre, *After Virtue: A Study in Moral Theory*, 3rd ed. (Notre Dame, IN: University of Notre Dame Press, 2007), 30.

Chapter 13: Becoming a Praying Leader

1. "[Jesus is in] daily, constant communion with God, manifested in the new and virtually unparalleled sense of intimacy with God expressed in Jesus' words, 'Did you not know that I must be in *my Father's* house?'" Sinclair Ferguson, *The Holy Spirit* (Downers Grove, IL: InterVarsity Press, 1996), 44.
2. In 2005, *Time* magazine named John Stott one of the hundred most influential people in the world. Quotes from Richard Trist are taken from Richard's talk at Ridley College, Melbourne, May 24, 2011.
3. Timothy Dudley-Smith, *John Stott: The Making of a Leader; A Biography of the Early Years* (Downers Grove, IL: InterVarsity Press, 1999), 251.

4. John Stott, *The Living Church: Convictions of a Lifelong Pastor* (Downers Grove, IL: InterVarsity Press, 2011), 145.
5. This was when I was associate director of World Harvest Mission, now called Serge. The New Era Foundation's collapse affected over 180 churches and nonprofits. The immensely helpful consultant was Allen Duble, along with his son Troy, of Canaan Group.

Chapter 14: Praying Big

1. I tell the story in Paul E. Miller, *A Praying Life: Connecting with God in a Distracting World*, 2nd ed. (Colorado Springs: NavPress, 2017), chap. 22.
2. John Newton, "Come, My Soul, Thy Suit Prepare" (1779), The Cyber Hymnal, www.hymntime.com.
3. Again, following Richard B. Gaffin Jr., *Resurrection and Redemption: A Study in Paul's Soteriology* (Phillipsburg, NJ: P&R, 1987), 80–92, and Geerhardus Vos, *The Pauline Eschatology* (Grand Rapids, MI: Eerdmans, 1961; repr., Phillipsburg, NJ: P&R, 1994), 164–67, I've translated *spiritual* as *Spiritual.*
4. Geraldine Taylor, *Behind the Ranges: The Story of J. O. Fraser* (Littleton, CO: OMF International, 2012), 165–66.
5. Taylor, *Behind the Ranges*, 198–99.
6. Taylor, *Behind the Ranges*, 197.
7. Archives of the Yunnan Academy of Social Sciences, vol. 412, sec. 20; cited in Ju-K'ang T'ien, *Peaks of Faith: Protestant Mission in Revolutionary China* (Leiden: Brill, 1993), 73.

Chapter 15: The Prayer Triangle

1. The prayer cards are as I wrote them at the time, with Scripture sometimes from the NIV, sometimes paraphrased, sometimes quoted from memory.
2. Geraldine Taylor, *Behind the Ranges: The Story of J. O. Fraser* (Littleton, CO: OMF International, 2012), 127.

Chapter 16: Avoiding the Pitfalls of Prayer

1. *National Lampoon's Christmas Vacation*, written and coproduced by John Hughes, directed by Jeremiah S. Chechik, released December 1, 1989.
2. *Glory*, screenplay by Kevin Jarre, directed by Edward Zwick, released December 15, 1989; see "Men of the 54th Regiment Prayer Meeting," Movie Speeches, https://www.americanrhetoric.com.
3. C. John Miller, "Love Received: Receiving Love Comes from Giving Love," 3–4 (chap. 3 of unpublished manuscript, October 7, 1987), the C. John Miller Manuscript Collection, PCA Historical Center, St. Louis, MO, box 3.

Chapter 17: Beginning Low and Slow

1. Megan Hill, *Praying Together: The Priority and Privilege of Prayer; In Our Homes, Communities, and Churches* (Wheaton, IL: Crossway, 2016), 80.

Chapter 19: Restoring Prayer to Sunday Morning

1. Alan Kreider, *The Patient Ferment of the Early Church: The Improbable Rise of Christianity in the Roman Empire* (Grand Rapids, MI: Baker, 2016), 205. I've summarized Kreider's chap. 7.
2. Basil of Caesarea (AD 350) said that the artisans and laborers who had to work urged the preacher "to be brief." Kreider, *The Patient Ferment*, 197.
3. Kreider, *The Patient Ferment*, 204.
4. Kreider, *The Patient Ferment*, 213.
5. Augustine, *The City of God*, quoted in Peter Brown, *The Ransom of the Soul* (Cambridge, MA: Harvard University Press, 2015), 40.
6. The idea of praying saints in heaven became corrupt, eventually leading to the idea that departed saints have extra merit that can be credited to us. Nevertheless, the New Testament rule that "what happens to Jesus happens to us" means that it is entirely possible that departed saints are now, like Jesus and the Spirit, in a posture of continual prayer. See Rom. 8:26, 27, 34; Heb. 7:25 on the intercession of Jesus and the Spirit.
7. Lausanne Occasional Papers, "Evangelism and Social Responsibility: An Evangelical Commitment," Lausanne Movement (website), 1982. https://lausanne.org/content/lop/lop-21.
8. Tertullian, *Apology* 39, trans. S. Thelwall, http://www.logoslibrary.org.
9. I treat Hebrew laments extensively in Paul E. Miller, *A Praying Life: Connecting with God in a Distracting World*, 2nd ed. (Colorado Springs: NavPress, 2017), where I added chaps. 22 and 23. See also Miller, *A Loving Life: In a World of Broken Relationships* (Wheaton, IL: Crossway, 2014), chaps. 3 and 6.
10. Thanks, again, to Jimmy Agan for this insight via personal correspondence, February 2022.
11. To listen to Tim's prayer, see "Prayer February 20th, 2022," YouTube, https://www.youtube.com/watch?v=W9V_x1wQw80.
12. Jeremy D. Smoak, "Words Unseen: The Power of Hidden Writing," *Biblical Archaeology Review* 44, no. 1 (2018), https://www.baslibrary.org.
13. I discuss gnosticism's impact on the church in *A Praying Life*, 104–7, 179–80; and stoicism, which is the "cultural face" of gnosticism, in Miller, *J-Curve: Dying and Rising with Jesus in Everyday Life* (Wheaton, IL: Crossway, 2019), 39, 62–63, 101, 140, 197, 209, 231.

Chapter 20: On a Resurrection Hunt

1. I examine this pattern extensively in pt. 4 of *J-Curve: Dying and Rising with Jesus in Everyday Life* (Wheaton, IL: Crossway, 2019).
2. I explore this pattern of Jesus in Paul E. Miller, *Love Walked among Us: Learning to Love Like Jesus* (Colorado Springs: NavPress, 2001), pt. 1.

Chapter 22: The Prayer Menu

1. These three sides of Jesus match the three ancient offices of Israel: the priestly office (compassion), the prophetic office (honesty), and the kingly office (dependence on God and submission to him). I explain these three sides in depth in Paul E. Miller, *Love Walked among Us: Learning to Love Like Jesus* (Colorado Springs: NavPress, 2001), pts. 1–3.
2. David Hackett Fischer, *Paul Revere's Ride* (New York: Oxford University Press, 1994), 154, 158, 168, 273.

Chapter 23: Constant in Prayer

1. Thanks to Jimmy Agan for the reflection on culture (personal correspondence, February 2022).
2. David Powlison, *God's Grace in Your Suffering* (Wheaton, IL: Crossway, 2018), 56.
3. David Powlison, "A 'Moderate' Makeover," *Journal of Biblical Counseling* 26, no. 3 (2012): 3.

Chapter 25: Turbocharging Our Prayers

1. John Fiske, quoted in Amy Belding Brown, "Feasting and Fasting in Puritan New England," *Collisions* (blog), November 28, 2016, https://amybeldingbrown.wordpress.com.
2. While one early manuscript adds "and fasting" to the end of Mark 9:29, most scholars today believe that it was not original to the Gospel of Mark. See Bruce M. Metzger, *A Textual Commentary on the Greek New Testament* (London: United Bible Societies, 1975), 101.
3. For a summary of the early church fathers, see Kent Berghuis, *Christian Fasting: A Theological Approach* (n.p.: Bible Studies, 2007), 77–118.

Conclusion

1. Peter Brown, *The Rise of Western Christendom: Triumph and Diversity, A.D. 200–1000* (Malden, MA: Blackwell, 2003), 470.
2. David Hackett Fischer, *Paul Revere's Ride* (New York: Oxford University Press, 1994), 158.
3. Shenoute of Atripe (385–466), the great abbot of the White Monastery at Sohag in Middle Egypt, quoted in Brown, *The Rise of Western Christendom*, 118. Italics are mine.

General Index

Aaronic blessing, 195
Abraham, called upon the name of the Lord, 34
Acts
  devotion to prayer in, 39–41, 177–78
  management by prayer in, 118
Agan, Jimmy, 261n4, 262n2 (chap. 5), 262n4, 264–65n8
Allums, Bob, 147–48, 150, 165, 233
Anna, 59, 123, 169–75
  praying in the temple, 169–75
answered prayer, takes shape of dying and rising, 112–13
anticipation, and prayer, 173–74
Apostles' Creed, 190
Arab world, centrality of prayer in, 41
armor of God, 81–83
asking, 198
attentiveness to one another, in prayer, 183–85
Augustine, 63, 190

beauty, 201
Benedictine Rule, 129
blessing, 66, 195–96
  as church's power train, 67
boasting, 160–62
boldness in prayer, 154
Brooklyn Tabernacle Church, 171, 179, 180, 195

celebrity culture, 58–59
charismatics, on the work of the Spirit, 105
childlike confidence, 187
Chosen, The (film), 150
Christian life, living by the power of the Spirit, 29–30
Christlikeness, 58
church
  as house of prayer, loss of, 41
  as Spiritual business, 24
  as three-dimensional Spiritual community, 17
Church at LifePark (Charleston), 170–71
church attendance, 54
church fathers, on fasting, 249
church power train, 138
Clausewitz, Carl von, 82
communication in warfare, 82
communion of saints, 190
compassion, 217
consumer mentality in the pew, 78
consumers, church attenders as, 74
continual prayer, 239
corporate prayer, 126–27, 129, 133–34, 144, 189–90
  at end of service, 193–94
corporate sin, 248–49
covenant love, 156
"cover prayer," 197

COVID pandemic
  exposed disordered love, 63
  and prayer, 145–46
culture of prayer, 123
Cymbala, Jim, 179, 180, 195
cynicism, 20, 239–40

David
  prayer and fasting of, 252
  sin of adultery, 86
day of fasting and prayer, 248, 253
decreasing, art of, 91–92
departed saints, prayers of, 190, 268n6
desire, 219
discipline structure, 57
discouragement, 210, 212
disordered love, 63–65, 107
divine community, 185–86
drama-filled prayers, 163–66
dying and rising, 101, 104

early church, prayer at center of worship, 189–90
Edwards, Jonathan, 163
Elizabeth, 59
enjoyment of God, 217
Enlightenment, 15, 18
equipping errors, 57–61
evangelical church, model for "doing church," 70–71
evening prayer services, 185

facts and feelings, 16–18
faith, 174
  and prayer, 187
fake spirituality, in prayer, 156–57
fasting, 244–53
  for corporate repentance, 247–49
  and dying and rising of Christ, 246, 249
feeding on Christ, 63
feeding people church, 62–63, 263n1
feelings, 215–17
First Evangelical Free Church (Fullerton, California), 196
Foundation for New Era Philanthropy, 127, 267n5 (chap. 13)

Fraser, James O., 139–43, 145–46, 152–53
friends, praying with, 231–33
frontline warriors, 50, 59

Gaffin, Richard B., Jr., 25, 27, 73–74, 264n1
Gethsemane, 39, 55, 112
Glory (film), 157–58
gnosticism, in prayer, 197
God, as Father, 38
Greatest Showman, The (film), 91

Hallesby, Ole, 172–73, 177
Hannah, 172
haystack prayer meeting, 9
health concerns, dominate prayer time, 208
Heppe, Bob, 103, 104–5
heresy, as truth out of balance, 54
hidden ministry of prayer, 173
hiddenness of the Spirit of Jesus, 101
hiddenness of the Spirit's work, 104
Hill, Megan, 174
Hollywood, caricatures of prayer, 155–58
Holy Spirit. *See* Spirit
honesty, 218
honesty in prayer, 207–13
hope, 174
  and prayer, 187
Hori, Jon, 107, 165, 221, 264n3
humility, 166
hypocrisy, 20

idolatry, 110, 266n3 (chap. 11)
imagination explosion, 101, 102, 103, 136
incarnate, in prayer, 230
individualism, 229
International Justice Mission, 179
Israel, as house of prayer, 34–36

Jackman, Hugh, 91
J-curve, 106–9, 113, 115, 128, 138, 142, 198

grandest prayers of, 138–39
model for doing church, 70–71
prayer habits of, 178
prayer in prison, 175
prayers over Ephesians, 65–67
on resurrection, 199–200, 205
summary of the Spirit's work, 105
vision of the church in Ephesus, 52–53
on weakness, 210, 212
personal liturgies of prayer, 129–33
personal prayer, enriches prayer meetings, 186
Peter, preaching of, 40
Pharisees, 117
pietism, 156, 160
pitfalls of prayer, 155–66
planning by prayer, 114
power train, of the church, 25, 27, 40, 53, 68, 95, 113, 151, 170
Powlison, David, 84, 231–32, 264n8
prayer
  accesses the Spirit of Jesus, 23, 25–26, 30–32
  as armor, 81–84
  as breathing, 7, 76–77
  in community, 256. *See also* corporate prayer
  constant in, 67–68, 227–34
  as conversation, 214
  deepens friendship, 102
  as dying and rising, 107–13
  for faith, 69
  lack of training in, 42–43
  without love, 162–63
  as mere therapy, 17
  as mini-sermons, 197
  for prayer, 146–48
  pride of place in worship, 188
  for problems, 203–4
  as real life, 6
  as slow and mysterious, 111
  and soft idolatry, 63
  as solitary activity, 13
  and temptation, 335–41
"prayer chair," 163

prayerlessness, 13–14, 90, 239
prayer meeting
  killing of, 12–21, 188
  overtalking in, 111, 134, 184, 186
  resurrection feel of, 6
prayer menu, 214–24
prayer resistance, 47, 60
prayer time, as resurrection, 5–6
prayer tithe, 177
prayer triangle, 144–54
praying church, 7–9, 25
  and power of the Spirit, 30–32
praying leaders, 123–34
Praying Life Ministry, 147–48
preaching, and prayer, 54–57
preaching resistant, 57
pride, 110
private prayer, 129, 133–34
prophets, 36
Psalms, as Israel's book of prayers, 34
public laments, 192–93
Puritans, days of fasting and prayer, 248

quenching the Spirit, 102, 163
quietness in prayer, 165

Ratzinger, Joseph, 116, 266n1 (chap. 12)
recruiting by prayer, 119–20
Reformation, tension on how church functions, 77
Reformed, on the work of the Spirit, 105
repentance, 101, 104, 218, 247
resurrection, 73–74
resurrection hunt, 199–201, 205–6
Revere, Paul, 224, 256
Robertson, Pat, 161

Sadducees, 117
saint lumber, 52–53
saints, 47
  as consumers, 54
  become forgotten, 59–60
  marginalized, 59–60
  as prickly, 173, 191, 264n5
saints in motion, 47–50, 75–76

"saints vision," 51
Satan, seeks to discourage and destroy, 210
Schaeffer, Edith, 18–19
Schaeffer, Francis, 18–19
secularism, 114
  killed the prayer meeting, 14–18
secular liberalism, 157
seeJesus (ministry), 5, 9, 115, 119–20, 129, 149, 176, 180, 250
self, dying of, 246
self-confidence, as barrier to prayer, 151–52
senior pastor, vision for prayer, 171
Serge, 108, 176
sexual temptation, 235–41
shame, 236, 242
silence, 165–66, 224
Simeon, 59, 123, 174, 175
simplicity of prayer, 256
social media, 111, 152
soft idolatry, 63–65
Solomon
  at dedication of the temple, 35
  prayer of, 42
song, as prayer, 194
Sonship Course, 108
Spirit, 22–31
  carries Jesus to us, 28
  depersonalized, 95–96
  outpouring on last days, 22–23
  shapes a praying community, 95
  surprising work of, 118–19, 233
Spiritual body, 97
Spiritual gift, as personal gift from personal God, 96
Spiritual person, in step with the Spirit, 96
spiritual-physical division, 15–16
spouse, praying with, 230–31
Stott, John, 125–27
strategy, 144–46
structured times for prayer, 176–80
suffering, and prayer, 137–38, 142
Sunday morning prayer, weakening of, 188

surprise
  in prayer meetings, 182
  by Spirit's work, 100, 103
Swindoll, Chuck, 196

tactics, 144–46
teaching to equip, 57–58
temple, as house of prayer, 35
temptation, and prayer, 235–41
ten-day prayer meeting (Acts), 39–40, 42
Tertullian, 192
"text-prayer meetings," 238
thanksgiving, 198
therapeutic church, 78
therapeutic vision, 51
tithing, 177
Trinity, 32–33
Trist, Richard, 125–27
turbocharging prayers. See fasting
typical church, weak on prayer, 23–24

unbelief, 95, 102
under-spiritualizing in prayer, 158–60

vision, 144–46
vision for prayer, 171
Voboril, Liz, 262n1 (chap. 5)
Vos, Geerhardus, 261n2

waiting and praying, 115, 151, 175
watching, 213, 219–20
weaker brother or sister, 223
weak faith, as barrier to prayer, 152–53
weakness
  God's power in, 247
  power of the Spirit in, 210–13
weariness with prayer, 206
Westminster Theological Seminary, 107
Westminster Shorter Catechism, 217
Whitefield, George, 77
wind of the Spirit, 97–98
wisdom, in prayer, 224
World Harvest Mission, 108
written pastoral prayers, 197

Zechariah, 59, 151

Scripture Index

Also Available from
Paul E. Miller

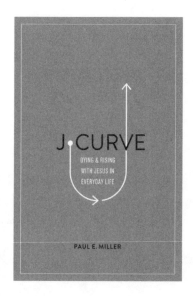

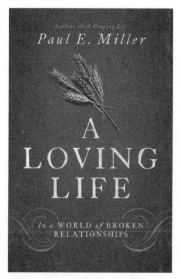

For more information, visit **crossway.org**.

Discover

seeJesus is a global discipling mission passionate about equipping the worldwide church to reflect all the beauty of Jesus. We invite you to learn more about our books, Bible studies, and seminars:

 Subscribe at info@seejesus.net

 Listen at seeJesus.net/podcast

 @_PaulEMiller

 Facebook/seeJesus.net

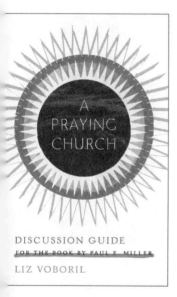

DISCUSSION GUIDE
FOR THE BOOK BY PAUL E. MILLER

LIZ VOBORIL

DISCUSSION GUIDE

This discussion guide teaches **you*** how to start the life-changing practice of praying together, right where you are.

*Whether your community is a small group, a family, a Sunday school class, or an entire church, you can begin to cultivate a praying community.

seeJesus.net/APrayingChurch

HOST A SEMINAR

Bring the Spirit back to the center of your community and watch him enliven the world's most powerful spiritual force—the everyday saints around you.

This new seminar, from the team who brought you the A Praying Life Seminar, will give you a vision for and practical experience in praying as a community.

see Jesus

seeJesus.net/APrayingChurch

BECOME A PRAYING CHURCH

Through a combination of seminars, cohorts, and coaching for your key leaders, A Praying Life Ministry can help you make this vision a reality.

Year 1: A Praying Life
Church members develop
their personal prayer lives.

Year 2: A Praying Church
Church members learn
to pray in community.

Year 3: A Culture of Prayer
Your church becomes a
self-sustaining praying community.

see Jesus

pathways@seejesus.net
seeJesus.net/APrayingChurch